Bloom's Modern Critical Interpretations

Bloom's Modern Critical Interpretations

Arthur Koestler's
DARKNESS AT NOON

Edited and with an introduction by
Harold Bloom
Sterling Professor of the Humanities
Yale University

CHELSEA HOUSE
P U B L I S H E R S
A Haights Cross Communications Company
Philadelphia

©2004 by Chelsea House Publishers, a subsidiary of
Haights Cross Communications.

A Haights Cross Communications ◀─┼─ Company

Introduction © 2004 by Harold Bloom.

Printed and bound in the United States of America

10 9 8 7 6 5 4 3 2 1

Library of Congress Cataloging-in-Publication Data

Darkness at Noon / edited and with an introduction by Harold Bloom.
        p. cm — (Bloom's modern critical interpretations) Includes
bibliographical references and index.
    ISBN 0-7910-7580-X (Hardcover)
    1. Koestler, Arthur, 1905– Darkness at noon. 2. Moscow Trials,
Moscow, Russia, 1936–1937—Historiography. 3. Totalitarianism and
literature. 4. Soviet Union—In literature. I. Bloom, Harold. II.
Series.
  PR6021.O4D3 2003
  813'.52—dc21

                                                        2003009466

Contributing editor: Janyce Marson

Cover design by Terry Mallon

Cover: © Bettman/CORBIS

Layout by EJB Publishing Services

Chelsea House Publishers
1974 Sproul Road, Suite 400
Broomall, PA 19008-0914

www.chelseahouse.com

Contents

Editor's Note

My Introduction ponders *Darkness at Noon*'s place in the unhappy Pantheon of Period Pieces.

Annett Edwards Platt centers upon Rubashov's toothache, which at least is not jargon, while Goronwy Rees insists upon the book's revelance as "a terrible vision of evil."

To Mark Levene, *Darkness at Noon* was Koestler at high-tide, the ebb coming with his "scientific writings," while Sidney A. Pearson, Jr. sees *Darkness at Noon* as another sequel to Koestler's *The Gladiators*.

Mark Levane returns to examine the psychology behind the trials, after which W. Marshall considers Koestler, along with the now-forgotton Victor Serge, as another annalist of Stanlinist terror, while Howard Fink contrasts the novel with *Nineteen Eighty-Four*.

The "political novel" is invoked as genre by Reed B. Merrill, while Anders Stephanson refutes William Pietz by pointing out that the Fascists were the true heirs of colonialism.

Robert Sutherland mediates upon "eternity" in *Darkness at Noon*, after which David Cesarani expounds the genesis of the novel. Martine Poulain concludes this volume by examining the reception of *Darkness at Noon* in post-war France.

Introduction

Arthur Koestler's *Darkness at Noon* (1940) is an eminent instance of one of my favorite sub-literary genres, the Period Piece. Koestler himself (1905–1983) is now a Period Piece: I recall reading him, with growing indifference, for a number of years, giving up for good when he proclaimed that all East European Jews were Tartars, not Semites, because descended (according to Koestlerian "science") from the medieval Khazars, who evidently accepted Judaism before they were overwhelmed by Christian and Moslem neighboring states.

Except for *Darkness at Noon*, I have only dim recollections of Koestler's novels, and rereading the story of Rubashov's martyrdom (to call it that), is certainly not an aesthetic experience. Koestler had no gift for characterization: "Rubashov" is just a name upon a page. I have no desire to break a butterfly upon a wheel: Koestler achieved fame during the Cold War era, which in the first decade of the twenty-first century is now remote, if not archaic. For Koestler, Soviet Communism was the God that Failed, and he went off whoring after even stranger Gods, settling finally for the God of a weird, personal Evolutionism.

Period Pieces frequently last up to three generations, and then vanish forever. Recognizing a Period Piece as such is always a test for the literary critic, though it never renders a critic popular. An ideological, politicized age like ours is particularly vulnerable to the enshrinement of Period Pieces. Nearly everything on our current academic scene, from grade schools to graduate schools, is one more Period Piece. Since we have only an interval, and then our place knows us no more, I urge my own students to learn to avoid Period Pieces, no matter how they are praised in the media or promoted in schools.

I give the last word on Period Pieces to my hero, Dr. Samuel Johnson, greatest of all literary critics, ever:

> Nothing is more common than to find men whose words are now totally neglected, mentioned with praise by their contemporaries, as the oracles of their age, and the legislators of science ... Every period of time has produced these bubbles of artificial fame, which are kept up awhile by the breath of fashion, and then break at once, and are annihilated.

ANNETTE EDWARDS PLATT

The Function of Rubashov's Toothache in Koestler's Darkness at Noon

In the context of modern political history, one of the most interesting themes of Arthur Koestler's *Darkness at Noon* is that of ends and means, of whether or not the end of collective good justifies means that involve the sacrifice of the individual. Involved, as Robert Gorham Davis termed it, is the conflict of "humane individualism and utopian inexorableness."[1] This conflict is presented through the protagonist Nicholas Rubashov and manifests itself tellingly through the "grammatical fiction" and the "oceanic sense," terms relating to concepts of the individual self and of the self in the cosmos. The entire novel may be viewed as Rubashov's ordeal in coming to philosophical grips with the concept that the end justifies the means when political expediency is concerned. This ordeal eventually leads him to throw off the "grammatical fiction," to acknowledge its contrary, and to embrace and be embraced by the "oceanic sense." Koestler uses the device of a recurring toothache to accentuate the struggles, pain, and final resolution that accompany Rubashov towards a new emotional and philosophical awareness.

Rubashov, an early leader and hero of the Revolution, is in the present action a political prisoner who must grapple with the "grammatical fiction," an idea perpetuated by the Party and translated into absolute policy. Essentially, the "grammatical fiction" is the elimination of the first person

From *McNeese Review* 23 (1976–77). © 1976 by McNeese State University.

singular. It calls for the effacement of self in favor of the collective interest of the Party. Rubashov "had christened it the 'grammatical fiction' with that shamefacedness about the first person singular which the Party had inculcated in its disciples."[2] By Party logic, it is the "I" itself that is fiction, its being replaced by the "we" of collectivism turned totalitarian. "The infinite was a politically suspect quantity, the 'I' a suspect quality. The Party did not recognize its existence" (p. 208). To adhere to the "grammatical fiction," its exponents must suspend or pervert pure logic, for the "Party denied the free will of the individual—and at the same time it exacted his willing self-sacrifice" (p. 208). In the realm of ethics, the "grammatical fiction" is the foundation for "the basic principle that a collective aim justifies all means, and not only allows, but demands, that the individual should in every way be subordinated and sacrificed to the community—which may dispose of it as an experimentation rabbit or a sacrificial lamb" (p. 128).

In conjunction with the denial of self and the doctrine of sacrifice of the individual, there is also the denial of any humanitarian impulses. For the Party, "humanism and politics, respect for the individual and social progress, are incompatible" (pp. 128–9). For the individual, "one may not regard the world as a sort of metaphysical brothel for emotions. That is the first commandment.... Sympathy, conscience, disgust, despair, repentance, and atonement are … repellent debauchery" (p. 124). In this area, "Rubashov was hesitant, uncertain and changeable. There was a soft spot in his carapace, and his sentiments were exposed.... Rubashov could not accept the price exacted by the means."[3]

Despite Rubashov's imprisonment and the relentless inquisition to which he is subjected, the conflict is more internal than external in nature. It lies in his initial intellectual acceptance of the pragmatic "grammatical fiction" with its related idea that the end justifies any means, as opposed to his instinctive and almost unconscious rejection of that same concept. As Edwin M. Moseley wrote, "His journey of learning is chiefly a solitary journey of retrospect and contemplation though each of the main sections of the book ends with his journeying literally and figuratively to face an official judge. As in all true stories of learning, the final judge is himself in more ways than one."[4]

Rubashov's covert rejection of the "grammatical fiction" and all that its implies manifests itself physically in the form of a recurring toothache. Although neither Rubashov himself nor Koestler, through the narrator, directly relates the toothache to this rejection, a definite pattern may be traced throughout the novel. Each time Rubashov denies the "I" that is his essential self for the cold and often brutal "we" of the Party and each time that confused or humane feelings for individuals of integrity or idealism whom he has helped to sacrifice intrude, the toothache is an automatic accompaniment. It is as though the toothache serves to accentuate the "I" of his individual self. The pangs of the tooth seem to be a manifestation of the proverbial pangs of conscience, and the more intense his feelings become, the more intense the pain. As traumatic memories pale or questions are resolved, the toothache invariably subsides.

Rubashov's toothache is not presented as pure metaphysical concoction of the author in juxtaposition with guilt feelings. It is given logical, physical explanation. In one of the many flashbacks through which Rubashov reviews his past, he relives the physical abuse he suffered in a foreign nation when arrested for Party activities. "He had kept silent when they beat him up, kept silent when they knocked the teeth out of his head, injured his hearing and broke his glasses. He had kept silent, and had gone on denying everything and lying coldly and circumspectly" (p. 48). Rubashov had, in effect, at that time submitted himself to the "grammatical fiction" and suffered, among other abuses, the broken teeth.

The first mention of the toothache is on Rubashov's first day in prison as a suspected enemy of the Party, a time of deep stress and inner searching. He complains of the toothache and cites it as the cause of his apathy toward prison regimen. For this, Rubashov is treated contemptuously by the prison warders. It is ironic that the toothache, whose origin lay in Rubashov's suffering for and subjugation to the Party, seems to symbolize for the warders the inner weakness that has characterized his recent thinking and conduct, caused an apparent rejection of the "grammatical fiction" and branded him a counter-revolutionary. The physical explanation for the toothache is reinforced through Rubashov's visit to the prison dentist:

> "There it is," said the doctor. "The root of the right eye-tooth
> is broken off and has remained in the jaw."
> Rubashov breathed deeply several times. The pain was throbbing
> from his jaw to his eye and right to the back of his head (p. 62).

The denial of anaesthetics to prisoners reminds Rubashov of the many aspects of prison torture, and he declines the dentist's offer to extract the root.

It is, however, the psychological origin of the toothache that takes precedence over the physical. In this context, the pain is in direct proportion to the guilt Rubashov feels about his past activities in behalf of the Party, particularly in regard to three persons he has betrayed. These three who haunt his memories are Richard, an intense and intellectual Communist worker in the Germany of the 1930's; Little Loewy, a leader of Party dock-workers in a port city of Belgium; and Arlova, Rubashov's secretary and mistress during his tenure in a diplomatic position. As Ivanov, his former comrade and now his jailer, attempts to obtain a confession from Rubashov of political crimes against the Party, he recalls Rubashov's role in Arlova's trial. "Rubashov was silent, and noticed that his tooth was aching again. He knew her fate. Also Richard's. Also Little Loewy's. Also his own" (p. 71). During that same session with Ivanov, Rubashov had previously centered his thoughts on Richard. "In the same instant a spasm of pain throbbed from his jaw up to his forehead and ear. For a second he shut his eyes. 'Now I am paying,' he thought" (p. 67). The toothache that invariably accompanies remembrances of his past adherence to the "grammatical fiction" by denying the "I" of himself and others for the expediency of the "we" of the Party seems to symbolize the pain of unexpiated guilt.

That Rubashov instinctively rejected the "grammatical fiction" is indicated by the fact that the toothache does not originate in remembrances of his acts of betrayal, but accompanied those acts. In the episode with Richard, Rubashov had been sent for the express purpose of denouncing the young worker. The source of the Party's displeasure with Richard was that, in the pamphlets he produced and distributed, he wrote openly of a recent defeat suffered by the Party rather than following central propaganda that claimed victory. At the initiation of their meeting, Richard knew only that

> Rubashov, who was a comrade from the Central Committee of the Party, was to be trusted like a father; but that one must not show this feeling nor betray any weakness. For he who was soft and sentimental was no good for the task and had to be pushed aside—pushed out of the movement, into solitude and the outer darkness (p. 29).

Richard was devoted to the cause of the Party. He was nineteen. His wife was seventeen and pregnant; for her Party activities, she had been arrested by the Nazis the night before the meeting with Rubashov. Richard was unaware that his wife had been having an affair with a comrade whose purpose was to spy on him. He was also unaware that Rubashov, despite his hallowed position, was not to be trusted like a father. As his interview with Rubashov progressed, Richard came to realize that its purpose was his condemnation. He argued for honesty as a means to the ultimate good and integrity of the Party. "'I only know,' said Richard, 'that one must tell people the truth, as they know it already in any case. It is ridiculous to pretend to them'" (p. 33). Yet, Richard's arguments were ineffectual against the unyielding wall of Party policy and the "grammatical fiction." "'The Party can never be mistaken,' said Rubashov. 'You and I can make a mistake. Not the Party'" (p. 34). As Rubashov listened to Richard's impassioned defense before pronouncing the inevitable sentence, his tooth began to ache. "Rubashov felt for the aching tooth with his tongue. He felt the need to touch it with his finger before pronouncing the decisive word, but forbade himself" (p. 36). After he told Richard of the Central Committee's decision to expel him from the Party, the toothache worsened. Rubashov heard Richard's plea, "'Comrade—b-but you couldn't de-denounce me, comrade...'" (p. 37). The cause Richard had believed in and sacrificed for rejected him, with Rubashov as its agent. Richard was without friends and wanted by the opposition. Without looking back, Rubashov left him standing in the street; "the affair with Richard had to be concluded, his tooth was aching" (p. 39). Both Richard and Rubashov in their own ways were being absorbed by the "grammatical fiction"; the pain from Rubashov's tooth was the only sign of his rebellion against it.

In the present action of the novel, Rubashov's imprisonment affords much opportunity for remembering the past. On the night that he most vividly recalls his association with Little Loewy, "His tooth also had started to ache again—the right eye-tooth which was connected to the eye-nerve orbitalis" (p. 46). Just as Rubashov had been the respected Party agent who betrayed the naive trust of Richard, so also was he the agent who betrayed Little Loewy and the sense of decency inherent in the dock-worker. Although Little Loewy lived and served the Party as leader of the dock-workers in a Belgian city, he was originally from Germany. Subversive activities on behalf of the Party had made him a political exile, and help from the Party, though promised, was not forthcoming. For years Little Loewy had been shuttled back and forth between France and Belgium by the police. Much of this time had been spent in prison. He had finally made contact with a fellow prisoner who was also a Party member. Papers were arranged for Little Loewy through this friend, and he begun to work on the docks and for the Party.

On the occasion of Rubashov's visit, only Little Loewy knew his identity, although he was almost recognized by an old worker who said, "'You look very like old Rubashov.' 'That I have often been told,' said Rubashov. 'Old Rubashov—there's a man for you,' said the old man, emptying his glass" (p. 50). The congeniality of the group, which had gathered at the local bar, lessened as the reason for Rubashov's visit became clear. Party ships with vital supplies for the newly established Nazi dictatorship were on their way to the port served by Little Loewy and his fellow workers. This was in opposition to the European boycott, and dock-workers had vowed to strike before handling goods destined for Nazi

Germany. As the workers were told of the coming of the ships, one exclaimed, "'The comrades Over There must know what they are about. We, of course, must continue to work for the boycott. You can trust us. In our port nothing will get through for the swine'" (p. 58). Only Little Loewy understood what Rubashov was asking of them, that they compromise their principles and work the docks at Party directive. Little Loewy said, "'The Comrade speaker has just explained to us the reasons for this business: if they do not deliver the supplies, others will. Who else wishes to speak?'" (p. 59).

As the workers railed against the proposal expressed by Rubashov, he applied as his argument the concept that is the basis for the "grammatical fiction." "'Comrades, the interests of our industrial development Over There come before everything else. Sentimentality does not get us any further. Think that over'" (p. 60). Little Loewy took the side of those who upheld the boycott. Rubashov informed the Party, Little Loewy was expelled and denounced as an *agent provocateur*, and he hanged himself soon afterwards. Rubashov, lying sleepless on a prison bed, relived the episode with Little Loewy:

> ...his tooth was throbbing. He had the sensation that all the association centres of his brain were sore and inflamed; yet he lay under the painful compulsion to conjure up pictures and voices. He thought of young Richard in the black Sunday suit, with his inflamed eyes "But you can't throw me to the wolves, comrade...." He thought of little deformed Loewy: "Who else wishes to speak?" There were so many who did wish to speak. For the movement was without scruples; she rolled towards her goal unconcernedly and deposed the corpses of the drowned in the windings of her course (p. 61).

The distaste Rubashov felt for his part in the affair with Little Loewy manifests itself at the later time of his imprisonment not only through the toothache, but through thoughts that express his view of the callousness of the Party as guided by the "grammatical fiction," that to which he had previously paid lip-service.

Rubashov's relationship with Arlova, unlike that with Richard or Little Loewy, was personal and of long duration. And his betrayal of her was also more personal and more blatant. Of all those whom Rubashov remembers from the past, it is Arlova who gives him the most pain and who most readily starts his tooth throbbing. "If anything in human beings could survive destruction, the girl Arlova lay somewhere in the great emptiness, still staring with her good cow's eyes at Comrade Rubashov, who had been her idol and had sent her to her death…. His tooth became worse and worse" (p. 72).

Rubashov met Arlova immediately after the episode with Little Loewy. He was assigned to a diplomatic post, and Arlova was his private secretary. As Rubashov thinks of Arlova, he remembers her docile attitude, her perfume, and her clothing, which consisted of "ridiculously high-heeled, patent-leather shoes with her pleasant, simple blouses and skirts" (p. 92). The early phases of their relationship were impersonal and office-oriented. Eventually, however, Arlova became Rubashov's mistress. On the first night that she spent with him, she said, "'You will always be able to do what you like with me'" (p. 93). Rubashov no more understood that simple statement than he did the "ridiculously high-heeled, patent-leather shoes." Arlova warned him against indiscreet asides he sometimes made about No. 1, the Party leader, or the Party itself. It was as though Arlova knew the dangerous fickleness of the Party better than Rubashov himself.

The Party appointed Arlova librarian with "political responsibility for the contents of the Legation library" (p. 96). Soon, during cell meetings, Arlova was being criticized for her handling of the library and was finally given a warning. A tension developed between her and Rubashov. "Rubashov stopped making personal comments while dictating, and that gave him a singular feeling of guilt" (p. 97). With one exception, Arlova's visits to Rubashov ceased. On that last intimate evening, it was as though Arlova wanted a commitment or declaration from him, one which she did not receive. When Arlova left, "He could not get rid of this tormenting sense of guilt; also his toothache had started again" (p. 97). News came that Arlova's brother and sister-in-law had been arrested for treasonous acts; at the next cell meeting Arlova was dismissed from her position with the library. "Rubashov, who was suffering from almost intolerable toothache, had excused himself from attending the meeting" (p. 98). Arlova's recall soon followed, and she was subsequently placed on trial. Despite Rubashov's knowledge of her innocence, he made a public disavowal of his former secretary and mistress. The principle of the "grammatical fiction" was at work in that he sought to save himself so that he might continue to serve the Party.

In the present action, it is not only Rubashov who questions his conduct in Arlova's case, but also Ivanov, Gletkin (who replaces Ivanov) and, eventually, the prosecutor of his own trial. The following excerpt from Gletkin's interrogation of Rubashov typifies his reaction:

> …The pressure in his eye-sockets radiated over all the nerves in the right side of his face. He noticed that his tooth had started to throb again.

"You know that Citizen Arlova had constantly called on you as
the chief witness for her defense?"

"I was informed of it," said Rubashov. The throbbing in his
tooth became stronger.

"You doubtless also know that the declaration you made at that
time, which you have just described as a lie, was decisive for the
passing of the death sentence on Arlova?"

"I was informed of it."

Rubashov had the feeling that the whole right side of his face
was drawn into a cramp (pp. 155–156).

It is not only the toothache that tortures Rubashov. He imagines how Arlova
must have looked being dragged to her death in her high-heeled, patent-
leather shoes and how the back of her neck must have looked to the
executioner who shot her in the head. "His consciousness of guilt ... could
not be expressed in logical formula—it lay in the realm of the 'grammatical
fiction'" (p. 121).

Although Rubashov's rejection of the "grammatical fiction" as
manifested through the toothache is most pronounced in his agonies over his
relationships with Richard, Little Loewy, and Arlova, there is also a broader
connotation. He reviews the history of the Revolution with its ideals that
have turned to cold brutality. He has seen the decline of the political
theorists and the rise of the Gletkins, the Neanderthals of the movement. He
has witnessed and contributed to an attempt at responsible politics that has
been translated into more of man's inhumanity to man. Early in the chronicle
of his imprisonment, the toothache is seen in conjunction with Rubashov's
questioning of the effects of the Revolution. "It is the orbitalis, he said to
himself; it comes from the broken off root of the eye-tooth. I will tell the
doctor about it tomorrow, but in the meantime there is still a lot to do. The
cause of the Party's defectiveness must be found. All our principles were
right, but our results were wrong" (p. 47).

Near the end of his imprisonment, Rubashov, in the presence of the
interrogator Gletkin, is confronted by another prisoner previously known to
him only from a distance and as Hare-lip. During the confrontation, "the
dull hammering in his head started again" (p. 160). Hare-lip, a young man
made old and warped by torture, is the son of a former companion of
Rubashov, an idealist already executed by the Party. Hare-lip becomes
Rubashov's accuser in his claim that, as a boy, he had been inspired by
Rubashov's political ideology and encouraged by him to assassinate No. 1,
the Party leader. The truth, untruth, or half-truth of the accusation is at this
point all but irrelevant to Rubashov. "The essential point was that this figure

of misery represented the consequence of his logic made flesh" (p. 167). Rubashov renounces the precept of the infallibility of the Party.

The toothache suffered by Rubashov emerges as a symbol of repudiation of the "grammatical fiction." During his probing of his past life and present consciousness, Rubashov discovers a new part of himself which he terms his silent partner, the "I" element of his being:

> ...it remained dumb, and its existence was limited to a grammatical abstraction called the "first person singular." Direct questions and logical meditations did not induce it to speak; its utterances occurred without visible cause and, strangely enough, always accompanied by a sharp attack of toothache. Its mental sphere seemed to be composed of such various and disconnected parts as the folded hands of the *Pieta*, Little Loewy's cats, the tune of the song with the refrain of "come to dust," or a particular sentence which Arlova had once spoken on a particular occasion (p. 89).

This emergence of the first person singular in Rubashov, though completed in prison, had begun long before. It was the "I" in Rubashov in opposition to the "we" of the Party that made it impossible for him to accept without physical pain the fates of the Richards and Loewys and Arlovas of the world. And it was when this first person singular aspect of Rubashov became evident to others that he became suspect. In his first prison interview, he is told that "There is one thing I would like to point out to you. You have now repeatedly said 'you'—meaning State and Party, as opposed to 'I'—that is, Nicholas Salmanovitch Rubashov" (p. 66).

At a later time, Ivanov scornfully characterizes what the acknowledgement of the first person singular has done to Rubashov. "He has discovered a conscience, and a conscience renders one as unfit for the revolution as a double chin. Conscience eats through the brain like a cancer, until the whole of the grey matter is devoured" (p. 122). The pain of the toothache, the voice of the silent partner, has made real the "grammatical fiction" for Rubashov and awakened his conscience in such a way that he sees his former acts and the course of the Party as perversions of the original ideals of the Revolution. Gletkin becomes the embodiment of this perversion for Rubashov. "Massive and expressionless, he sat there, the brutal embodiment of the State which owed its very existence to the Rubashovs and Ivanovs. Flesh of their flesh, grown independent and become insensible" (p. 185).

With his new awareness of self, Rubashov feels a sense of expansion rather than contraction. He no longer thinks of himself only in terms of the

Party, but in relation to the cosmos; he experiences the "oceanic sense." Robert Gorham Davis explains the "oceanic sense" through Koestler's autobiographical account in *Dialogue with Death* of his own imprisonment in Spain during the time of the Spanish Civil War, a time when Koestler was convinced that death was imminent. He overcame fear of the firing squad by the quasi-mystical experience of identification with the passive misery of the world, the merging of his individual misery with that of the universe itself so that he was not alone, but a part of the whole. This, Davis asserts, is the "oceanic sense" experienced by Rubashov.[5] Through this experience, Rubashov responds to all about him:

> ...the greatest and soberest of modern psychologists had recognized this state as a fact and called it the "oceanic sense." And, indeed, one's personality dissolved as a grain of salt in the sea; but at the same time the infinite sea seemed to be contained in the grain of salt. The grain could no longer be localized in time and space (p. 207).

Despite this mystical experience and even with his trial, conviction, and impending execution, Rubashov retains some remnants of the Party's pragmatism. In reference to an exaltation he feels in reading an account of his statement at his trial, Rubashov thinks,

> —the "oceanic sense" had swept him away. Afterwards he had been ashamed of himself. The Party disapproved of such states. It called them *petit-bourgeois* mysticism, refuge in the ivory tower. It called them "escape from the task," "desertion of the class struggle." The "oceanic sense" was counter-revolutionary (p. 208).

As Rubashov waits in his cell to be taken to his execution, he thinks "Perhaps later, much later, the new movement would arise—with new flags, a new spirit knowing of both: of economic fatality *and* the 'oceanic sense'" (p. 211). As John Atkins comments, Rubashov rediscovered his inner voice, his recognition of and consideration for the individual. Rather than forsaking the Marxist theories for which he had worked and sacrificed, he hoped that at some time in the future his new concepts concerning individual feeling might be applied within the Marxist framework.[6] At such a point there would be no necessity for the "grammatical fiction." Instead, there would be "the joining of a million individuals to form a new entity which, no longer an amorphous mass, will develop a consciousness and an individuality of its own, with an 'oceanic feeling' increased a millionfold, in unlimited yet self-contained space" (p. 211). With the "grammatical fiction" exposed, the "oceanic sense" acknowledged, there would be no necessity for the toothache that makes up the voice of the silent partner of men such as Rubashov.

As Rubashov is led toward his execution, he wonders about the revolver that will end his life, whether it is still in its case or hidden in the executioner's sleeve, "like the dentist, who hid his instruments in his sleeve while bending over his patient?" (p. 215). Rubashov also thinks of the toothache that no longer plagues him:

> Strange that his toothache had ceased in the minute when that blessed silence had closed around him, during the trial. Perhaps the abscess had opened just in that minute. What had he said to them? "I bow my knees before the country, before the masses, before the whole people..." (p. 215).

Rubashov confessed his crimes, not against the Party, but committed in the name of the Party against humanity. In so doing, Rubashov still displays vestiges of cynicism. He may doubt the maturity of the masses in contributing to responsible government, he may wonder if there is a Promised Land, he may feel the necessity for the Gletkins he abhors, but it is as though he has made his personal peace with the world. Rubashov achieves a tragic dignity in that "he comes to understand that despite his physical defeat he has his own little place ('the grammatical fiction I') in the vast order of things ('the oceanic sense')."[7] In a confession of guilt to a particular charge levied against him, Rubashov had stated, "I plead guilty to having placed the idea of man above the idea of mankind..." (p. 153).

Rubashov's statement at his trial provided the expiation for his guilt. There was no longer the necessity for the toothache; Rubashov's albatross disappeared into the "oceanic sense," just as Rubashov was to dissolve into the "oceanic feeling" at the moment of his death: "A second, smashing blow hit him on the ear. Then all became quiet. There was the sea again with its sounds. A wave slowly lifted him up. It came from afar and traveled sedately on, a shrug of eternity" (p. 216).

NOTES

1. Robert Gorham Davis, "The Sharp Horns of Koestler's Dilemmas," *The Antioch Review*, 4 (Winter 1944–1945), 504.

2. Arthur Koestler, *Darkness at Noon* (New York, 1975), p. 205—this edition hereafter cited in text.

3. John Atkins, *Arthur Koestler* (New York, 1956), p. 185.

4. Edwin M. Moseley, *Pseudonyms of Christ in the Modern Novel* (New York, 1962), p. 190.

5. Davis, p. 509.

6. Atkins, p. 69.

7. Moseley, pp. 192–193.

GORONWY REES

Darkness at Noon *and*
the 'Grammatical Fiction'

*H*abent sua fata libelli; books have their own destinies. No doubt this is true of all books, but there are some, of which *Darkness at Noon* is one, to which the phrase seems to have particular relevance. They are those books which, for some special reason of time or circumstance, from the moment of publication seem to assume a life of their own, almost independent of their author's original intentions, so that henceforward the world takes possession of them and makes of them whatever it wishes or pleases.

It would be hard to say what common quality confers upon such books their appeal to all kinds and conditions of men and women, of all times and in all countries. But even if we cannot define their secret, they have certain characteristic features which are worth noticing, and these *Darkness at Noon* also shares. One, paradoxically enough, is that though their appeal is not limited by time or space, they have their origins in a narrowly circumscribed historical situation, sometimes indeed in a particular historical incident which by now has been long forgotten. It is hardly possible to understand the references in *Pilgrim's Progress* or *Gulliver's Travels* or *Robinson Crusoe* without a fairly thorough acquaintance with the ideas and controversies which agitated Englishmen in Bunyan's and Swift's and Defoe's day; yet a child can read the books with delight though he learns nothing of their origins.

Again, and perhaps as a consequence of this paradox, it is a

From *Astride the Two Cultures: Arthur Koestler at 70*, ed. Harold Harris. Adapted from the introduction and appreciations in the Heron Books edition of *Darkness at Noon*. © 1976 by Random House.

characteristic of such books that they can be read as myths or fables of the human condition in its most universal form. For this reason, they concentrate on the life and adventures of a single person, for whom other characters are in the nature of foils, challenges, sometimes simply arguments. These are the hero's other possible selves, and his problem is to come to terms with them, which is in fact a way of coming to terms with himself. Since this is a situation of universal application such books make a very direct and personal appeal to us, and this is reinforced because the stories they have to tell, the events they narrate, are in essence simple and uncomplicated, even though the hero's reaction to them may vary between the extremes of naivete and sophistication.

Darkness at Noon is, then, both a historical novel and a spiritual and intellectual biography. It is very firmly rooted in a particular time and place in history, the Russia of the Great Purge conducted by Stalin from 1936 to 1938. It is true that Koestler never names Stalin in his book, in which he is referred to throughout simply as 'No. I', nor the Soviet Union, nor does he give precise dates to the events of his story, but there is never any doubt about what those events were, nor when and where they occurred. Indeed, we can identify them precisely because the trial of Koestler's hero, Nicolai Salmanovitch Rubashov, follows very closely the scenario devised by the Soviet secret police, the GPU, for the trial in 1938 of Nikolai Bukharin, the last and in many ways the most brilliant of the Bolshevik Old Guard, 'the darling of the Party' as Lenin described him.

Darkness at Noon is also primarily the story of a single individual, who, under the circumstances of exceptional pressure and strain, both personal and political, tries to draw up a balance sheet of his life and to explain why it is that, at the end of it all, there is something wrong with the accounts. Its hero tries to solve the problem by introducing into the figures of profit and loss a factor which he has hitherto ignored, as inadmissible in strict accounting procedures. He calls it by a number of different names, and makes use of a number of analogies, often mathematical, to illustrate its nature and behaviour; but he never succeeds in identifying it to his complete satisfaction, chiefly because its mere existence, once admitted, seems to make nonsense, or worse, of his entire life and of everything it has been devoted to. At the same time, he has to confess to himself that only by accepting its existence can he understand how it is that he, and the revolution which he has helped to make, should have been reduced to the disastrous condition in which they find themselves at the moment when, without hope and without faith, he goes to meet his executioners.

It might be said that the dilemma in which the hero of *Darkness at Noon* found himself was one that had become distressingly familiar to its author,

Arthur Koestler, in his own life; and though in Rubashov's case it acquires a political, and a philosophical, significance which transcends any purely personal experience, the autobiographical element in the novel is a very strong one and no doubt contributes to the intensity with which it is written. Koestler's life, up to the period when he wrote *Darkness at Noon*, provides the background of the experiences out of which the novel is made; at the same time, his early life was so much a product of the characteristic social and political conflicts of the first half of this century that it has a wider interest than the biographical material which helps to explain the origins of most novels. The two volumes of his own autobiography, indeed, *Arrow in the Blue* and *The Invisible Writing*, form an invaluable contribution to the history of our own times.

In December 1931 Koestler applied for membership of the KPD, and in July of 1932, having resigned from the Ullstein Press, in which he had made a spectacularly successful journalistic career, he left Germany for the Soviet Union with an assignment to write a book and a series of articles which would present the Fatherland of Socialism in the best of all possible lights to the liberal bourgeoisie of Western Europe.

It would be difficult to analyse the reasons, conscious and unconscious, for Koestler's conversion to Communism. They would include the breakdown of the capitalist system under the strain of the world economic depression; the threat of war and dictatorship implicit in the rise of Fascism in Germany, and the inability of the democratic parties to offer any effective resistance to National Socialism. But commitment to Communism also involved irrational and emotional elements which were deeply rooted in Koestler's character; a deep sympathy with the down-trodden and oppressed, the 'wretched of the earth', with whom he identified himself; a yearning for a discipline as of some monastic order which would subjugate the warring impulses of his own nature, a desire for self-sacrifice and self-abnegation which would assuage his sense of guilt; the hope and belief that in the ranks of the Communist Party he would renew that sense of fellowship, of 'belonging', which he had only previously found as a member of his *Burschenschaft*, the student duelling society which he had joined at his university in Vienna.

But in addition there was also the attraction of Communism as a closed and all-inclusive intellectual system which not only offered a complete answer to all the problems of human existence but claimed to show that the answer could be applied in practice. Communist policy had the same relation to Marxist theory as applied science to pure science, and in both Koestler found an answer to his search for the Absolute. Communism reconciled Science with Faith, Thought with Action, the Individual with the

Community, and in each of these aspects it made a profound appeal to Koestler's deepest instincts.

Its appeal, indeed, was so powerful, so much a matter of emotional need, that it made of his visit to Russia something very nearly approaching a farce. At that time, the Soviet Union, as a result of Stalin's policy of collectivizing the land, was experiencing a crisis which was even more acute and severe, and with far more terrible results in human suffering, than the parallel economic crisis in the capitalist world. But of all this Koestler apparently saw nothing, or if he saw refused to believe the evidence of his eyes, though his travels took him from Kharkov, in the Ukraine, into Georgia, Armenia and Azerbaijan, across the Caucasus and through Turkestan down to the Afghan border, up to Bokhara, Samarkand and Tashkent and through Kazakstan. He travelled through a land in which millions of people were dying of starvation and in some areas had been reduced to cannibalism, while other millions were being forcibly deported to the most intemperate regions of the Soviet Union; and yet nothing disturbed his conviction that in this vast and tormented territory he had at last arrived in the Promised Land.

Thus his visit was more in the nature of a hallucination than a journey through a real country, and he himself notes that not a word of the reality of life in the Soviet Union escaped into anything that he wrote about it, which differed in no way from the work of any Party hack. But he also notes that beneath the frozen crust of ideology which protected his illusions, in the darkness of the subconscious, the seeds of doubt had already been planted, though it was to be many years before they germinated and came to harvest.

Koestler left the USSR in the summer of 1933. By that time Hitler had come to power in Germany, the Reichstag fire had taken place, and the Communist Party of Germany had been driven underground and had ceased to have any existence as an organized political force; this total defeat and destruction of a party which even a year earlier had commanded over 6000 000 votes was described in official Communist propaganda as a 'strategic retreat'. In the new Germany of Adolf Hitler there was no place for Koestler. Though still a devoted and active member of the Party, and faithfully performing the tasks assigned to him, he was in fact the prey of obscure impulses which fought a long and protracted struggle with the orthodoxies imposed on him by his beliefs. Some unconscious instinct of self-preservation prevented him from becoming a paid functionary of the Party, though his entire life was bound up with it, and being at the same time almost totally isolated from bourgeois society, he was debarred from any regular form of employment.

The years which he spent in Paris, from 1933 to 1936, were years of desperate poverty and at times of semi-starvation and homelessness. Yet they were also particularly fruitful years, in which his long protracted adolescence finally came to an end and his strangely divided personality gradually came to terms with itself and he began to realize his true vocation, not as a journalist, but as a writer. Nevertheless, his day-to-day activities continued to be dominated by the Party. In 1934 the Comintern, reversing its previous policy of refusing all collaboration with other parties, embarked upon the policy of a Popular Front of all radical and progressive forces in the struggle against Fascism. Its most effective agent in the West was the great Communist agitator and propagandist Willy Muenzenberg, who as head of the powerful IWA (International Workers Aid) and of the western section of AGITPROP, the Comintern's department of agitation and propaganda, founded a bewildering variety of Communist front organizations through which to conduct the Popular Front's struggle against Fascism; his activity was so multifarious and ubiquitous that in a sense it would be true to say that the great anti-Fascist crusade of the thirties was an invention of Muenzenberg's.

From 1934 to 1936, Koestler worked in close collaboration with Muenzenberg and with his assistant, Otto Katz, alias André Simon, and his association with these two remarkable men both deepened his understanding of the intellectual processes of the dedicated Communist revolutionary and of that curious combination of moral fervour, selfless devotion and lack of scruple which is the basis of Communist ethics. The success with which Muenzenberg prosecuted the Party's policy of collaboration and alliance with everyone willing to fight under the banner of anti-Fascism was all the more remarkable because, in the Soviet Union itself, Stalin, having in all probability instigated the assassination of Kirov in 1934, was preparing for the Great Purge of the Communist Party which so completely exposed the hollowness of the Soviet Union's pretensions to be the champion of democracy and freedom.

On August 31st there opened in Moscow the first of the great series of State trials which culminated in 1938 in the trial of Bukharin; by a further irony, 1936 also saw the promulgation of the new Soviet Constitution, 'the most liberal constitution in the world', largely drafted by Bukharin and Radek, who, together with almost every other member of the original leadership of the Bolshevik Party, were themselves to become victims of the Purge. Thus the period of the Soviet Union's collaboration with the radical and middle-class opponents of Fascism was also the period in which the dictatorship of Stalin assumed its most savage and ruthless form.

It was Koestler's privilege, or misfortune, to observe this process from within the ranks of the Communist Party, to watch its progressive deterioration as the Purge assumed more and more hideous forms and follow its repercussions as they penetrated down to the Party's smallest cells, not only in the Soviet Union but abroad. Yet, once again, his 'closed system' of beliefs for some years more proved impervious to the Great Purge as it had been to the Great Famine; the truth is that it so completely circumscribed his intellectual and emotional life that he could not conceive of existence beyond its limits.

It was to survive one more test. On July 18th, 1936, General Franco raised the flag of insurrection against the legitimate Republican government of Spain, and his revolt was followed by one of the most curious and tragic episodes in modern European history. On the one hand, it inspired a heroic struggle by the Spanish people to defend their liberty and independence against the reactionary forces, both internal and external, which were allied to destroy all their hopes for the future. On the other hand, it also inspired what might be called a Children's Crusade of volunteers, from all over the world, who saw in the Civil War the last chance of halting the triumphant advance of Fascism and to avert the world war to which it was the preliminary. It was the policy of the Soviet Union to place itself at the head of that crusade, to bring it under its own control, and to use the Civil War itself as a means to advancing its own foreign policy and to winning for the Communist Party the monopoly of political power in Spain.

Koestler, like thousands of other members of the Party, hastened to join the crusade. For him, as for others, the issues in Spain were so absolutely clear that the Civil War offered an opportunity, perhaps the last, for the Party to demonstrate that, in spite of the mutilations and deformations it had suffered, it was still the only force capable of defeating Fascism. In Spain, however, the policy of the Party revealed the same contradictions, the same conflict between propaganda and reality, the same combination of moral fervour and cynical hypocrisy, the same perverted logic, as it had already shown in Germany and in the Soviet Union itself. Its degeneration had proceeded so far that it transformed even the Civil War into an incident in an internal party struggle, of which the final victims were those of its members who had most wholeheartedly believed in the cause they thought they were defending in Spain.

Yet it was not the realization that the Party had become a hideous travesty of everything that it professed to be which provoked Koestler's final break with it. To abandon a faith, it is necessary to discover the means of living without it, if one is to go on living in any real sense at all. In Spain, Koestler underwent an experience which provided at least the basis for such an hypothesis. His own part in the Spanish Civil War took the form, after consultation with and direction by Willy Muenzenberg, of becoming an agent and observer for the Comintern under the cover of an accredited correspondent to the Franco forces of the liberal English newspaper the *News Chronicle* and, somewhat precariously, of the reactionary *Pester Lloyd* of Budapset. The operation was conceived in a curiously clumsy and amateurish fashion and five months after his arrival in Spain, in February 1937, Koestler was arrested and condemned to death as a spy. He spent three months in solitary confinement, in daily expectation of execution, before he was released in exchange for a Franco hostage in Republican hands.

The confrontation with death which Koestler underwent in his cell in Seville is closely related to the experience of Rubashov in his cell in Moscow. It was significant, not because it provided any further evidence of the corruption of the Communist Party, but because it released in him feelings, instincts, perceptions, which had been rigidly excluded from the boundaries of the 'closed system' of Marxist ideology. In this respect, Koestler's own experience offers a close parallel to that of Rubashov in *Darkness at Noon*. In both cases, what is significant is the sudden and explosive eruption into consciousness of experiences which hitherto have been successfully repressed in the interests of a system of thought with which they cannot be reconciled.

It might be said that those experiences were, in both cases, the product of the abnormal psychological condition induced, in Koestler and Rubashov alike, by the shock of arrest, solitary confinement and imminent confrontation with death. This may well be so. But the truth is not a function of psychological states, and the validity of any experience is not to be judged by the conditions by which it has been induced. The dilemma of Koestler-Rubashov in his cell is precisely what kind of validity to attribute to an insight which threatens to shatter the coherence of a system of thought on which the whole of his life has been based. His dilemma is intensified by a heightened receptivity stimulated by a sense of release from a burden of guilt which has been borne for too long. In his cell in Seville, Koestler recognized that there was a kind of rough justice in his sentence to death, not only because he was in fact, as his judges claimed, a spy, but even more because he had for years, in his role as a convinced and committed Communist, been impersonating a character in which he fundamentally did not believe. He had become one of those 'people in prison who revalue their lives and discover that they are guilty, though not of the crimes of which they are accused'. Like Rubashov, he almost felt relief in the admission: *I must pay.*

The history of a loss of faith is a long and complicated one, and it was not until 1938 that Koestler formally resigned from the Communist Party.

In March of that year there took place in Moscow the last of the great

State trials of the Bolshevik Old Guard, including Nikolai Bukharin, President of the Comintern, Christian Rakovsky, Krestinsky, Rykov, and Yagoda, head of the Soviet security police, the GPU. This last trial was a kind of monstrous *reductio ad absurdum* of the Great Purge, in which it was proved to everyone's satisfaction that not only the whole of the original leadership of the Bolshevik Party had become spies and traitors but that the case against them had been conducted by one who shared in exactly the same crimes. *Darkness at Noon*, which is an account of the historical process of which this trial was the culmination, was begun in the Autumn of 1938 and was finished in April 1940, a month before the German invasion of France; in the meantime Koestler had been arrested, and released, by the French police, and the page proofs of the book were delivered to him in Pentonville, in England, where he had been imprisoned after the fall of France and his subsequent escape across the Channel.

Much of the material of the novel is drawn from Koestler's own experiences, and from the experiences of friends and acquaintances within the Communist Party. It is important to remember that the tragedy which was enacted in Russia in the thirties was one which penetrated to every level of the Party; for every case, like Rubashov's, which was exposed in the glare of publicity of a State trial, there were thousands of others, including those of many of Koestler's friends and colleagues, which were conducted in silence and in darkness.

The tragedy which was thus enacted had two distinct acts: the Great Famine and the Great Purge, and the second act was in some respects the logical consequence of the first, because it was in the Famine that the Party discovered and adopted the methods of repression which were brought to perfection in the Purge. Gletkin, the interrogator in *Darkness at Noon*, describes how he discovered almost by accident during the famine the technique of extracting a false confession from a recalcitrant and uncooperative prisoner.

At the time of Rubashov's arrest, such techniques had been developed into a universal system of terror, of a scope and violence which had never previously been seen in Europe, even in the Germany of Adolf Hitler; the legitimacy of terror as a political weapon is of course one of the problems which pre-occupy Rubashov in his meditations in his prison cell. Terror had been recognized as a legitimate political means since the French Revolution, and had been accepted as such by Marx and Engels and by Lenin himself. But in the Great Purge, and even earlier, not merely terror, but torture had become an established and approved instrument of government, and this was something which was unique to the Soviet regime, until it found a willing disciple in the National Socialist government of Germany.

The use of physical torture as a political weapon plays a large part in Rubashov's meditations in prison, because it raises problems which are almost insoluble within the terms of his own revolutionary beliefs. There is the question whether its universal application during the Great Purge is merely an aberration due to No. 1's sadistic instincts, or rather a logical consequence of a doctrine which holds that revolution is an end which justifies every means. There is the irrepressible feeling that, however logical and rational its operations, a regime in which torture is not the exception but the rule has achieved something new and unique in the degradation of man by man. There is an even more difficult question: whence do such feelings arise, and with a force which cannot be ignored? For by the dialectic of the revolution, they should be judged as merely sentimental weaknesses which serve to disguise the vestiges of bourgeois moral prejudice. At the beginning of *Darkness at Noon*, Koestler has placed a quotation from Dostoyevsky: 'Man, man, one cannot live quite without pity'. For a revolutionary, what kind of meaning can such a sentence have?

The question of physical and mental torture is of crucial importance in *Darkness at Noon*, for several reasons. In the first place it provides the most striking demonstration of the degeneration of the Soviet State, and how and why this could have come about is one among the most urgent questions with which Rubashov torments himself in his prison cell. In the second place, it vitally affects the nature of the 'confessions' made by Rubashov himself, and by the accused in the Soviet State trials, on which his own is modelled. *Darkness at Noon* has frequently been interpreted as offering a 'psychological' explanation of the confessions, so bewildering to the Western mind, based on the inability of the accused, as convinced and devoted Communists, to resist the authority of the Party, even when what it demands of them is the sacrifice, not merely of their lives, but of reputation, honour, dignity and self-respect.

Certainly such a motive plays a large part in Rubashov's final surrender to Gletkin, but it is only one motive among many others, and Koestler makes it abundantly clear that, in inducing his final decision, the relentless physical pressure brought upon him by Gletkin, the lack of sleep, the deprivation of the privileges accorded him by Ivanov, the blinding glare of the lamp, have also had their effect. Indeed, it is an essential part of Gletkin's creed, as a representative of the new 'Neanderthal' type of the Soviet man, that a person like Rubashov cannot be brought to capitulate without the use of such methods. Gletkin's armoury includes a multiplicity of weapons, which can be adjusted and combined to suit each particular case. What they have in common is the manipulation of the human being as material for use and a subject for experiment.

The importance of torture in *Darkness at Noon* is that it exposes in its most naked form the fundamental problem with which the novel is concerned. That problem, at its simplest, is: how far is it justifiable to use human beings as a means and not as an end? And it is because this question has a universal application that Koestler's novel has a certain timeless quality which is independent of the particular place and time of the story it has to tell. Even to ask such a question is to assume a utilitarian ethic in which both ends and means can be quantified in a universal calculus which assigns only an infinitesimal value to the experiences of the invididual. From his own Marxist, Communist, point of view Rubashov can see no escape from this conclusion; and both his interrogators, Ivanov and Gletkin, are agreed with him in this, which is why he can find no answer to their arguments. It is important to realize that even before he has been surrendered into the merciless hands of Gletkin, Rubashov has already capitulated to the 'vivisection morality' of Ivanov: the difference between them is that out of old affection and friendship, Ivanov wishes, if he can, to save Rubashov's life. This is a sentimental weakness on Ivanov's part, and it is a part of the logic of the novel that therefore Ivanov should be shot and Rubashov be handed over to Gletkin.

One of the great merits of *Darkness at Noon* is that Koestler should have been able to reduce the enormous complexity of his material, historical, political, and psychological, to an almost classical simplicity of form and structure; and indeed there are other elements in the story, of Fate, of Hubris, of the individual entangled in a more-than-human conflict, which recall the classical parallel. The three long sections which form the main part of the narrative unfold like the three acts of a play, each with its appropriate curtain; the short final scene of Rubashov's public trial and confession is simply an epilogue to a tragedy that has already been played out. Within this severe structural scheme, the narrative, varying continually and with great subtlety between the objective and the subjective plane, advances with compelling force, and like Rubashov himself one is caught up in a storm of events, memories, feelings and ideas which is only finally resolved in the peace of death.

The sheer pace of the narrative, indeed, is so exhilarating that one is almost tempted to overlook, or at least to underestimate, one element in the story which is of equal importance with the political problem which it presents for our consideration, though it is in a sense the key to its solution. Formally, the drama of the story is compressed into Rubashov's three confrontations with his interrogators; in the intervals between them, in the silence of his cell, Rubashov recalls incidents of his past which have a particular and sinister reference to the ordeal to which he is being subjected.

Yet in addition to Rubashov, Ivanov, Gletkin, there is always present another principal actor in the drama, who, while having no name or, in the proper sense of the word, personality, has a decisive influence in its development; one might almost call him, not Rubashov, its hero. He is like that shadowy character whom the disciples encountered on the road to Emmaus, shapeless and featureless in the dusk and yet, as they all felt, the real centre of the great event in which they have taken part.

'Who is that third who always walks beside you?' This character never, or hardly ever speaks directly, except in certain phrases which involuntarily force themselves to Rubashov's lips in his long monologues in his cell, in particular the recurrent phrase: *I must pay*. The phrase makes no logical sense to Rubashov; but it is accompanied by a sense of being at peace, as if it contained a promise of release from suffering. He hardly knows where the phrase comes from, but it transforms his meditations into a monologue *à deux*, in which the other partner cannot be identified.

To this presence, a kind of *Doppelgänger* which reverses all Rubashov's normal processes of thought, he finally gives the name of the 'grammatical fiction', the first person singular denoting the 'I', the self, to which the Party refuses to attribute any significance because it appears to have, or to claim, an existence independent of any social reality, which is the only reality which the Party recognizes. Of its nature or its mode of being, its ontological status or its psychological or intellectual procedures he knows nothing; it has something of the amorphous, floating character of the Latin poet's *animula blandula vagula*, the 'simple soul', the passive recipient on which experience imprints itself as on a photographic plate. Yet gradually he becomes uneasily aware that by his refusal to recognize its existence he may have betrayed himself, and millions of others—and for this treachery also, *I must pay*. As much as any of the arguments used by Gletkin, it is this recognition of guilt which finally persuades him to accept the shameful role for which he is cast in the scenario prepared for him by Gletkin and his superiors, and it is this recognition which finally brings him a kind of peace before the bullet in the back of his head finally puts an end to him; his last hours he reserves for converse with the 'grammatical fiction'.

The intermittent, yet decisive, appearances of the 'grammatical fiction' make of *Darkness at Noon* something of a Hamlet without the Prince of Denmark. They also introduce into it, and especially into Rubashov's tenacious but futile struggle with his interrogators, a certain note of ambiguity. For the mute but major premise of Rubashov's argument is suppressed; the 'grammatical fiction' has no existence in Gletkin's vocabulary or syntax, nor has Rubashov himself any means of introducing it into their murderous interchanges. If, in the end, Rubashov surrenders to the idea that the Party still has a use for him, it is because, blinded by the confusion of his own mind and feelings as much as by the glare of Gletkin's lamp, he no longer has the strength of mind or will to reject the temptation out of loyalty to something whose existence he still hardly acknowledges and whose nature he has not had time to understand. It is at this point that we realize, with sympathy, that Rubashov is old, that he is intellectually and emotionally exhausted; that he is, in fact, beaten.

The 'grammatical fiction' also involves a noticeable, though perfectly justifiable, distortion of the historical material on which Koestler based his novel. This is indeed one of the reasons why we feel it to be fiction, or a work of art, rather than a political *roman à clef*, to be judged primarily by its fidelity to the particular historical situation which was its direct inspiration. Koestler tells us that Rubashov is deliberately based on the early leaders of the Bolshevik revolution. His personality and even his physical appearance, the pince-nez, the wispy beard, the incisive gestures, come from Trotsky and from Radek; the sophisticated dialectical processes from Bukharin, who had a scintillating intelligence which melted the mind and the heart even of Lenin. In his dedication to the novel, Koestler says that 'N. S. Rubashov is a synthesis of the lives of a number of men who were victims of the so-called Moscow trials. Several of them were personally known to the author.' Indeed, he follows his model Bukharin so closely that Rubashov's confession at his trial very nearly repeats *verbatim* Bukharin's at his. But there is nowhere, so far as I know, any evidence in any documents of the revolutionary period, or of the Great Purge, that any of the veteran leaders of the Bolshevik Old Guard ever fell a victim, like Rubashov, to the seductions of the 'grammatical fiction'. Its introduction into the novel is a brilliant feat of imagination on Koestler's part.

Rubashov's interrogation by Gletkin, however, is conducted entirely in terms of the revolutionary dialectic of which they are both, in their different ways, masters. The difference between them is that while Rubashov applies it as a living body of thought, capable of new insights and new developments, for Gletkin it is strictly an instrument for use, in this case in a singularly brutal way. But he is not, for that reason, any less skilful in applying it than Rubashov; indeed, he shows himself more consequent than Rubashov in pushing it to its conclusions, so that in the struggle between them Rubashov meets with total and unconditional defeat and the last vestiges of his self-respect are stripped away from him. There are readers of *Darkness at Noon* who have come away from it with the feeling that, in the end, Gletkin's arguments are so irrefutable that Koestler has acted as a kind of devil's advocate who has succeeded in making the bad cause appear the good.

To feel this is only to acknowledge the nightmare quality, the Alice-in-Wonderland kind of reality, with which Koestler has endowed his novel. This feeling is intensified by the admirable economy of detail with which its physical context is portrayed; the huge beehive of a prison, with its two thousand prisoners, each thinking his own thoughts in the solitary confinement of his own cell and each equally exposed at any moment to physical mutilation or final extinction; its long corridors where the lights forever burn nakedly and dimly and the silence is only broken by the shuffling of a jailor's shoes, the clanging of cell gates and the screams of those who are tortured in the night; it is as if one had been admitted to some vast laboratory designed to strip the skin from the flesh of its human guinea pigs and expose to pitiless examination their raw and bleeding nerves.

All this is admirably suggested; but despite the screams of the victims, the whimpering cries in the night, it is not physical brutality which Koestler dwells on, but the torture which can be inflicted by ideas, of which physical brutality is a consequence. One of the triumphs of the novel, and one which is very rarely achieved in fiction, is to make ideas living, real and actual as if they were as vital to those who thought them as the circulation of the blood. It is also a part of its horror that in it ideas are so deeply imbued with the smell and taste of blood; but it also offers a saving grace by which, perhaps, their stain can be washed away.

Proust says that it takes a very long time for a truly original work of art to be properly understood, and certainly, in the case of *Darkness at Noon*, there was a long delay before the full significance of the novel was realized. Indeed, it required a world war, and the profound changes it brought about in political attitudes in the West, before men's minds became receptive to what it had to say. By the end of the war the hidden contradiction between the aims of the Soviet Union and those of its allies had already begun to make itself felt, and after the war the Soviet Union and the indigenous Communist parties of liberated Europe showed that the nature and the methods of Communism were indeed such as Koestler had described them in *Darkness at Noon*. For the first time, Western countries learned by bitter experience what it was to live under Communist rule, and it confirmed in every detail the terrible picture which Koestler had drawn in his novel.

Within the Soviet sphere of influence, Communism became the permanent way of life of the countries to which No. 1 had extended his dictatorship, but even beyond it, for a short time, Communist parties, and the partisan armies which they had inherited from the resistance movements, secured a monopoly of power over large areas; it is true to say that they exercised that power in a way which would have earned the complete approval of a Gletkin and did earn them the detestation of those who suffered under it.

In France, in the period immediately following the liberation, the Communist Party, and the resistance groups it controlled, for a short time enjoyed a liberty of action which they used to carry out, wherever possible, a ruthless purge of their opponents. *Darkness at Noon* was published there in 1946, when it was still doubtful whether General de Gaulle would succeed in establishing himself as the effective ruler of France, and the result of the forthcoming referendum on the French Constitution was in the balance. It was this situation which explains the immediate and spectacular success of the French translation of the novel, which sold over 400,000 copies and broke all pre-war publishing records in France. There were some who claimed that the novel had a decisive influence on the Communist defeat in the referendum.

Since that time *Darkness at Noon* has established itself as one of the essential documents of the political life of our time, and it has maintained that position in spite, or perhaps because of, the immense increase in recent years in our knowledge of the particular period of Russian history with which it is concerned. But *Darkness at Noon* does not only refer to the past; it has had the peculiar distinction of appearing to predict and influence the future, as if even Communists had accepted it as a scenario by which to direct their behaviour.

Some fifteen years after the Great Purge, there took place in Prague a re-enactment of the drama which was played out in Moscow in the thirties; and the imitation repeated with a sickening fidelity the details both of the original and of the account given of it in *Darkness at Noon*. Indeed, by a strange concatenation of events in which nature seemed to imitate art, at one point it appeared as if Rubashov himself had returned to life to repeat the message of the novel.

The culmination of the purge in Czechoslovakia was the trial in 1952 of Rudolf Slansky, general secretary of the Czech Communist Party, Vlado Clementis, the Foreign Secretary, and twelve other defendants, who all duly confessed to the charges falsely brought against them and were condemned to death or life imprisonment. Among the accused was Koestler's friend and former colleague in the 'Muenzenberg trust', Otto Katz, alias André Simon; his public confession of guilt was an ironic parody of Rubashov's final speech at his trial, which in turn was a repetition of Bukharin's confession in 1938. Simon's last words were: 'I ... belong to the gallows. The only service I can still render is to serve as a warning example to all who by origin or character are in danger of following the same path to hell. The sterner the punishment...' At this point his voice became inaudible. According to

Koestler, Simon's parody of Rubashov was both an indication, for those who could understand, of the falsity of his 'confession', and perhaps a last desperate appeal to his friends outside Czechoslovakia to organize the kind of rescue operation by which he and Muenzenberg had helped to save Koestler's life in Spain.

It was not only Simon's confession which recalled *Darkness at Noon*. Our knowledge of the proceedings in, and the preparations for, the Slansky trial has by now been greatly enlarged as a result of information published during Czechoslovakia's tragic bid for freedom in the summer of 1968; some of that information has been summarized in an article entitled, significantly enough, 'Koestler Revisited', and introduced by a quotation from the Czech historian, Jaroslav Orpat: 'A remarkable novel exists, known all over the world except in our country, the novel *Darkness at Noon* by Arthur Koestler, which accurately describes the mechanism of the Soviet trials in the second half of the thirties, the logic of the interrogators, the judges, the prosecutors and the accused, who themselves become the collaborators of the investigators and the prosecution ... The most tragic thing is that a decade later these events repeated themselves with the force of a natural law.'

A natural law; the phrase emphasizes that *Darkness at Noon* not only describes a particular stage in the development of the Soviet Union, but is also an analysis of certain essential features of Communism wherever it establishes itself in power. It is a story of the past which remains valid in the present and foreshadows the future. 'Koestler Revisited' also emphasizes that the use of terror as a political instrument is not an exclusively 'Russian' phenomenon but is applied with equal ruthlessness wherever Communism judges it necessary. Indeed, it shows that, if anything, Koestler has understated rather than exaggerated its merciless inhumanity. All the weapons in the armoury of a Gletkin were applied to the victims of the Slansky trial. They were held without trial in solitary confinement. They were beaten into insensibility. They were subjected to arbitrary and bizarre methods of punishment that disorientated them in time and space. They were exposed to starvation and alternations of intense cold and intense heat. Their personality was disintegrated by the use of hallucinatory drugs and forms of degradation designed to reduce them to the status of animals; they were placed in Kafkaesque situations created in order to induce a sense of the unreal and the absurd.

Reading of such experiences, one can do no more than repeat Kurtz's exclamation after his reversion to savagery in Conrad's *Heart of Darkness*: 'Oh, the horror ... the horror!', and it is this same sense of a vast and unnameable evil which one feels in reading *Darkness at Noon*. What is remarkable is that Koestler achieves this effect, not by dwelling on physical horrors, but by exposing the moral evil which it reflects. It is an effect, not of documentation, but of art. The physical horrors occur in the honeycombed cells and corridors which lie beyond Rubashov's field of vision between his prison bars. The screams in the night go unheard; it was precisely the triumph of *Darkness at Noon* that it made the world listen to them.

Darkness at Noon, says Koestler, was the second in a cycle of four books devoted to examining the morality of revolutionary ethics. The first was *The Gladiators*; the third and fourth were *Arrival and Departure* and *The Yogi and the Commissar*. With the completion of the cycle, Koestler turned away from the problems of political morality which had been the main inspiration of his writing, as if he had exhausted the subject by the very intensity of his experience and by the finality of his rejection of Communism both in theory and in practice. Thereafter, his main interest has been in science, which has inspired a long succession of books. It is worth noticing, however, that despite his withdrawal from politics and the reversal of interests which it involved, there is, in one respect at least, a marked continuity between his early and his later works; just as, indeed, his later writings are inspired by a revival of the scientific interests which were so important to him in childhood and youth, before politics ever touched him.

For in our day, it is not only totalitarian political systems which threaten, or deny, the existence of that 'grammatical fiction', the self, which forced itself into Rubashov's consciousness while in prison. It is equally threatened, or dispensed with, by forms of scientific thinking which refuse to take cognizance of any experiences which cannot be quantified, and, more especially in the field of experimental psychology, reject the hypothesis that there is anything in human nature which cannot be identified by the normal processes of scientific observation and, potentially, cannot be changed as a result of scientific research.

There are indeed Neanderthalers of the laboratory as well as of the torture chamber, inspired by the same 'vivisection morality' as Gletkin. Koestler's later writings have been very largely an attempt to defend the claims of the 'grammatical fiction' against those types of scientific thought which regard it as no more than an unnecessary hypothesis and human beings as no more than a collection of sense data. In essence, this is the same problem with which Rubashov wrestled in his cell; and it is because of his final, even though reluctant, awareness of the 'grammatical fiction' as a hypothesis without which human life ceases to have any meaning or value, that *Darkness at Noon* is not only a terrible vision of evil, but a vision also of the sources through which the evil may ultimately be exorcised.

MARK LEVENE

Arthur Koestler: On Messiahs and Mutations

We have Jehovah in our blood. We can't help it.
After all these centuries Jehovah lives in our
darkness like a worm in the intestines.
—Green, *The Honorary Consul*

The pre-eminent Cold War personality of the Forties, Arthur Koestler has been pronounced intellectually dead a number of times since he withdrew from political debate into what has seemed an increasingly idiosyncratic fascination with science. He was so completely identified with Europe's aborted revolutionary hopes and their bleak reflection in *Darkness at Noon* that when he began to claim prominence as a psychological and evolutionary theorist, many readers, particularly his admirers, could not make the transition with ease. In a review of *The Ghost in the Machine* (1967), Koestler's grim diagnosis of man's innate "schizophysiology," Leslie Fiedler remarks that the title is "terrifyingly apt" because Koestler, once an indispensable teacher and guide to the illusions of the Thirties, "is, and has long been, a ghost: the ghost of a man who died when his god failed."[1] Because he assumes that Koestler's "god" was finally buried by the German-Soviet Pact of 1939, Professor Fiedler fails to see that a distinct, if ungraceful, line extends from the early political novels to the encyclopaedic works on science.

From *Modernist Studies: Literature & Culture 1920–1940* 2, no. 2 (1977). © 1977 by the University of Alberta.

At least a segment of this line corresponded to the experience of many other intellectuals in Europe and America during the early Thirties. For Koestler as for Spender and Auden, Romain Rolland and Malraux, Malcolm Cowley and Sidney Hook, liberalism was ethically bankrupt, bourgeois society was disintegrating daily, and Communism was the solitary power capable of eradicating Fascist brutality from the future of mankind. However, analyses of this kind were rational and therefore, Koestler insists, generally secondary to Communism's ultimate appeal as a coherent doctrine and faith. Silone and Spender have also stressed the mystical, devout, congregational feelings evoked by the Party, and Orwell completes his indictment of the Marxist poets of the Thirties by declaring: "It was simply something to believe in. Here was a church, an army, an orthodoxy, a discipline.... All the loyalties and superstitions that the intellect had seemingly banished could come rushing back under the thinnest of disguises."[2]

If there was a profound religious quality in the revolutionary fervour of the period, then for a time Koestler was indeed, as he has frequently claimed, a "typical" member of the Continental intelligentsia. But Communism, although obviously his most intense and durable commitment, was only one expression of his "absolutitis," one incarnation of what Nicola Chiaromonte calls the "utopian will" inherent in radical zealotry.[3] Well before Koestler decided that Communism was civilization's remaining hope, he was emotionally predisposed to accept an all-embracing ideology. He had already experienced the brief excitement of Bela Kun's revolutionary government in Hungary and in the Twenties had gone to Palestine supported by nothing more than a belief in the messianic vision of Zionism.

In his autobiography Koestler pictures himself with pride and defensiveness as "a Casanova of Causes," a rebel, an enthusiast, though not a fanatic, and sees the origin of his utopian obsession in the secularism of Western culture:

> It was the same quest and the same all-or-nothing mentality which drove me to the Promised Land and into the Communist Party. In other ages aspirations of this kind found their natural fulfilment in God. Since the end of the eighteenth century the place of God has been vacant in our civilisation; but during the ensuing century and a half so many exciting things were happening that people were not aware of it. Now, however, after the shattering catastrophes which have brought the Age of Reason and Progress to a close, the void has made itself felt. The epoch in which I grew up was an age of disillusions and an age of longing.[4]

This description accounts for the initial phase of Koestler's intellectual life, but we must understand that his entire career has been dominated by a succession of failed and reconstructed social gods. The same quest and temperament led him from Communism to his visionary socialism of the war years, from politics and art to the world of science. Although Koestler's bitter intimacy with the Marxian Zion did not destroy his utopianism, it produced a fervid independence which he has nurtured for thirty years and which too often he has transformed into polymathic eccentricity or arrogance.

Because of this independence, he did not draw upon a conventional religious ideology to help him overcome his disillusionment with the Communist Party, nor has he found much social value in existing forms of meditative release. The moral re-location from the Commissar to the Yogi position which other writers sought in escaping the Thirties appalled him. Their easy recovery from the psychological blows inflicted by Stalinism represented to him an unforgivable betrayal of intellectual responsibility. Koestler subsequently took the much-travelled route to the East, but returned to argue in *The Lotus and the Robot* (1960) that "both India and Japan seem to be spiritually sicker, more estranged from a living faith than the West" (p. 276). Caught between his rejection of precast ideologies and the impossibility of withdrawing from the public world into the private byways of the psyche, Koestler's remarkable solution was to design his own doctrines, a compulsion that has made him perhaps the purest, certainly the most tenacious, ideologue of faith in our time.

There are both heroic and lamentable elements in his career as novelist-turned-natural philosopher. For almost half a century he has relentlessly pursued an understanding of the human condition, and we respond with startled admiration to his fierce sense of public involvement. He changed languages, forms of writing, and despite acute frustrations, he has continued to insist that his perceptions could help mankind recognize its great splendours of creativity and its more prevalent diseases. Of his contemporaries only Koestler has fought for a strategic position in the glare of the world's future redemption. Malraux withdrew into personal style and the patronage of de Gaulle; Silone returned to an unmilitant piety; and Orwell died leaving generations in fear of his vision. Our admiration for Koestler's utopian confidence is shaded with considerable regret, however. By allowing his personal messianism to develop unchecked, he relinquished the literary power intrinsic to his first novels, *The Gladiators* and *Darkness at Noon*, that rare balance of imagination and morality which marks their enduring value as political art. Spartacus and Rubashov are Koestler's objectively conceived messianic figures; through them he explores the essentially religious basis of revolutionary commitment. In the Forties, however, as the political situation in Europe accelerated through the war with Germany to the menace of Soviet expansionism, Koestler's perception of ideological faith gave way to the intense need for his own secular belief, a need that has continued to erupt not as art, but as varieties of prophecy, an almost unending series of discourses on new faiths, ethical changes, and evolutionary mutations.

But there are no suggestions of prophetic urgency in *The Gladiators* (1939). Important as the novel was for the growth of Koestler's political understanding, it has remained among the least didactic of his works. Unlike Howard Fast and J. Leslie Mitchell in their renderings of the Slave Revolt, Koestler never allows Spartacus to speak as though he were at the Finland station. Although analogies with Stalin's "revolution from above" become intrusive at points, for most of the novel Spartacus is an integral part of an authentic pre-Christian world drawn with great attention to the imaginative use of historical detail. But it is a world and a social upheaval with significant implications for an understanding of revolutionary ethics throughout history.

Although Spartacus exhibits a degree of egalitarianism in his appeals to the Italian peasantry, his first concern is the survival of his army. But when he encounters an Essene who addresses him as the "liberator of slaves, leader of the disinherited" (p. 68) and recounts prophecies of the coming of "One like the Son of man" (p. 69), Spartacus suddenly takes his place in the "gigantic relay race" (p. 76) which, the novel suggests, includes Plato, Saint-Just, Lenin, and Koestler himself. Always "one man stands up and receives the Word, and rushes on his way with the great wrath in his bowels" (p. 76). For Koestler, "the Word" is not the Logos, but a process of anointment, of conversion, by which a thoroughly secular messiah is initiated into a utopian quest. The "Word" may be the Essene's cryptic stories, the *Communist Manifesto*, or it may be Koestler's own ethical testaments as they appear in *Arrival and Departure* and *The Ghost in the Machine*.

Like the French and Russian members of the great revolutionary family, Spartacus has embraced a belief in mankind's age-old ideal of equality, tolerance, and freedom. But his utopian adventure is similarly doomed because of what the novel views as the inexorable "law of detours" (p. 130), the necessity of violence and expediency. Koestler ascribes the entire collapse of the revolution to the refusal by Spartacus to order the massacre of a dissident tribe. In fact, the gladiator's failure was his inability to translate his own messianic feelings into a doctrine, a new religion, his followers could share. On the other hand, his clear success was in the realm of the political imagination. As the Essene prophesied, he has become a parable in the mythological structure of revolution. Nicolai Rubashov, Koestler's next moral courier, became a haunting figure within history itself.

Darkness at Noon (1940), Koestler's masterful novel about the consequences of revolutionary faith, prompted its readers to reaffirm or alter their own beliefs concerning the nature of politics and human behavior. In 1946 the French translation, *Le Zéro et l'Infini*, encountered the kind of social "ripeness" Koestler later theorized about in *The Sleepwalkers*, but which he would never again experience.[5] In the context of the power held by the postwar French Communist Party, his portrait of an Old Bolshevik's confession to fabricated charges during the Moscow Trials divided families, provoked hard-line Stalinists to malicious attacks on Koestler's personality, and compelled the non-Communist philosopher, Maurice Merleau-Ponty, to an impassioned rebuttal of the novel. Although decades later the reactions it elicits are no longer so intense, *Darkness at Noon* is still the subject of historical controversy. Whereas Solzhenitsyn claims that the novel is an accurate reflection of the Purge, especially Bukharin's part in it, Stephen Cohen argues in his political biography of Bukharin that Rubashov has absolutely no historical validity.[6]

But however one regards the Trials, the novel itself apart from any external frame of reference affords an understanding of Rubashov's confession and the quality of mind he cannot repudiate. In essence, his doubts about the infallibility of a Party led by "No. 1," his fragmentary sense of conscience and selfhood, are insufficient to destroy the forty years he has devoted to the Revolution's secular messianism, too frail to erode the rationalistic habits of mind through which his faith becomes calcified. Though in speaking about the Party Rubashov alternated between mathematical terms and the language of religion, the goal he had given his identity to was not economic reorganization, but an earthly Land of Promise. Yet since man cannot lead himself or recognize the true good, he must "be driven through the desert" and prevented from "worshipping golden calves" (p. 100). With this justification Rubashov sent dissident Party members to their death, acquiesced in the execution of one who loved him, and accepted policies which betrayed the selfless commitment of other believers.[7]

While Rubashov's religious allusions suggest a militant, coercive faith, he is ultimately judged by a different kind of belief—a gentle morality, a compassionate grasp of human suffering represented by the *Pietà* he glimpsed on a mission in Germany, by his brief acquaintance with his silent, inner self, and primarily embodied by the old porter who served under Rubashov in the Civil War. When Vassilij hears the official account of the trial, the two objects he worships, a greasy, tattered Bible and a now forbidden portrait of Rubashov, merge in his mind: "And the soldiers led him away, into the hall called Praetorium … and they smote him on the head with a reed and did spit upon him; and bowing their knees worshipped him" (pp.

235–36). Out of compassion and love he identifies Rubashov with the suffering Christ; however, Rubashov's Christ is the heart of the Party's unyielding body: "The old man with the slanting Tartar eyes ... was revered as God-the-Father, and No. 1 as the Son ... From time to time No. 1 reached out for a new victim amongst them. Then they all beat their breasts and repented in chorus of their sins" (p. 64). Symbolizing contradictory beliefs, these images of Christ mirror the static nature of Rubashov's situation. Dominated by his intellectual rigidity, he can do no more than isolate his rudimentary conscience and repent as his past and No. 1 demand.

Because Rubashov has habitually subordinated all personal feeling to his devout rationalism, the "philosophy" of logical consequence, he must now restrict his guilt-ridden memories to an isolated level of consciousness. They are imprisoned in his mind just as he is encaged in the unfathomable mind of No. 1 and the mysteries of historical process. Once he has, by confessing, bound himself again to the Revolution, Rubashov returns to the silent partner, the voice of his hidden emotions, and frees it from the purity to which it was condemned. He devotes his last living hours to the questions it raises about the suffering created by the Party's messianism, but his thinking is still dependent on syllogistic patterns and hypothetical propositions.[8] Like his maker, Rubashov finds little solace in a clumsily immediate liberalism and looks to the future for a new moral energy:

> Perhaps later, much later, the new movement would arise—with new flags, a new spirit knowing of both: of economic fatality *and* the "oceanic sense". Perhaps the members of the new party will wear monks' cowls, and preach that only purity of means can justify the ends. Perhaps they will teach that the tenet is wrong which says that a man is the product of one million divided by one million, and will introduce a new kind of arithmetic based on multiplication: on the joining of a million individuals to form a new entity (p. 249).

Unlike his character, Koestler has yet to find relief from the burden of this frail compelling hope.

At least in the first years after his separation from the Party Koestler could respond with largely unimpeded imagination to his narrative subjects. At this time the messianic revolutionary was a perception of political behaviour in an externalized world, not a mirror image of Koestler himself reflecting on an indefinite, but desperately needed future perfection. One reason he was able to approach his first novels with relative detachment was the sense of exhilaration he experienced in creating and pursuing his own mental structures after years of intellectually rigid propaganda work. Yet this imaginative freedom was itself possible because his political isolation was by no means total.[9] Consciously or not, he transformed the religious fervour of his Communism into an emotional, diffuse belief in the development of a revitalized, independent socialist movement which in the early Forties he saw as the only force capable of reviving "the values on which Western civilisation is based" ("Illusion," *Yogi*, p. 201). He argued that the violent betrayals of the socialist ideal by the Soviet "vanguard" did not preclude progressive action in Europe, but the kind of action he envisaged was necessarily vague. The Left had to "wean" itself from spiritual contact with Communist ideology, then create "a new fraternity in a new spiritual climate, whose leaders are tied by a vow of poverty to share the life of the masses, and debarred by the laws of fraternity from attaining unchecked power" ("Illusion," *Yogi*, p. 204). While his arguments clarify his distance from conservative politics in the war years, the religious note of this rhapsodic untheoretical programme originally sounded by Rubashov also marks his first movement away from historical concreteness.

In *Humanism and Terror* (1947), Merleau-Ponty justifiably accused Koestler of being "a mediocre Marxist."[10] On a philosophical level Koestler is an equally mediocre socialist. But the reason for this is neither the frailty of his intelligence nor Merleau-Ponty's clinically byzantine view that "for fear of having to forgive, he prefers not to understand" (p. 167). He has simply never been concerned with the precise intricacies of a theoretical system. Whatever the area of debate—politics, psychology, biochemistry— and however lucid or misconceived his analyses are, Koestler ultimately measures every structure for its secular redemptive value. In his work after *Darkness at Noon* we are not, again in Merleau-Ponty's terms, "dealing with a philosophy in retreat" (p. 164), but rather with incantations in the form of literature or scientific discourse. If anything, it is philosophy in a constant state of millennial anticipation. Unlike Dr. Johnson he does not kick the rock of human experience, and unlike Sisyphus he does not push it. Averting an apocalyptic shadow, Koestler jumps from stone to stone, believing all the time that each gap is a grace he is about to see. He ends his diagnosis of socialism with an assertion worthy of *The Possessed*:

> The age of enlightenment has destroyed faith in personal survival; the scars of this operation have never healed. There is a vacancy in every living soul, a deep thirst in all of us. If the socialist idea cannot fill this vacancy and quench our thirst, then it has failed in our time. In this case the whole development of the socialist idea since the French Revolution has been merely the

end of a chapter in history, and not the beginning of a new one ("Illusion," *Yogi*, p. 204).

Inevitably, his hopes for a regenerate, messianic socialism were uprooted by reality. "If ever there was a chance for socialism in Britain, it was in the period from Dunkirk to the fall of Tobruk.... This was only a link in the chain of socialism's missed opportunities" ("Fraternity," *Yogi*, p. 102). The uninspired pragmatic character of the postwar Labour Government would add yet another link but in 1943, before his disillusionment with the Left was complete, he was already forming an ethical alternative. After enumerating the repeated failures of the socialist movement in Europe, Koestler then expresses the belief, which he admits some readers may find "crankish," "that the day is not far when the present interregnum will end, and a new global ferment will arise—not a new party or sect, but an irresistible global mood, a spiritual spring-tide like early Christianity or the Renaissance" ("Fraternity," *Yogi*, pp. 103-104). The nature of this force is even more elusive than Koestler's almost mystical socialism. He restricts the announcement to the feeling that "the new movement will re-establish the disturbed balance between rational and spiritual values" and will not lead to Huxley's Brave New World ("Fraternity," *Yogi*, p. 104). Koestler was initially wary of placing too much hope in this prophecy, but it reshaped his role as a novelist nevertheless. When it became clear to him that the Left was incapable of an essential transformation, the notion of a new moral energy grew to dominate his imagination and eventually drove him to the biochemical prescriptions in *The Ghost in the Machine*.

The unequal battle between the prophet and the novelist begins in *Arrival and Departure* (1943). At the expense of both narrative and intellectual coherence, Koestler directs the central figure, in whom he invests considerable personal feeling, towards a new god, a new age in the life of the human race. But before Peter Slavek reaches this apotheosis, he undergoes a process of strict Freudian therapy which reveals that his revolutionary commitment and even his heroic silence under torture were efforts to expiate the childhood guilt he incurred in trying to blind his infant brother. The novel suggests a limited endorsement of the orthodox Freudianism represented by Sonia, Peter's Junoesque analyst; Peter's unhealthy interest in boat-hooks clearly drives him to search for atonement through extreme political action. However, prompted no doubt by his own spiritual pursuit and urgent claims on the future, Koestler must reject not only Sonia's insistence that moral beliefs are "mere pretexts of the mind, phantoms of a more intimate reality" (p. 119), but also her dogmatic identification of this "reality" with neurotic motives. Just as Peter is about to leave an embattled

Europe to join his lover in America, he suddenly casts the meticulous therapy aside and rushes to enlist at the British Consulate. Much to the consternation of Koestler's readers at the time, particularly Orwell, the threat Fascism poses to civilization is not the novel's overriding concern, even though Peter has actually witnessed the slaughter of aged Jews. Through Peter's intuitive compulsion Koestler affirms that transcendence and faith are inherent in man and cannot be reduced by a rationalist system of explanation.

Because both the source and goal of Peter's newly perceived realm of faith are highly ambiguous, Koestler depends upon a concentration of symbols to refute Sonia's mocking reduction of the messianic temperament. Peter is not even allowed the semblance of a rational decision. He hears the "call" (p. 155) of a new priesthood and an enigmatic redeemer, receives his "sign," and embraces "the invisible cross" (p. 177) which appears to him in a dream and which is no longer the emblem of the messianic revolutionary as we have known him in Koestler's earlier novels. It will become visible only with the emergence of the "global ferment" Koestler has prophesied. Just before Peter is flown behind the lines of his own country, he announces the imminent arrival of "a new god" (p. 188) and speaking as one of Koestler's fraternity of short-term pessimists, hopes that somehow, parachuting through the night, he is assisting in its birth. What he is not permitted to realize, however, is that he is going to land in precisely the area of his country where he had watched the Jews being gassed. This striking lapse of memory eliminates an accessible morality and is the ultimate indication the novel provides of how attached Koestler has become to his recent religious intimation.

His more mundane hope in 1943 was that after the war Europe would have "a breathing space of perhaps a couple of decades, with at least a chance of averting the next fatal plunge" ("Knights," *Yogi*, p. 97). But Soviet expansionism severely restricted this possibility and, in his view, threatened to suffocate Europe as a whole. Political malaise or impending anarchy confronted him throughout Western Europe. It was increasingly difficult to hold to the advice he had given Peter Slavek and himself, the most notable members of the "fraternity": to renounce "radical solutions" and await, without despair, "the first signs of the new global movement" (*Yogi*, p. 105). For a while the situation in Palestine helped to relieve Koestler's scrutiny of the horizon. Survival for the Jews meant nationhood, not the delivery of a new god, and political action could be limited and decisive without involving questions of ideology or mysterious currents of historical change.

The impulses behind his renewed involvement in Zionism were an uneven mixture of frustration with Europe's lack of spiritual energy, a persistent hostility towards ghetto-bred "Jewishness," and simple horror at the success of the Nazi concentration camps. Yet he did not reaffirm the messianic Zionism of his youth; in 1945 his expectations were "limited, resigned, and utilitarian" (*Writing*, p. 462). Palestine presented the only hope for the survival of the displaced and brutalized Jews of Europe. Koestler's main weapon in arguing the case for partition was *Thieves in the Night* (1946), his most avowedly propagandistic novel. A rambling documentary-like narrative, it chronicles the building of a communal settlement and in an apparent reversal of his earlier attitudes to political violence portrays the necessity of selective Jewish terrorism. Koestler insists that faced with British indifference and Arab violence, Palestinian Jews were driven to "the ethics of survival" (*Thieves*, Postscript, p. 335). Although morally disquieting, *Thieves in the Night* is Koestler's most relaxed work of fiction. In its scope, its unworried techniques, the novel displays none of the ideological solipsism that constrains his narratives of redemption. He was only temporarily sharing his characters' nationalistic aspirations and knew that the role of prophet was inappropriate to the struggle in the Holy Land.

But Koestler immediately turned to challenge the "moral insanity" of postwar France and with an often terrible violence of feeling narrowed his prophetic outlook ("Virtue," *Trail*, p. 25). With its powerful Communist Party and influential fellow-travellers France, the country where he had felt most at home during the Thirties, was close to an upheaval which would resound throughout Europe. The only hope for liberty, he maintained, was the unqualified acceptance by the French of American support, an attitude which the leftist intelligentsia found repugnant. Despite the remarkable effect *Darkness at Noon* had on French political opinion in 1946, his personal experience there was a lacerating failure. The Paris "mandarins" he was most concerned to persuade would not accept his prophecies. They declined to choose between Russia and America and, unlike Koestler, they still saw literature as socially valuable. Under the pressure of what must have been intolerable frustration and disillusionment, Koestler wrote *The Age of Longing* (1951), a startling document which vilifies Europe's spiritual emptiness, its moral vulnerability, and with Rubashov only a dim memory pays a bitter tribute to Stalinist zeal.

The Age of Longing is less a novel than a series of uncontrolled mental projections, a prolonged rite of exorcism and compulsive revenge. Although he attempts to parody notable leftists like Merleau-Ponty, de Beauvoir, and of course Sartre pictured as the creator of "neo-nihilism," "a piquant technique of intellectual masturbation" (p. 207), Koestler's more effective though repellent weapon is the language of disease. He victimizes his characters with a bizarre recurrence of tics, scars, unhealthy skin, limps, heavy legs, incongruous eyes, oily mouths, and foul breath, all of which seem designed to prove a Cold War neoplatonism, that the faithless are unworthy of physical dignity. Julien is the character with the greatest assortment of afflictions and he argues, as Koestler does later in *The Ghost in the Machine*, that the nature of one's faith is the primary question, that it is preferable to have no belief than to be committed to a brutal or illusory creed.

But it is Hydie, an ex-Catholic, who voices Koestler's desperate feeling in the late Forties that any faith is stronger, hence better, than spiritual vacuity. Her affair with Nikitin, an ideologically and sexually potent (Soviet) Commonwealth agent, not only confirms this proposition, but is also meant to demonstrate that Communism is the regrettably legitimate heir of the church militant. When Hydie reflects on her first orgasm with Nikitin, she realizes that the only other man who she instinctively knew could bring her to physical climax was her confessor at the convent. Nikitin serves the brutal Stalinist God, but since he is the only figure Koestler is prepared to recognize as capable of impersonal devotion, he escapes the metaphorical degradation inflicted on all the other characters. Neither the Son of man nor midwife for a shapeless deity, Nikitin is the embodiment of pure faith divorced from a humane messianic purpose by Koestler's own bleak longings and hatreds.

Since faith bestows on the devotee the aura of Christ and the mark of Cain, Koestler could never bring himself to give his unrepentant Parisian leftists the stature of being included among the honourable faithful. Instead, they displayed symptoms of political "masochism," "nymphomania," and sectarian "incest," aberrations that produced a dangerous "moral insanity."[11] Koestler initially voiced his concern about a clinical insanity inherent in the structure of the human brain a few years before his encounters with the French intelligentsia ("Anatomy," *Yogi*, pp. 109-111). The "perversions" of their world expanded and strengthened his diagnosis. In *The Age of Longing* Julien says almost triumphantly:

> Have you ever doubted that a hundred years hence they will discover that we have all been insane—not metaphorically, but in the literal, clinical sense? Has it never occurred to you that when poets talk about the madness of homo sapiens they are making not a poetical but a medical statement? It wouldn't be nature's first blunder either—think of the dinosaur. A neurologist told me the other day that in all probability the snag lies somewhere in the connections between the forebrain and the interbrain. To be precise, our species suffers from endemic schizophrenia … Our misfitted brain leads us a dance on a permanent witches' sabbath. If you are an optimist, you are free to believe that some

day some biological mutation will cure the race. But it seems infinitely more probable that we shall go the way of the dinosaur (p. 365).

After sixteen years of attempting to reconcile his incurable optimism with the very clear shadow of the dinosaur on human history, this passage ultimately developed into *The Ghost in the Machine*. Equally important, though, is the relation of his own passions to Julien's announcement. As a man of faith, perhaps Koestler found immunity in associating madness with what he believed at the time was modern man's crippling lack of spiritual fervour. Yet it is startling that even a growing assurance of racial insanity did not give him pause to reflect upon his impulse to condemn, mutilate, and brutalize the godless.

To meet the world's moral recalcitrance, Koestler made an essential alteration in his view of the future. As Julien's medical report suggests, around 1950 he began to think in terms of "a biological stimulus ... which will release the new mutation of human consciousness" ("Dilemma," *Trail*, p. 194). The process of change he foresaw remained spontaneous, but as a "mutation" was clearly more difficult and involved transitions on levels different from the smooth arrival of "an irresistible global mood." In "The Trail of the Dinosaur" (1955), his first extensive discussion of this modified belief, Koestler tries to explain what he means by mutations of consciousness or interest, but by limiting himself to instances from social history the analysis diminishes once again to the rhythms of prophetic hopefulness. His main example is the shift in the seventeenth century from religious to national consciousness and the emergence of the new philosophy. A mutation, in this context, is a modification in all essential patterns of individual and social existence, but our understanding is unsettled by Koestler's insistence on the necessity of purposeful hierarchical change. The new mutation, harmonizing human reason and "cosmic awareness" (p. 251), must be a movement to a higher plane of life; however, in its present from the cultural evidence from the past cannot justify such an assumption. Koestler himself implies as much in his grief over the spiritual impoverishment which has endured since the time of Galileo and Newton (pp. 247–48).

Whether or not Koestler was fully aware of this logical problem, he began to formulate a solution by transferring his energies from man's moral future to the history of science. The general argument of *The Sleepwalkers* (1959) is that scientific progress is neither linear nor constant. "The philosophy of nature evolved by occasional leaps and bounds alternating with delusional pursuits, *culs-de-sac*, regressions, periods of blindness and amnesia" (p. 513). The momentous fertile discoveries were "mutant" theories "selected" by the needs of their particular age; "among the multitude of new concepts which emerge only those survive which are well adapted to the period's intellectual *milieu*" (p. 515). According to Mark Graubard, Koestler's approach has been invaluable to contemporary historians of science.[12] What concerns us here, though, is less the book's objective merit than its strategic importance for Koestler's momentarily dormant sense of mission.

The concept of creative mutations not only liberated him from a strictly hierarchical perspective on social evolution, it also meant that given certain "pre-conditions," such as the "ripeness" of the times (p. 519), a new phase in man's development could arise spontaneously assisted by the necessary vision and visionary. Because *Darkness at Noon* became part of French political history and *Thieves in the Night* influenced members of a United Nations Commission deliberating the future of Palestine, Koestler, more than most writers, succumbed to a belief in the world's malleability. Although the responsiveness of the age has remained beyond his control, the other requirement specified in *The Sleepwalkers* could be fulfilled through intellectual perseverance and moral devotion: "A new evolutionary departure is only possible after a certain amount of de-differentiation, a cracking and thawing of the frozen structures resulting from isolated, over-specialized development" (p. 518). If they have not yet prompted a change in social evolution, Koestler's syntheses of information from various regions of scientific theory and research are expressions of a remarkable temperament and reflect his conception of the creative act itself, a drawing together of previously unrelated "ideas, facts, frames of perceptions, associative contexts" (*Ghost*, p. 184).

It is not clear exactly when Koestler decided that the natural emergence of an ethical mutation was a flimsy hope and that only an artificial process to "supplant biological evolution" could retrieve mankind from the trail of the dinosaur (*Ghost*, p. 327). We cannot know, therefore, whether his trilogy on the "life sciences" was a carefully planned sequence of arguments designed to converge in the pharmaceutical cure proposed by *The Ghost in the Machine*. Nevertheless, it is evident that each volume leads inevitably to the next. The investigation of scientific discovery in *The Sleepwalkers* is followed by an exploration of the biological mechanisms fundamental to the artist, and having concluded *The Act of Creation* (1964) with the argument that the sources of imaginative structures "are in the phylogenetically and ontogenetically older, underground layers" of the mind (p. 659), Koestler proceeds to maintain in *The Ghost in the Machine* that man's paranoid, collectively murderous behaviour derives from the same neurological areas.

Furthermore, although these works represent a relentless accumulation of detail, his basic attitudes to the nature of creativity and man's endemic insanity were formed years earlier. *Insight and Outlook* (1949) is Koestler's preliminary analysis of the creative process, and his suspicion, or knowledge, that an evolutionary flaw in the structure of the brain is responsible for our madness dates at least from "Anatomy of a Myth" (c. 1944). In *Twilight Bar* (1945) he projects neurology into the cosmos. An extra-terrestrial creature comes to investigate Earth's right to survive in the universe and explains that "an evil curvature" (p. 26) splits the galaxy into distinct moral and immoral parts. The difference between this play and *The Ghost in the Machine* is strictly one of vocabulary. Whatever Koestler's design for his encyclopaedic trilogy was, the result, as Stephen Toulmin aptly described it, was a Manichean picture of all human endeavour.[13]

In *The Sleepwalkers* Kepler is the major figure in the portrait Koestler constructs of the scientific theorist as visionary, a creative being whose insights are evoked by irrational beliefs or intuitions, then confirmed by reason. This conception is central to *The Act of Creation* as well but is cast in ostensibly different terms. Here Koestler deploys an array of biological analogies to prove that such "regression" as Kepler displayed is inherent in all feats of the imagination. Every from of life, Koestler insists, is capable of responding to a "traumatic" challenge or crisis with the release of creative potentials. Under the pressure of damage to limb or brain, animals "return to a more youthful or primitive condition" (p. 455), then regenerate their structures and functions. Man exhibits this process of *reculer pour mieux sauter* (p. 461) chiefly in the sphere of the mind. Disturbed by a particular problem, the artist or scientist regresses from conscious levels to the psychological underworld, the older regions of the brain, but surfaces with at least the beginnings of a previously unknown solution or synthesis. These acts of "self-repair," Koestler says in *The Ghost in the Machine*, "result in biological or mental progress" (p. 173). Having equipped himself with the argument for ubiquitous, creative energies in nature, Koestler was prepared to confront mankind with its greatest challenge—the urgent need for an "adaptive mutation" (*Ghost*, p. 336), a secular grace translated into the language of science.

"Art is a school of self-transcendence; but so is a patriotic rally, a voodoo session, a war dance" (*Ghost*, p. 245). Out of the need to be part of something "higher," to share in the infinite, the artist and scientist evolve the great achievements of the race. But as Koestler has always known, man is more prone to murder than creativity. Only "the happy few" (*Ghost*, p. 242) are capable of a constructive return from the nether mind, of transforming their "transcendent" drives into imaginative splendour. Most people find satisfaction for their sense of "partness" in "primitive or perverted forms" of identification (p. 243), in such creeds as militant Christianty, the Millennial Reich, and Stalinism which thrive on man's delusional "immersion in the group mind" (p. 248). The crusader and rabid nationalist were earlier masks worn by the messianic Prometheus whose moral derangement is even more dangerous now since he possesses "power over life on the planet *as a whole*" (p. 322). In 1950 the alternative to an ethical mutation was the Soviet Army; here it is genosuicide.

Drawing extensively on Paul MacLean's research, Koestler presents a fuller diagnosis of our neurological disability than he did in *The Age of Longing*. Because of an evolutionary mistake in the co-ordination "between the phylogenetically old areas of our brain, and the new, specifically human areas" (p. 273), reason and awareness are at the mercy of primitive instinct. The fanatic's terrible achievement is the use of (neocortical) language to rationalize his complete regression into the affect-world of the old brain. The results are impervious, often brutal "closed systems" of belief (p. 263). From this perspective, Koestler's Zionism and Communism, his Rubashov and Sonia, are examples of clinical insanity. And in *The Call-Girls* (1972) Koestler suggests that even his plea for an induced reconciliation between faith and reason may also be tainted. But there is no self-conscious interruption in the messianic climax of *The Ghost in the Machine*. "Since we cannot in the foreseeable future expect the necessary change in human nature to arise by way of a spontaneous mutation," and since creative leaps are a universal principle of life, "we must induce it by artificial means" (pp. 326-27). In the Forties history offered little justification for the anticipated arrival of an emergent redemption; twenty years later the objective evidence was again absorbed by Koestler's sense of moral urgency. The modest conclusion his mentor, Paul MacLean, drew from the available data was the hope that education and improved communications will prevent us from choosing deranged political leaders.[14] But for Koestler in his prophetic vigil, the solution had to be less haphazard. He seems to have had no doubt that chemical tools would produce his long-sought mutation, not a monster worse than anything yet known.

Unnerving as this confidence is, one is inevitably saddened by the weary, defeated mood of *The Call-Girls*. Ostensibly an attack on learned meetings like the Alpbach Symposium Koestler chaired in 1968, the narrative is a muffled coda to *The Ghost in the Machine*. He distributes his major arguments between a psychologist and a neurosurgeon. During a conference called "Approaches to Survival" Harriet Empson declares that "loyalty and devotion ... make the fanatic" (p. 116), and Dr. Valenti discourses on man's endemic insanity (p. 143). But through these characters

Koestler trivializes his ideas and for the first time in his published work wonders aloud about the purity of his own moral passion. However exact her understanding of the human condition is, Harriet's inclinations are sexual not political, and her lesbianism is designed as symbolic proof of her personal inadequacy. Valenti is a Dr. Strangelove-figure whose equipment is faulty and whose experiments in controlling mental imbalance are dangerously prone to failure. Moreover, he is a pious though secret Catholic and therefore dominated by the primitivism of the "old brain." Solovief, who convened the conference out of despair for the plight of the world, endorses Valenti's argument for an "engineered" mutation, but asks himself: "Where had he gone off the rails? When he had let himself be carried away by the idea of 'biological tampering.' *If* there was a road to survival, it pointed in that direction. But did he really believe in that 'if?'" (p. 170). These doubts, the hesitation and sense of loss which pervade the novel, do not amount to a clear repudiation of *The Ghost in the Machine*. They represent a degree of unresolved disillusionment and mark yet another change of course in Koestler's intellectual life.

Blocked by the collusion of an unresponsive world and his personal uncertainties, Koestler has withdrawn from the "mutant" theory he devoted such immense efforts to construct. But he is still unwilling to retreat from the appeal of an ultimate vision. In *The Roots of Coincidence* (1972) we find him speaking of parapsychology "as the highest manifestation of the integrative potential of living matter" (p. 121), a pre-eminence he recently claimed for the creative process. A room dedicated to automatic dice and invisible cards is a meagre substitute for an earthly paradise. Too small to contain Rubashov's memories, it may unfortunately be large enough for Koestler's battered and diminished prophetic energies.

NOTES

1. Leslie Fiedler, "Towards the Freudian Pill," *New Statesman*, 74 (27 October, 1967), 549.

2. George Orwell, "Inside the Whale," *The Collected Essays, Journalism and Letters*, ed. Sonia Orwell and Ian Angus (London: Secker & Warburg, 1968), I, 515.

3. Nicola Chiaromonte, "Letter to Andrea Caffi," *The Worm of Consciousness and Other Essays*, ed. Miriam Chiaromonte (New York: Harcourt Brace, 1976), p. 202.

4. Arthur Koestler, *Arrow in the Blue* (1952; rpt. London: Hutchinson, 1969), p. 69. Page references and, where possible, abbreviated titles will appear in the essay. The texts used are in the Hutchinson Uniform Edition, except for the following: *The Age of Longing* (London: Collins, 1951), *Darkness at Noon*, tr. Daphne Hardy (London: Jonathan Cape, 1940), *Insight and Outlook* (Lincoln: University of Nebraska Press, 1949), *The Lotus and the Robot* (1960; rpt. New York: Macmillan, 1961), *The Trail of the Dinosaur & Other Essays* (London: Collins, 1955), *Twilight Bar* (London: Jonathan Cape, 1945).

5. See Koestler, *The Invisible Writing*, Ch. xxxvii and *The Sleepwalkers* pp. 519–20.

6. See Solzhenitsyn, *The Gulag Archipelago*, tr. Thomas P. Whitney (New York: Harper & Row, 1974), I–II, 412–19; and Stephen F. Cohen, *Bukharin and the Bolshevik Revolution* (New York: Vintage, 1975), p. 372.

7. Cf. Peter Axthelm, *The Modern Confessional Novel* (New Haven: Yale University Press), pp. 101-09.

8. Cf. Jenni Calder, *Chronicles of Conscience: A Study of George Orwell and Arthur Koestler* (London: Secker & Warburg, 1968), p. 129.

9. *Ibid.*, pp. 209–11.

10. *Humanism and Terror*, trans. John O'Neill (Boston: Beacon Press, 1969), p. 23.

11. "A Guide to Political Neuroses," *Trail*, p. 228 and "The Right to Say 'No,'" *Trail*, p. 201.

12. "*The Sleepwalkers*: Its Contribution and Impact," *Astride the Two Cultures: Arthur Koestler at 70*, ed. Harold Harris (London: Hutchinson, 1975), p. 32.

13. "The Book of Arthur," *The New York Review of Books*, 11 April, 1968, p. 20.

14. "The Paranoid Streak in Man," *Beyond Reductionism*, ed. Arthur Koestler and J. R. Smythies (1969; rpt. Boston: Beacon Press, 1971), p. 275.

SIDNEY A. PEARSON, JR.

Darkness at Noon

*D*arkness *at Noon* has been rightly recognized, both at the time of its original publication in 1941 and ever since, as one of the truly powerful works of twentieth century political literature. The passage of time has not in the least diminished its appeal. If anything, the novel has grown in stature because of the truth of its portrait of the ideological basis of totalitarian movements. The powerful combination of logic and passion make it a compelling masterpiece.

The central theme of *Darkness at Noon* is an exploration of the other side of the revolutionary dilemma discussed in *The Gladiators*—how and why revolutions fail when the end comes to dominate the means. Unlike the remote historical setting for *The Gladiators*, however, Koestler chose his own contemporary experience with the Russian Revolution and Communism as the basis for his novel. It reflects the fundamental tension in his own mind between thought and action and between ends and means. It must be understood that while he regards the revolution of the commissar as a failure, it does not follow that he regards the ethics of his opposite to be preferable. When a crucial decision must be made between the two, Koestler reluctantly casts his lot with the commissar. His critique of the commissar must therefore be viewed in this light.

Because *Darkness at Noon* is the best known and most influential of

From *Arthur Koestler*. © 1978 by Twayne Publishers.

Koestler's work it is also the most controversial and has provoked the greatest response, both favorable and unfavorable. An adequate discussion of the novel will therefore have to take into account both aspects—the argument of the novel itself, as well as the reaction to it. This chapter will focus on the novel and the final chapter will consider some of the controversy it has spawned.

I *The Structure of the Novel*

The setting for *Darkness at Noon* is dramatically different from that of *The Gladiators*. Rather than a remote historical background, it is set in the bureaucratic underworld of a modern revolutionary state. It is the world of the commissar made politically manifest. The question raised is still the same as in the first novel: why do revolutions fail? The answer still turns on the issue of ends and means, but here the revolution fails because the vision of the end is allowed to overshadow the means to that end. Could Spartacus' revolution have succeeded had he not followed the law of detours? Koestler's answer is "No."

The bureaucratic setting is Russia during the infamous Purge Trials of the 1930s. To much of the outside world, the purge of the old Bolsheviks was inexplicable, but to Koestler it reflected the inner logic of the revolutionary movement at its deepest level. What his novel did was to give to the trials a rational basis in the context of Marxist theory and practice that shocked and horrified its readers. Indeed, it is the very rationalism of the revolutionary terror that remains the true horror of *Darkness at Noon*. If the terror were irrational it would not be lacking in raw power, but would perhaps leave the impression that it could be tamed by reason. In the account by Koestler, however, the consequences of revolutionary logic may be deplored but the end result in no way alters the structure of its rationale. Who wills the end wills the means, Koestler says, and if you accept the commissar's vision of the end you cannot rationally refuse his means.

In *Darkness at Noon*, the reader's attention is directed toward the psychology of a single individual rather than the broad sweep of history that prevailed in *The Gladiators*. The effect of the change is to focus Koestler's points more sharply. But in the person of that single individual, Commissar Rubashov, the whole universe of revolutionary symbolism and theory is concentrated. His intellectual biography is the story of the revolution. In him all of the contradictions and consistancies of the ends-means dilemma find a home. In contrast with *The Gladiators*, there is very little physical action to distract attention from the theoretical argument.

The physical action of the novel is slight. It consists of the arrest, interrogation, trial, and execution of one Commissar Rubashov during the Moscow Purge Trials. Since the final fate of Rubashov is scarcely in doubt from the opening pages, the full attention of the reader is directed toward the reasons behind Rubashov's personal story rather than the fate of the particular individual. Furthermore, given the obvious though unstated reference to the Moscow trials, even the final confession itself can be surmised. All of this helps to make the theoretical logic of the outcome all the more fascinating. What the reader wants to know is "why" so many of the old guard freely confessed to crimes they never in fact committed. What Koestler supplies is the reason.

Because the rationale behind the confessions is the central theme, the most crucial aspects of the work deal with the interrogations of Rubashov. It is here that the ideological logic of the revolution is worked out. The interrogations are by two other commissars, Ivanov and Gletkin. Symbolically they do not represent different persons so much as Rubashov's own alter ego at different stages of ideological development. They are, therefore, always throwing back on him his own arguments, his own thoughts. The interrogations are thus more in the nature of a series of arguments Rubashov has with himself. There is no indication that Ivanov and Gletkin are other than different phases of Rubashov's own argument.

These modern commissars are the natural heirs of Spartacus but have learned the lesson of his mistakes. They have the same vision of a utopian end but are determined to keep it in view and not be sidetracked by the law of detours. It would be an anachronism for Koestler to have placed a modern revolutionary in a context such as that of Spartacus. The modern commissar is a theorist of ends, not means. The failure of modern revolutions, as distinguished from ancient ones, must be understood as failures of ends-dominated theories.

II *Who is Rubashov?*

The person of Rubashov poses one of the most difficult problems in any interpretation of *Darkness at Noon*. This is because he is both a symbolic figure and one whom Koestler intends to be interpreted literally. Koestler assembled Rubashov as a composite protrait of several acquaintances whom he knew personally and a number of old Bolsheviks whom he did not know on a firsthand basis. It is important to keep these twin aspects of Rubashov separate since the inability to do so has led to a number of misinterpretations.

Closely tied to the problem of *who* Rubashov represents is *what* he is in the novel. Literally, he is one of the last of the original revolutionaires who had made the revolution in his mind long before it had become an historical fact. As such, he is also one of the few to know from personal knowledge that a shadow has fallen between the dream and the reality of the revolution. Partly for this knowledge, perhaps even exclusively because of it, he is to be liquidated by No. 1, a euphemism Koestler reserves for Stalin. But while the reasons for liquidation are obscure, the rationale behind the public trial is not. He has been selected for an open, public trial precisely because he knows the ethics of the dream-end. He is a true believer. Were he not a true believer he could never be trusted to confess publically and would instead be unceremoniously murdered in private. Only the most trustworthy could be counted upon to play their assigned role as scapegoat for the regime in public and of their own free will. Above all, there must be no doubt by the party that he might suddenly recant his confession in public and thereby cast suspicion on the revolutionary purity of the party itself.

For Rubashov, the reason of the party is the source both of his greatest strength and of his fatal weakness. His rationalism is of a highly abstract order. His arguments on ends and means are cast in a purely theoretical foremat, and he has difficulty making the transition from theory to practice, even though the memory of that practice is the source of his own doubts. The practices of the revolution are constantly in the background, but only in the background. The working assumption of all the commissars is that it is ideas that are ultimate reality and the tangible fruits of those ideas are trivial by comparison. What follows, therefore, in Koestler's analysis is the testing of reason itself in pursuit of the revolutionary ideal.

In the literal interpretation of Rubashov, he is portrayed not as a real person, but a composite of real persons. In his physical appearance and biographical background, he bears a striking resemblance to Trotsky and Bukharin, respectively. While this has led many critics to see in Rubashov a fictional version of Bukharin in particular and to evaluate *Darkness at Noon* in terms of the literal congruity between the two, this similarity has too often been overdrawn. While Rubashov is intended by Koestler to be taken literally, there is more to it than that alone. Rubashov is a synthesis of persons, no doubt with some of Koestler's own personality thrown in for good measure. Physical similarities with actual persons, or the lack thereof, in no way destroys Koestler's argument. It is true enough to note that there may never have been a single victim in all the Purge Trials who embodies all of Rubashov's physical and mental traits. But the inability to find an exact historical counterpart cannot be taken as a serious rebuttal to the fictional Rubashov. Such criticisms would be more valid if Koestler had not intended Rubashov to posess a symbolic quality more important than the literal one.

At the symbolic level, Rubashov is more than merely a composite figure pasted together by an imaginative writer. First of all, it must be recalled that

Koestler is chiefly concerned with ideas rather than with persons as such. His interest is in the logical consequences of theoretical notions. These ideas cannot be separated from the persons who hold to them, but neither does Koestler intend that the reader's attention should become overly absorbed in the individual to the exclusion of the idea. Rubashov's realism is not derived exclusively from a physical and/or biographical similarity to any actual person. It is also derived from the truth of the ideas he argues and how they shape his behavior during the interrogations and after. What Koestler is saying is that if the logic of the commissar is carried to its final conclusion, a Rubashov will be the result—and that there are individuals prepared to follow the commissar logic, even at the sacrifice of their own lives. What Rubashov believes and argues is what any true Communist would have to believe and argue in order to accept and justify the Moscow trials at their face value.

Symbolically, then, Rubashov is the embodiment of the idea of the perfect commissar. He is the modern materialistic rationalist stripped down to his political essence. In this symbolic construction of Rubashov, there is no doubt that Koestler has left himself open to certain telling criticisms. For example, the intense intellectualization of Rubashov's motives robs them of the more human elements of personality. As a fictional character, he is a person the reader can look at with sympathy or horror but seldom with a strong sense of personal identification. In part this is a result of Koestler's own proclivities as a writer. He is a master of description for pure ideas, but decidedly weaker in relating actions or emotions. Actions and emotions are distractions in Koestler's work, and it is a strength of Rubashov, as well as his weakness, that he is reduced to almost pure thought.

For the revolutionary personality, which Koestler has described as pure action-oriented, Rubashov's exclusive preoccupation with theory may seem incongruous. It may seem less so if two points are kept in mind. First, the yogi-commissar spectrum was conceived as an attempt to rationally interpret what would otherwise be irrational. When Rubashov argues the commissar's position, it is for the purpose of theoretical clarification and not action-oriented demonstration. Secondly, the fact that forces Rubashov into a position of pure thought is his imprisonment. Unable to act politically, he has little alternative but to think. In this inability to act, Koestler is able to dramatize the theoretical aspects of revolution more clearly than he did with *The Gladiators*. The modern split between theory and practice is more intensified. It is not that Rubashov does not have an active side. The reader is constantly reminded of Rubashov's past actions in behalf of the party through a series of flashbacks. But these are always in the context of highlighting the sharp contrasts between idealized theory and a practice that is all too real. It is one of the basic features of *Darkness at Noon* that Koestler wants to put as much distance between theory and practice as the nature of the problem will permit in order to focus on the theoretical side.

Because the focus of the novel is on ideas, the truth of Koestler's work is very much dependent on the truth of the theoretical dilemma described. To understand Rubashov as Koestler intended him to be understood means that the theoretical symbolism must be preeminent over the literal representation.

At the symbolic level of interpretation, Rubashov is a split-personality. On the one hand he is the prototype commissar. But in addition, he is also representative of a type of secularized Christological symbolism. The Christ like features of Rubashov build throughout the novel in a variety of subtle ways until they reach a crescendo in the closing pages. This symbolism is, as has been noted, an extension of the same sort found in *The Gladiators*, but it is handled much more deftly in Rubashov than with Spartacus. The Purge Trials take on certain qualities of the trial and execution of Christ, but without the resurrection. But the trials in both cases can only be understood from the perspective of the totally dedicated individual—in this case the secularized revolutionary saint. Only a person with Rubashov's revolutionary insight into the higher truth of the will of the party would be expected to see the logic in the confession.

Rubashov represents the modern perversion of reason, but it remains a form of reason nonetheles. It is as a rationalist of the materialist mold that he is led to "think his thoughts through to their logical conclusion." Physical torture would only serve to divert attention away from the ideas of the movement. The confession to crimes that he never committed is not intended to cast Rubashov outside the revolution, but just the opposite. Confession is the only way that he can return to the fold. The confession serves to reunite the victim with the executioner in the common purpose of serving the revolution. Shortly after his arrest, Rubashov asked Ivanov, "Did I arrest you or did you arrest me?" There is more than just irony involved here. Their two roles could quite easily be reversed. So long as Rubashov either does not or cannot disassociate himself from the revolution he has, for all practical purposes, sanctioned his own arrest.[1] Since his personal life and the life of the revolution are inseparable, to deny the right of Ivanov to arrest and interrogate him would mean to deny the justice of the revolution and of his own life and actions as a part of it.

Had Rubashov confessed for reasons of physical torture, Koestler's novel might have more closely resembled Orwell's nightmare *Nineteen Eighty-Four*. It might have been easier to understand the trials in one sense if the confessions were forceably extracted, but the revolutionary unity of theory and practice would have been obscured. The freely given confession points toward an entirely different order of ideas in the service of revolution than does a tortured one. Although Rubashov presents the reader with the revolution in terms of almost pure reason, Koestler does not lose sight of the close relationship between the theory and practice of the revolutionary tradition. Here we can also see more clearly why Rubashov is not the "typical" victim of the trials but rather the "atypical" victim; the dilemma of ends and means for intellectual revolutionaries could not be explored otherwise. The final confession is necessary in order to keep the theoretical question clearly in view. Rubashov is a martyred saint of the revolution, not just another faceless nonentity. He is a faithful servant of the new god, who follows the laws, the reasons, the acts of the movement to their final and inevitable end. Ivanov, the first interrogator, knows instinctively that Rubashov is not really an outsider: "We both grew up in the same tradition and have on these matters the same conception.... Put yourself in my place—after all, our positions might equally be reversed."[2]

Ivanov knows that Rubashov will confess because of the logic of the party's, position, not by torture. He tells Gletkin, "When he has thought everything out to its logical conclusion he will capitulate ... it won't be out of cowardice, but by logic."[3] This is one of the most crucial points in the novel about Rubashov and the confession. Unless it is understood that Rubashov confesses for reasons of logic and not fear, the point Koestler is making will be lost. Later, when Gletkin kills Ivanov and takes over supervision of the interrogation, he thinks that it is his brutal methods that finally breakdown Rubashov's will-power. But that is a by-product of his own theoretical illiteracy and action-oriented character. Rubashov knows that he confessed because of the logic of Gletkin's position and not because of its brute force. It is explicitly described as a "last service to the Party" and does not have a great deal in common with Winston's confession, for example, in *Nineteen Eighty-Four*. The terror in *Darkness at Noon* is not the physical terror of Orwell, but rather is the terrible logic of an idea—the idea that the end will justify the means. Ultimately it is not the party that destroys Rubashov, except in the physical sense. His real destruction is as much symbolic as literal and comes from his own hand as he lives out his idealized, theoretical life in a polluted world. His destruction follows the attempt to weld an abstract image of perfection together with a real and imperfect man. In the process, both are destroyed. It is reflective of the tragedy of the modern world in Koestler's eyes that this is so.

III *The Interrogations*

The interrogation of Rubashov first by Ivanov and then by Gletkin takes place in three separate and distinct phases. Each phase has a symbolism and meaning of its own even as they are tied together in a single flow of reasoning. The three persons of the novel, Rubashov, Ivanov, and Gletkin, may be said to represent respectively the party past, the party present, and the party future. As the interrogators question Rubashov, it can be seen as arguments of the past attempting to come to grips with arguments of the present and future. All of these phases are crucial links in the chain of causality that begins with the past and progresses to the logical culmination. In this process, past, present, and future are separable for analytic purposes only and not in logic, as each phase is implicit in the other. Gletkin thus is not only a perfect commissar of the future, he is also implicitly what Rubashov already is as potential.

The three figures of the novel that surround the interrogation should be seen as a single piece. They are different but related aspects of the dilemma of ends and means. In this, Rubashov is presented at first as one who has lost faith in the revolution of the present because it does not seem to accord with his original dreams. The physical terror that has come with the revolution was not what he and his fellow theorists intended. But could the end in Gletkin have been avoided? Having willed the end, could he avoid willing the means? The answer is already suggested by the structure of the interrogation, but is incomplete until Rubashov thinks his thoughts through to the end. He knows at the outset that the present difficulty is a result of having abandoned morality as means: "As we have thrown overboard all conventions and rules of cricket-morality, our whole guiding principle is that of consequent logic. We are under the terrible compulsion to follow our thoughts down to its final consequence and act in accordance with it. We are sailing without ethical ballast."[4]

Rubashov's shaken faith in the revolution ought not to detain the reader for long. He has committed his life to the proposition that the end will justify the means, and though his appearance of doubt is real enough, it is primarily a literary device Koestler uses to begin his train of thought. The subsequent development of the logic of the dilemma is the process by which apologists for the purges also overcame their doubts. Rubashov's doubts are not merely his alone, but also those of an entire generation of Western intellectual revolutionaries.

Although Rubashov has separated ends from means in his mind, the question of means continually intrudes into his otherwise rational calculation of ends. It is an unwanted intrusion, lacking in reason, but it will not go away.

It is part of what he dubs the "grammatical fiction," the fact of an unexpected discovery of conscience. While ends and means can be kept analytically separate, they cannot be kept practically separate. Although in his essay "The Yogi and the Commissar," Koestler maintained that pure thought and pure action were at opposite poles, few of his literary creations have ever been able to keep the two totally apart.

In the interrogation, Ivanov and Gletkin may also be seen as figures who move closer and closer to the ideal commissar as pure, unreflective action. They are Rubashov's alter ego whose task it is to mold him into the perfect commissar. What happens as a result is that a rift is opened up in his personality between his idealized self and his real self. It produces a definite neurosis in his personality. In turn, this neurosis in Rubashov is his personal link to the moral defect of the revolution. The neurotic revolutionary personality is born of the rupture between an idealized image of the self, capable of realization only in the party, and the real self that is full of doubts. His denial of his imperfect self corresponds with a denial of genuine morality as means. "Perhaps the heart of the evil lay there," he thought to himself, "Perhaps it did not suit mankind to sail without ballast."[5] But as the interrogation eventually leads him to accept the end of the revolution sailing without ballast, it must be said that he knowingly and willingly accepts the evil means that go with it.

IV *The Logic of the Confession*
and the "Grammatical Fiction"

Darkness at Noon opens with a deliberate link between the Communist and Fascist revolutions. The link is not at the theoretical level, but at the practical level of means. In order to oppose the Fascists, the Communists have become just like them in practice. When the party comes to arrest Rubashov, he is asleep. As he awakens, he has difficulty deciding who it is that has come for him. Is he asleep and dreaming of being arrested in a Fascist country, or is he awake and actually being arrested in the country of the revolution? What follows until the end of the novel could have been duplicated with only a slight variation in a Fascist state. Furthermore, since neither Communism nor Stalin are ever mentioned by name, it is always relatively easy to substitute one regime for another in the double-edged symbolism. At the end, after he has been struck by one of the two fatal bullets in the back of the head, Rubashov looks up at a picture of No. 1 and is uncertain whether it is Hitler or Stalin he sees: "But whose color-print was hanging over his bed and looking at him? Was it No. 1 or was it the other—he with the ironic smile or he with the glassy gaze? ... what insignia did the figure wear on the sleeves and shoulder-straps of its uniform—and in whose name did it raise the dark pistol barrel."[6]

This powerful symbolic effect of tying Communist terror to Fascist terror at the practical level is no doubt one of the principle reasons for the timelessness of the work. It is also Koestler's reminder to the reader that the dilemma of ends and means is not exclusively a Marxist problem. Furthermore, it must be understood that it is only at the practical level that Communism and Fascism appear to be the same. At the theoretical level, Fascism is unreflective evil whereas Marxism seeks to justify its deeds. Gletkin could be as Fascist, but Rubashov could never be one. Whether this is a difference that makes a difference is a question Koestler never pursued. He did raise the issue again briefly in *Arrival and Departure*, but he never developed the logic of it.

The logic of the confession does not turn on the objective guilt or innocence of Rubashov on the specific charges. The reader knows he is innocent in the usual meaning of the term. But of what, if anything, can he justly be considered guilty? Here it seems that Koestler intends the answer to depend upon the level in which such judgement is made. At the ideological level of party reasoning, he is guilty of counterrevolutionary heresy for harboring doubts about the revolution. At the personal level, Rubashov has the nagging feeling that he is indeed guilty of having used means to further the end of the revolution that are vaguely immoral, though he has no basis other than the end sought from which to decide moral questions. The knowledge that he has destroyed countless lives to further the goal of the revolution weighs heavily on a newly discovered conscience. There is a profound tension between these two poles of guilt in the eyes of the party and guilt in his own eyes. Rubashov finally resolves the tension by deciding in favor of the party, symbolizing the final triumph of ends over means. But the reader is left with an awareness that his real self is also guilty of sins of commission in means.

For the party there is only one crime—"to swerve from the course laid out: and only one punishment: death."[7] The party does not believe in or follow the law of detours. It does not argue that there may be separate roads to the same end or that some compromises along the way may be necessary. The party line "is sharply defined, like a narrow path in the mountains. The slightest false step, right or left, takes one down the precipice."[8] What matters to the party are not "subjective" motivations, but the logical consequence of ideas that are of their nature "objective." For the party it is sufficient that Rubashov has experienced a single twinge of doubt. If he no longer wills the end, he must will means that are destructive of that end. From a single fleeting doubt, the party can logically construct his intention to undermine the revolution.

The first interrogation by Ivanov brings out this point dramatically. The charges that he is an active agent of certain counterrevolutionary elements is patently false, at least in terms of overt actions. But when he admits to Ivanov that for some time he has harbored doubts about certain party actions, he is caught in an ideological web from which there is no escape. Ivanov confronts him with the logic of his doubts: "You now openly admit that for years you have had the conviction that we were ruining the Revolution; and in the same breath you deny that you belonged to the opposition.... Do you really expect me to believe that you sat watching us with your hands in your lap—while, according to your conviction, we led the country and Party to destruction."[9]

Ivanov could never have confronted Rubashov with this line of reasoning had not both agreed beforehand that actions logically follow thought and that the two are intrinsically in harmony. Rubashov knows this and agrees that Ivanov has reason on his side; "Logically you may be right," he says. What Rubashov refuses to link together at this point in the interrogation is the praxis between theory and practice. A confession will necessitate an acceptance of that cause-effect relationship. It will require an acceptance of his idealized self at the expense of his real self. This has suddenly become an important consideration for Rubashov, because in his jail cell he has, for the first time, discovered that he has two selves. He calls this new self, his conscience, the "grammatical fiction."

Rubashov's guilt at the practical level, the level where means are most important, is presented in the form of what Koestler calls this grammatical fiction.[10] It is a dimension of reality discovered in prison that is entirely unknown to the previous conception of the commissar's rationalism. It is an inner voice, an unwanted and wholly unexpected discovery of individual existence that is distinct from corporate existence in the party form of class consciousness.

It is in the nature of this grammatical fiction that it defends the individual against the collective conscienceness. Koestler raises this notion to the highest possible level of symbolism. In one form or another, it became the moral touchstone of most of his subsequent writing. It was the basis upon which he engaged in later battles against behaviorists, psychologists, materialist philosophies, and any other examples of modern thought that tend to deny this notion of the reality of the individual soul. As Koestler conceptualizes it, there is a strong hint of a Kantian sort of distinction that seems to be wholly compatible with the yogi-commissar continuum. It has, alternatively, been the basis of Koestler's humanism and his defense of political means while theoretically siding with the ethic of ends in politics.

Rubashov experiences this grammatical fiction as something that seems to have taken possession of him against his will. That it is an integral part of his personhood, however, there is no doubt. Contrary to all the rules of grammar, it persists in addressing him as "I" instead of "You," as his materialist philosophy would have it. It is a silent partner that speaks even when he does not want to listen and without any visible pretext for starting the conversation. Rubashov fights it, unsuccessfully because it is a reminder of the gap between the theory and practice of the revolution as he originally conceived it. It threatens to upset all of his previous notions about the mechanical nature of reason as it reminds him of the problem of means.

The party, of course, does not recognize the existence of a grammatical fiction. Implicitly, however, the party does recognize something of the sort as one of the major obstacles standing in the way of the confession. For the party, there is no "I" in their vocabulary, but only the plural "We." The Party of "We" is at war with the individual.[11] Ivanov sees the heresy of Rubashov's continual referal to the party as "You," implying that he has an existence apart from it. The interrogation and Rubashov's final confession represent a struggle to subordinate the "I" to the "We" and to return to the logic of ends over means.

The logic of the commissar eventually overwhelms the grammatical fiction. In part this is because Rubashov cannot reduce it to a rational thing and dissect it scientifically. The voice of conscience thus appears to be something outside of reason. Of all the things in his world, the grammatical fiction is the one uncaused effect. He cannot argue with it, as it claims an autonomy independent of reason alone.

At times this voice of conscience is cast symbolically as Rubashov's toothache. The toothache is a result of a Fascist beating. It comes and goes whenever his conscience ought to be bothering him during the interrogation. It is finally assuaged only at the end of the novel when he confesses. When the "I" disappears and only the "We" remains, the toothache and the grammatical fiction are no longer part of Rubashov's life. It is the end of the struggle between theory and practice.

The confession is built on the supression of the grammatical fiction, but it also involves the creation of an historical fiction—the idea of the progress of history. History is, as Koestler well knows, the god of revolution. He makes clear that this historicized world view is the product of Marxist thought. The party, as the inheritor of this tradition, knows nothing of conscience and toothaches. Scientific history knows only ends and the party as its prophet. As Rubashov recalls: "The Party is the embodiment of the revolutionary idea in history. History knows no scruples and no hesitation. Inert and unerring she flows toward her goal.... History knows her way. She makes no mistakes. He who has not absolute faith in History does not belong in the Party's ranks."[12]

History, like the commissar's ethic of ends, is morally neutral. When Rubashov puzzles over means, he has cast himself outside the stream of history as well as the party. The party is absolved of all sins, since it is merely the agent of the mechanistic god of a material universe. It is in the end impossible for Rubashov to hold either Gletkin or the party responsible even for his own death because they are merely the agents of the new god.

The final confession is Rubashov's "last service to the Party." At this point, the party needs villans as black as pitch and not heroes. Rubashov has his assigned part to play and can do no less than play it. There is a strong temptation to "die in silence," but that would be petty bourgeois morality. His subject guilt is real, in terms of the logic of both the party and himself. He "had followed every thought to its last conclusion and acted in accordance with it to the very end."[13] In confessing of his own free will, which the party has ironically denied, Rubashov is, as Koestler makes clear, the exception and not the rule among the victims of the purge. Most confessed because of torture, but "the best of them," meaning the saints of the revolution, did so as the "We" had its final triumph over the "I." They returned to the fold.

V *The Unity of Theory and Practice*

Unlike the revolution of Spartacus, the new revolution has come to power and held on to it. But it was a predictable failure all the same. It too is founded on an illusion. There is no utopia ordained by history or any other god. The attempts to build utopias inevitably end in tragedy, but not always for the same reasons. Spartacus failed because he followed the law of detours; the Russian Revolution failed because it did not. For Koestler, there is no middle ground, and the would-be revolutionary cannot escape failure. The Moscow trials were not, therefore, an aberrition of Marxism, but its very essence: "[The commissars] dreamed of power with the object of abolishing power; of ruling over people to wean them from the habit of being ruled. All their thoughts became deeds and all their dreams were fulfilled."[14]

The difficulty with the modern notion of praxis in revolution is that it is tied to a notion of reason that has become demonic in its consequences. Ivanov confronts Rubashov with this fact during the first interrogation: "In the old days temptation was of a carnal nature. Now it takes the form of pure reason. The values change. I would like to write a Passion play in which God and the Devil dispute for the soul of Saint Rubashov."[15]

But reason is not on the same side as God. It is the ally of the revolutionary and the enemy of the desert God of the Jews. The reason of the commissar is the Promethian reason of Marx and loses none of its appeal or power by siding with evil:

> Satan [is] ... a fanatical devotee of logic. He reads Machiavelli,
> Ignatius of Loyola, Marx and Hegel; he is cold and unmerciful to
> mankind, out of a kind of mathematical mercifulness. He is
> damned always to do that which is most repugnant to him ... to
> strip himself of every scruple in the name of a higher
> scrupulousness, and to challenge the hatred of mankind because
> of his love for it—as abstract and geometric love.[16]

Reason is thus not only on the side of Satan, but against means as well.
In any debate over ends and means that is conducted according to logic and
reason alone, the ends will always emerge triumphant. This is the true terror
of the revolution to Koestler—its alliance with reason. It is why the
grammatical fiction loses the debate with reason. It is Rubashov's inability to
argue against Ivanov and Gletkin that eventually brings him back into the
party's ranks voluntarily. The commissar wins the argument with the yogi.
Conscience may occasionally triumph, but only at the cost of reason: "*Apage
Satanas!* Comrade Rubashov prefers to become a martyr. The columnists of
the liberal press, who hated him during his lifetime, will sanctify him after
his death. He has discovered a conscience, and a conscience renders one as
unfit for the revolution as a double chin. Conscience eats through the brain
like a cancer."[17]

Ivanov does not silence Rubashov's conscience by logic alone, but he
does defeat it. The arguments of the party are those of the future, whereas
conscience belongs to the prehistoric past. Rubashov's doubts, representing
the party past, cannot answer the party present in Ivanov and thus succumb
to the party future in Gletkin. This future in Gletkin now appears to have
been ordained from the beginning, and Rubashov can no more deny the
logic of Gletkin than he could deny himself. During the last interrogation,
conducted by Gletkin, Ivanov has already forged the link that joins Gletkin
and Rubashov together like father and son. The unity of theory and practice
in Marxist praxis is one more established in Rubashov's mind. In Gletkin, it
is his future self that he confronts with the logical conclusion of his own
arguments and his own reason.

Gletkin's interrogation is a more harsh one than that conducted by
Ivanov, but that is because Gletkin is the "new man" of socialist consciousness.
Gletkin believes that it is his methods that get Rubashov to confess, but the
old commissar knows better. Gletkin is "a repellant creature, but he
represents the new generation." He is a more pure commissar than Rubashov,
"the generation which started to think after the flood. It has no traditions, and
no memories to bind it to the old, vanished world. It was a generation born
without an unbilical cord.... And yet it had right on its side."[18]

Compared to Gletkin, Rubashov, with his grammatical fiction, is described as an ape looking with ignorant scorn at the first man. Gletkin is "the barbarian of the new age which is now starting." But he is also the necessary first step along the evolutionary path toward the classless man of the future. He is Rubashov's ideological son and the rightful heir to the revolution. Though he is an unreflective individual, he was anticipated by the revolutionary theoreticians such as Rubashov. It is not in spite of his beastial qualities but because of them that he is now the right man in the right place at the right time to further the ends of the revolution. He has no scruples over ends and means—it is a nonexistent problem. As Rubashov prepares his final confession at the public trial, he thinks of Gletkin: "You don't understand the issue, but, did you understand, you would be useless to us."[19] The key here is that at the end Rubashov speaks of himself and Gletkin as "Us"—the triumph of the "We" over the "I."

VI *The Religious Symbolism in Darkness at Noon*

In *Darkness at Noon*, the god of revolution is history. It is an amoral, perhaps even immoral, god that determines the form of rational and ethical behavior. Like all gods, it demands certain sacrifices. With the party sacrifice of Rubashov to the new god go the last traces of what the West had always understood as the concept of the soul—here portrayed as the grammatical fiction. Koestler makes Rubashov into a secularized saint of revolution, and he does so by contrasting it with a more orthodox saintliness in the biblical tradition. It is an extension of the same symbolism found in *The Gladiators*.

Rubashov's story, from arrest to execution, is so closely tied to a form of reverse Christian symbolism that to overlook it would result in a misreading of the novel. That symbolism begins with the arrest scene. As Rubashov is getting dressed, he looks down at his own feet and recalls a verse from his early childhood "which compared the feet of Christ to a white roebuck in a thornbush."[20] The attention of the reader is thus drawn at the outset to compare Rubashov with Christ. Unlike Christ, however, Rubashov is not portrayed as innocent in any sense. Like Christ, he is innocent of the crime alleged by his accusors, but he is guilty of other crimes in his conscience. Absolution from past sins comes when he submits to the new god that is explicitly opposed to the desert God of the Jews and hence to Christians as well.

Even Rubashov's most conspicuous traits and habits take on a decidedly religious connotation. The connection between his toothache and his conscience has already been mentioned; but in addition, his nervous habit of rubbing his glasses on his sleeve throughout the interrogation is described by Koestler as an act similar to "praying with a rosary."[21] This modest action is a symbolic and reflexive prayer that assuages his toothache—conscience whenever Ivanov and Gletkin are tempting him with a Santanic reason. At the end of the novel, as Gletkin is taking him out to his ignominious Calvary, he drops his glasses and is lost without them. This has a double significance. Not only is his physical vision lost, but his spiritual vision as well.

During his confession at the public trial, the daughter of an old comrade reads the account to her father. Alternately, the reader hears the confession of Rubashov and the old man's recollections of the Gospel passages where Christ is executed. The confession, however, is also different than Christ's condemnation. In the end, Rubashov suffers the same fate as Spartacus. The fate of the yogi turns out to be the same as that of the commissar. Christian principles are no more effective in Koestler's view than those of the commissar. The trial of Christ is the mirror image of the Moscow trials; everything is reversed, including the guilt of the two accused—yet the result is the same, the death of each, without changing the nature of the human condition. They are opposites in all respects save one. They are both failures. One is a failure of means over ends and the other is a failure of ends over means, but at the practical level this does not seem to matter much. For Rubashov the grave is the end; there is no resurrection. There is no heaven on earth or anywhere else for that matter. The religious symbolism in Koestler thus creates a mood of hopelessness and pessimism. It is a conscious reversal of Christian symbolism but a continuation of the same themes from *The Gladiators*.

NOTES

1. Arthur Koestler, *Darkness at Noon* (Danube Edition, 1973), p. 82.

2. *Ibid.*, pp. 89, 93.

3. *Ibid.*, pp. 102–3.

4. *Ibid.*, pp. 99–100.

5. *Ibid.*, p. 248.

6. *Ibid.*, p. 254.

7. *Ibid.*, p. 77.

8. *Ibid.*, p. 49.

9. *Ibid.*, p. 90.

10. For an excellent discussion of the "grammatical fiction", see Goronwy Rees, "*Darkness at Noon* and the 'Grammatical Fiction'", in Harold Harris, ed. *Astride the Two Cultures–Arthur Koestler at 70* (New York, 1976).

11. On the opposition of the "We" to the "I", a suggestive novel that may have influenced Koestler on this point is Yevgny Zamyatin, *We* (New York, 1970).

12. *Darkness at Noon*, p. 48.

13. *Ibid.*, p. 243.

14. *Ibid.*, p. 62–63.

15. *Ibid.*, p. 146.

16. *Ibid.*, p. 146.

17. *Ibid.*, pp. 146–47.

18. *Ibid.*, pp. 178–79.

19. *Ibid.*, p. 180.

20. *Ibid.*, p. 20.

21. *Ibid.*, p. 20.

MARK LEVENE

The Mind on Trial: Darkness at Noon

Completing *The Gladiators* had helped Koestler bear the sense of "outer
loneliness and inner emptiness" he experienced in finally choosing to
dislocate his personal history from that of the Communist Revolution.[1] But
as a novelist, a reporter, and an individual whose very pulse seemed to be
political, Koestler's instinct was to stay closer to the ideological convulsions
of his own time, among the legacies of a bankrupt rationalism he saw
embodied in Marxism. With his second novel Koestler turned from the
relative comfort of historical emblems to the painful and immediate moral
pressure exerted on the European Left by the Moscow Trials, Stalin's
systematic and precisely orchestrated burial of the Bolshevik "old guard."

The novel was originally called *The Vicious Circle* and was to center on
a group of characters imprisoned in a totalitarian state. The real guilt they
share, Koestler says in the autobiography, is "having placed the interests of
mankind above the interests of man, having sacrificed morality to
expediency.... Now they must die, because their death is expedient to the
Cause, by the hands of men who subscribe to the same principles."[2] In the
actual writing of the novel, Koestler held to this conflict between means and
ends, but of the figures he planned to include, only one grew in his
imagination—Nikolai Salmanovich Rubashov—whose "manner of thinking"
was modeled on that of Nikolai Bukharin, the most notable defendant in the

From *Arthur Koestler*. © 1984 by Frederick Ungar Publishing Co., Inc.

Great Trial of 1938. Intellectually the most fascinating of the Bolshevik leaders, Bukharin had been "a ranking member of Lenin's original revolutionary leadership," the editor of *Pravda*, "and co-leader with Stalin of the Party between 1925 and 1928."[3]

Although during his own trial Rubashov echoes some of Bukharin's most eloquent words, his ancestry is also more general. In an important sense Rubashov represents an entire generation of "militant philosophers" who by the early 1930s had few resources left to withstand Stalin and Stalinism. What Koestler remembered most about the various members of the Soviet hierarchy he met in 1933, including Bukharin, was their fatigue:

> It was not only the effect of overwork, nervous strain and apprehension. It was the past that was telling on them, the years of conspiracy, prison and exile; the years of the famine and the Civil War; and sticking to the rules of a game that demanded that at every moment a man's whole life should be at stake. They were indeed "dead men on furlough," as Lenin had called them. Nothing could frighten them any more, nothing surprise them. They had given all they had. History had squeezed them out to the last drop, had burnt them out to the last spiritual calorie; yet they were still glowing in cold devotion, like phosphorescent corpses.[4]

They had not yet given everything; there was still to be a claim on their "cold devotion." Between 1935 and 1938 they and the rest of the revolutionary elite, the creators of the 1917 Revolution, confessed in open court to being saboteurs, assassins, thieves, and agents of foreign powers. The trials bewildered and frightened observers, those on the independent Left, fellow travelers, and Communist Party members throughout the world. If the accused were guilty, a generation of Bolshevik politicians and whole sections of Russian revolutionary history were tainted. If they were innocent, the current Soviet leadership was dedicated to a program of baroque vengeance and self-interest wholly incompatible with anything but the most dogmatic, inhumane revolutionary principles. After Koestler's death, the philosopher Sidney Hook remarked that only "*Darkness at Noon* was able to convey the sickening truth, overcoming by its psychological plausibility the initial doubts and resistance of Communist sympathisers."[5]

In his essay on Koestler, Orwell argued that "the common-sense explanation" for the confessions was that the accused "were tortured, and perhaps black-mailed by threats to relatives and friends."[6] Koestler did not discount this sort of pressure. In the novel itself and in numerous debates about Rubashov, Koestler agreed that some confessed in the hope of saving their families or their own lives. But in Rubashov Koestler dramatized a more complex motive which for years after the publication of the book proved to be highly controversial. "The best of them, the hard-core Bolshevik intellectuals" behind the creation of Rubashov "were great men, and it would be the final injustice to misinterpret the motives for which they died." They confessed and died "to do the Party a last service."[7]

With the exception of a few scenes, *Darkness at Noon* is concentrated in the mind of ex-Commissar of the People Rubashov: his meditations on political ethics, his memories, his debates with the interrogators, and ultimately his decision to acquiesce in the Party's demand on him. In the opening section, "The First Hearing," Rubashov is arrested by his own countrymen. With a detachment that comes from years of self-abnegation and ideological commitment, he surveys his body, contemplates the possibility of his execution, and assesses the power of No. 1 (Stalin is never named in the book). Rubashov wonders whether "that mocking oracle they called History" might prove that No. 1 was correct in his decimation of the "old guard."

But the workings of his own history refuse to remain so opaque. In the solitariness of prison Rubashov's memories become living presences. "The imploring gesture of the meagre, stretched-out hands" from a neighboring cell reminds him of a *Pietà* that hung in a German gallery. As head of an Intelligence unit, Rubashov had been sent to deal with "Richard," a German Party worker who had been distributing "defeatist" pamphlets. After explaining the need for unwavering faith and obedience, Rubashov expelled Richard from the Party and betrayed him to Hitler's police. When he left the gallery, Rubashov was aware not of guilt, but of a tormenting toothache.

This physical response, prompted by his rudimentary conscience, becomes even more acute while Rubashov paces in his cell and begins to voice doubts about the Party's infallibility: "We brought you truth and in our mouth it sounded a lie. We brought you freedom, and it looks in our hands like a whip." This meditation extracts another painful recollection: his explanation to a group of Belgian dockworkers that they should not prevent the shipment of goods to a Fascist state, since "the Country of the Revolution" had to increase its industrial capacity, not encourage "romantic gestures." The embargo was lifted, and after being "denounced in the official Party organ as an *agent provocateur*," the union leader, Little Loewy, hanged himself. Without belief in the Revolution and its heroes, he could not continue to live.

Between these memories Rubashov has conversations in code with his monarchist neighbor, No. 402, from whom he receives unexpected tobacco and emotional generosity. But there remains more common ground with his first official interrogator, Ivanov, an old comrade Rubashov had once persuaded on ideological grounds not to commit suicide. Ivanov points out that despite some reluctance, Rubashov has made various "declarations of loyalty" over the years in order to avoid expulsion from the Party. He argues that Rubashov's past and his need to remain within the Party logically dictate that he make a partial confession now. "The methods follow by logical deduction ... and in five years you will be back in the ring again." Although Rubashov says that he has had "enough of this kind of logic," Ivanov "had hit a tuning fork, to which his mind responded of its own accord. All he had believed in, fought for and preached during the last forty years swept over his mind in an irresistible wave."

In "The Second Hearing" Rubashov begins to make the acquaintance of the "grammatical fiction," the illogical realm of selfhood and personal conscience that had been stifled by his habitual submission to political expediency. The "silent partner," as he also calls his inner voice, has already drawn him to certain images: to the *Pietà* that had been partly hidden from his view as he excommunicated Richard and to the cats Little Loewy was forced to skin in order to survive for the sake of the Party. Now, through the memory of his lover's bent neck, it draws Rubashov to his most complete betrayal. While working at a trade delegation in a European country, Rubashov lived for weeks "in the atmosphere of [Arlova's] large, lazy body." During the day and at night he found her sisterly, sensual warmth more human than anything he had encountered before in his life. But when Arlova was "recalled" and accused of treason, he neither came to her public defense nor did he attempt to comfort her in private. Rubashov's simple calculation was that his own existence was more valuable to the Party.

Joining these images within Rubashov's "first person singular" is the sound of Bogrov—"Former Sailor on the Battleship Potemkin, Commander of the Eastern Fleet"—whimpering, crying for his old friend, as he is led past Rubashov's cell. Even after this horrifying example of No. 1's "objective" morality, Ivanov continues to argue that "sympathy, conscience, disgust, despair, repentance, and atonement are for us repellent debauchery." But Rubashov cannot throw him out, cannot reject his entire past which is carried in this echo of his own words and attitudes.

In "The Third Hearing" Rubashov proudly informs Ivanov and No. 402 that he is capitulating. A general recantation will, he has decided, allow him some "breathing-space" as well as time to formulate new theories of social utility and revolutionary ethics. But Ivanov has himself been arrested and another interrogator installed. Representing a new, "Neanderthal" generation, and sharing neither memories nor style with the old intelligentsia, Gletkin demands from Rubashov a complete public confession to crimes of treason and espionage. "You admit your 'oppositional attitude,'" he says to Rubashov, "but deny the acts which are the logical consequence of it." Rubashov has insisted that he cannot confess to crimes he has not committed. But gradually he submits to what Koestler's friend Raymond Aron calls "the perverse logic of those chain identifications ... that are the essence, the diabolical and fascinating essence of an absolute historical faith."[8]

Confronted with "Hare-lip," in whose presence years earlier he had mocked and condemned the Soviet leadership, Rubashov concludes that it is irrelevant whether the young man actually tried to assassinate No. 1: "The essential point was that this figure of misery represented the consequence of his logic made flesh." When Rubashov acknowledges to Gletkin that Harelip's confession "accords with the facts in the *essential* points," he "seals" his own confession. Although he could simplify the interrogation by admitting the entire indictment all at once, Rubashov contests every point; he must see the macabre dance of casuistical intellect through to the very end. He has tacitly agreed that if Gletkin could prove the accuracy of the "root" of a charge—"even when this root was only of a logical, abstract nature—he had a free hand to insert the missing details.... Neither of them distinguished any longer between actions which Rubashov had committed in fact and those which he merely should have committed as a consequence of his opinions." To complete the logic of the interrogation and at the same time to secure his bond with the past, Rubashov agrees to a ritualistic trial as his "last service" to the Revolution.

"The Grammatical Fiction" begins with an account of the public confession. Virtually every perception and thought in the novel has been Rubashov's, yet the trial, toward which he has inexorably argued himself and the elite of the "old guard," is conveyed through a newspaper description read to the porter, Vassilij. Denying Rubashov the direct narration of the event is remarkably effective. He has, in essence, relinquished both the ethical and aesthetic right to speak for himself. His perverse rationalism has temporarily canceled what individuality he possessed, and for the duration of the trial he is nothing more or less than a public creation of the Party. As a result, his direct reactions to the charges of the prosecution and the jeers of the audience are sadly irrelevant.

Having made his peace with history, Rubashov is free to contemplate the "grammatical fiction" and the questions it evokes about human suffering. He goes to his death unsure that there is any difference between No. 1 and the German messiah, but in the hope that perhaps a "new movement" will arise, driven by knowledge of both "economic fatality" and the "oceanic feeling" (the sense of infinity Koestler himself glimpsed while under sentence of death in Spain and which he called on again in his suicide note). "Perhaps," Rubashov thinks, "the members of the new party will wear monks' cowls, and preach that only purity of means can justify the ends."

But it was as a weapon, not as an expression of hope, that the book had such an extraordinary influence when the translation, *Le Zéro et l'Infini* appeared in France. Koestler maintains that the reason the book "broke all prewar records in French publishing history was not literary but political."[9] In 1946 the French Communist Party was extremely powerful, well-organized, and likely to increase its governmental control through a constitutional referendum. "In this oppressive atmosphere, a novel on the Russian Purges, though dealing with events that lay ten years back, assumed a symbolic actuality, an allusive relevance which had a deeper psychological impact than a topical book could have achieved. It happened to be the first moral indictment of Stalinism published in post-war France."[10]

Judging from the shrill attacks on Koestler's manhood and drinking habits as well as his "graveyard" politics, the novel produced considerable distress among the Party orthodox.[11] At the same time, it confirmed others in their anticommunism and swayed the uncommitted *either* toward or away from the Party. This paradoxical effect, which Koestler was very much aware of, but did not emphasize publicly, in his essays or autobiography, is rather startling evidence of his persuasive detailing of Bolshevik rationalism and argumentation. The novel also prompted in the eminent philosopher Maurice Merleau-Ponty an immediate and lengthy response to the concepts implicit in the portrayal of Rubashov. As a Marxist with little sympathy for Stalin's version of revolutionary terror, Merleau-Ponty believed that Koestler had at least approached the essential terms of contemporary political ethics: "Even if it does not pose the question properly, the book raises the problem of our times"—how to balance the human demands of social change with the inhuman temper of violence.[12]

Koestler cites the assertion in a Paris editorial that "the most important single factor which led to the defeat of the Communists in the referendum on the Constitution, was a novel, *Le Zéro et l'Infini*."[13] Even if only partly accurate, this statement gives Koestler's novel a place in an uncrowded area of literary history, among works that have had a direct and verifiable effect on a society's approach to its structures and principles. *Darkness at Noon*, like *Nineteen Eighty-Four* and *Uncle Tom's Cabin*, became a catalyst of public opinion by accident. Passions about slavery and Soviet communism absorbed these novels in a particular way at the right, the necessary, historical moment. But Koestler could not plan this necessity or foresee the postwar compulsions of France. Although he *hoped* to affect his readers' understanding of Stalinism, he wrote *Darkness at Noon* as though he had to be content with the traditional significance of imaginative forms—the slow and subtle alteration of a culture's mode of perception.

Koestler's intention to mold the subject of Rubashov's confession into a fully integrated and permanent artistic entity is evident from the first pages of the novel. After Rubashov has examined his cell and fallen asleep, we are taken back to his arrest at home an hour earlier. He is straining to wake himself from the recurrent nightmare of his initial arrest by the Gestapo. "He dreamed, as always, that there was a hammering on his door, and that three men stood outside, waiting to arrest him." Then Koestler explicitly binds the dream to the present reality:

> The hammering on Rubashov's door became louder; the two men outside, who had come to arrest him, hammered alternatively and blew on their frozen hands. But Rubashov could not wake up, although he knew that now would follow a particularly painful scene: the three still stand by his bed and he tries to put on his dressing-gown.

Vassilij, the old porter and Rubashov's follower, takes part in the translation of the nightmare; he is the third person standing by Rubashov's bed as he awakes. Koestler's literary self-consciousness is clearly exhibited here. Yet the deliberateness does not diminish the exceptional intensity in the identification of Rubashov's past and present.

Patterns of repetition and contrast are pursued throughout the novel. For instance, Rubashov becomes obsessed with the memory of a photograph of delegates to the First Party Congress. These men, among whom he sat, "looked like the meeting of a provincial town Council," yet "dreamed of power with the object of abolishing power; of ruling over the people to wean them from the habit of being ruled." Although the picture was once displayed prominently throughout the country, in embassies as well as in prisons, now there are only light patches on the walls. It epitomizes the past that No. 1 has repudiated, but which Rubashov cannot erase.

Rubashov reverses and is himself worshipped. To Vassilij the official portrait of Rubashov as a commander in the Civil War is a sacred possession, but it too must now be taken down and will survive only in the memories of the old. When Rubashov is arrested, his eyes have "the expression which Vassilij and the elder official knew from old photographs and colour-prints." Even the prison warder is reminded of "the colour-prints of Rubashov in uniform, which in the old days one used to see everywhere." Koestler's purpose is again accomplished with considerable neatness and precision.

These memories interact with Rubashov's own recollection of the Congress portrait to form an extensive metaphoric structure that confirms his alienation from the present regime and course of the revolution.

But the bond between Rubashov and an ostensibly more humane generation is not without qualification. The Rubashov Vassilij worships is "the little bearded Partisan commander who had known such beautiful oaths that even the Holy Madonna of Kasan must have smiled at them." The language of this Rubashov was spontaneous and full of human feeling, but has been abandoned for the grotesque and deadening rhetoric of Party dialectics. After the Civil War, Vassilij found Rubashov's formal Congress speeches nearly incomprehensible. Rubashov accuses the Party of forfeiting its understanding of the masses, "the great silent x of history," but because Vassilij, who represents this abstract factor in the flesh, never impinges on Rubashov's consciousness, it is clear that the responsibility belongs as much to Rubashov as to No. 1. Never does Rubashov conceive of his past the way Vassilij remembers it. The Party Congress and its vast design plague him, not the long-dead vitality of his own leadership.

Koestler's method of balancing characters in terms of similarities and differences is also apparent in Rubashov's relationship with his interrogator, Gletkin. Initially, despite the old Bolshevik's aversion to the barbarism of the new generation, he tries to persuade himself that the Gletkins must be accepted because they have right on their side and represent a necessary modification in the Party. When, during the investigation, Rubashov comes to reaffirm the supremacy of reason and logical consequence, his attitude toward the new breed alters. Gletkin is no longer an aberrant necessity, but actually the creation of the old guard: "Massive and expressionless, he sat there, the brutal embodiment of the State which owned its very existence to the Rubashovs and Ivanovs. Flesh of their flesh, grown independent and become insensible." Koestler also links Gletkin with Vassilij: both of them, the narrative emphasizes, received scars in the Civil War. The inevitable implication is that even Vassilij's loyalty enabled the Bolsheviks to develop and fulfill their dictum, that the end, when political, justifies the means.

Koestler's highly self-conscious and compelling artistry is evident not only in his alignment of characters but also in the overall structure of the novel. The beginning of the novel introduces patterns, like the photographs and the equation of religious and ideological faith, which are sustained throughout, and at the end the prominent threads are tied together, the final symmetry formed. Awaiting his execution, Rubashov expresses his sense of defeat in biblical terms. Moses at least saw "the land of promise," whereas "he, Nicolai Salmanowitch Rubashov, had not been taken to the top of the mountain; and wherever his eye looked, he saw nothing but desert and the darkness of night." He imagines his own executioner exactly as he did Bogrov's: a dentist who conceals his tools in his sleeve. We are meant to recall that when Rubashov went to Germany to excommunicate Richard, he was disguised as a salesman of dental instuments and that every guilty association in his mind has been accompanied by a toothache.

The memory of his arrest in Germany returns and with it the metaphorical identification of the Nazi and Soviet dictatorships. For the last time Rubashov smells fresh leather, a smell associated with the Gestapo agents, with the first chairman of the Communist International, and with Gletkin—a fraternity that for Koestler encompasses the horrors of European totalitarianism. Rubashov thinks he is back in his room and wonders "whose colour-print portrait was hanging over his bed and looking at him? Was it No. 1 or was it the other—he with the ironic smile or he with the glassy gaze?" In his autobiography Koestler says that the portraits of Stalin and Hitler appear at the beginning and end of the novel.[14] Curiously, the picture of Hitler is in fact described only once, in the instant before Rubashov's execution. One can only conclude that the symmetry of *Darkness at Noon* was intended to be even more complete.

But most readers have been less interested in the novel's narrative intricacies than in the validity of its psychological and historical interpretations. The Soviet dissident writer Alexander Solzhenitsyn has praised the novel as a "talented inquiry," which, more than any other document, has helped to clarify the "riddle" of the trials. He explains that Bukharin, the chief model for Rubashov, confessed out of total devotion to and need for the Party. "Bukharin (like all the rest of them) did not have his own *individual point of view*.[15] Yet in his political biography of Bukharin, Stephen Cohen argues that it was not a barren marriage with the soul of the Party that prompted his confession, but the hope of keeping his family alive. Cohen insists, moreover, that during the trial Bukharin managed to defend "Bolshevism's historical legacy."[16]

Literary critics, particularly those with a fundamental belief in the value of political literature, have also found Koestler's psychology "untrue to our sense of human behavior, even the behavior of Bolshevik politicians."[17] Indeed, it is true, as Irving Howe points out, that Koestler omits the "whole middle ground of Rubashov's experience, the gradual destruction of his will and integrity as he takes step after step toward acquiescing to the regime he knows to be vile."[18] This omission eventually calls into question Koestler's sense of history. But the process of the confession itself is not detached and "superimposed." Rubashov's unyielding belief in reason emerges in all his actions, and by the time of the last interrogations, we come to expect nothing from him but the most rigid, self-justifying logicality.

Before raising the issue of the confession, Koestler very skillfully depicts Rubashov's temperament in a variety of its manifestations. Rather than eliciting shock or fear, the arrest and imprisonment trigger Rubashov's habitual reliance upon his powers of logical analysis. He meets every detail of the situation with self-congratulatory expertise. When we first see him, he is inspecting his cell and making a mental inventory. He assesses the resonance of the walls and pipes: "So far everything was in order."

But Koestler weaves ironies into his responses, even during these early stages of isolation. Rubashov has correctly deduced that it is improbable "one had to get up here before seven in winter." Soon he hears marching in the corridors and expects the various sorts of torture to begin. Yet his anxiety is suddenly deflated by the appearance of "two orderlies dragging a tub of tea." Similarly, having fallen asleep in apparent control of himself and what is being done to him, Rubashov cannot will the movements of his hand. The real control is held by the guards who watch him twitch in his sleep. The arrival of the tea and the spasms of his hand are brief but powerful notations of the frailty at the heart of Rubashov's rational belief in himself.

There is no room in his makeup for unmitigated fear or prolonged surprise. The first scream of the tortured was usually terrible, he reminds himself, but then "one got used to it and after a time one could even draw conclusions on the method of torture from the tone and rhythm of the screams." Whereas this assessment is an evocative balance of human self-protectiveness and an almost inhuman reliance on reason and empirical data, his code-contacts with No. 402 demonstrate the self-deception, the absurd *hubris*, in his readiness to draw an idea out to its logical conclusion.

When No. 402 refuses his request for tobacco, Rubashov retreats into a precise, visual judgment of the monarchist prisoner: "He saw the young officer with the small moustache, the monocle stuck in, staring with a stupid grin at the wall which separated them." Comforted by this image, he deduces that between "you and us there is no common currency and no common language." But his proud logic crumbles because No. 402 suddenly decides to send some tobacco and because we realize that Rubashov had constructed his picture of an archetypal class enemy through a faulty process of logical inference. The monocle and moustache were hypothetical details that instantly became fixed in Rubashov's mind, made absolute by his syllogistic obsessions.

The pathos of his devout rationalism is also apparent in Rubashov's reactions to Arlova and Gletkin. After she is dismissed from her post, she desperately wants Rubashov to say or do something to affirm their bond; all he can sense is some urgency, but nothing of what it means. As a result, it is a relatively uncomplex decision for him to choose his own political survival over her life. But Rubashov has as much difficulty sustaining hate as love. His revulsion from Gletkin vanishes as soon as he lapses into the eminently rational habit of placing himself in his opponent's position. This tendency, which both annoys Rubashov and yet is the source of an eccentric pride, is highly selective. He can project himself into another's mind only if its perceptions are similar to his own. Because of their commitment to logical expediency, Gletkin and Ivanov, to some extent even No. 1, are open to his sensibility whereas the more emotional Arlova, Richard, and Little Loewy are essentially alien creatures to him.

Because Rubashov is an incomplete human being, even his discovery of guilt and selfhood is appallingly frail. The "closed system mentality" is so deeply rooted in him that his questioning and ultimately his renunciation of reason are either kept on the level of fragmentary memories or made abstract by being expressed in the language of reason. Jenni Calder remarks: "Even his doubts are sifted, categorised, channelled, by the habit of logical thought."[19] No genuine difference develops between Rubashov's articulation of his groping toward individuality, the claims of personal self, and the opposite side of the dilemma, the argument that feelings, privacy, and conscience are irrelevant to the inexorable sweep of the revolution. The rigid predictability of Rubashov's intellect erodes any hope we have for a fundamental change in his character.

The irony and sadness of his perceptions are most intense when he begins to reflect upon "the grammatical fiction," the realm of subjective reality. Forty years of political devotion and human denial have eliminated the use of "I" from his vocabulary. As a result, he is "shy" in the presence of his hidden self, ashamed to confront it directly: hence, the peculiar terminology. Initially Rubashov searches for the meaning of "the silent partner" with the impersonal curiosity that an unexpected problem in logistics or the appearance of something unusual under the microscope might arouse:

> He found out that those processes wrongly known as "monologues" are really dialogues of a special kind; dialogues in which one partner remains silent while the other, against all grammatical rules, addresses him as "I" instead of "you", in order to creep into his confidence and to fathom his intentions; but the silent partner just remains silent, shuns observation and even refuses to be localized in time and space.

There is an excitement and appropriateness in Rubashov's clinical appraisal of this novel sense of irrationality. The reader is bound to hope that the molecular vision will grow and reshape itself into an all-encompassing meditation. But Rubashov ultimately responds to the promptings of the inner voice with an unconscious process of classification. Because he is reluctant to defile the personal self by open contact with the facts of revolutionary violence and paradoxically because at the same time they threaten the validity of his past, Rubashov transfers his guilt-ridden memories to a sealed psychological vault where they remain until his transaction with the Party is complete.

The inevitability of Rubashov's confession is concentrated in the novel's most powerful episode, the scenes surrounding Bogrov's execution. One evening Rubashov senses "something unusual in the air" and is told that executions of his "sort" are imminent. With each detail passed from cell to cell, the intensity and Rubashov's awareness of his senses become unbearably acute. He wants the name of the victim and is finally told, "BOGROV. OPPOSITIONAL. PASS IT ON." We are not given Rubashov's reactions directly. To his neighbor he taps out his friend's full name, his distinction in the Revolution, and his fate. As Bogrov is carried before the cells, the prisoners' drumming grows to hypnotic force, and for an instant Rubashov ceases to be chained by his rigid intellectual patterns. He becomes, like the others, a primitive being pounding on the bars to reclaim part of himself lost to the shadows of political clarity.

But the essential horror is less in the image of Bogrov than in Rubashov's readiness to stop hearing the sound of his friend's broken voice. Barely minutes after the prisoners' tribal farewell, Rubashov again begins to argue with Ivanov: "He felt dully that the conversation had taken a turn which he should not have allowed ... he had not thrown out Ivanov. That alone, it seemed to him, was a betrayal of Bogrov—and of Arlova; and of Richard and Little Loewy." Even this perception cannot withstand the power Ivanov wields. Using many of Rubashov's own phrases, his appeal to Rubashov's past and his habitual logicality is bound to be effective because it evokes what is most deeply rooted in him. And Rubashov is not prepared to face the chaos and historical degradation that keeping silent would entail.

After the trial Rubashov turns again to the "silent partner" and frees it from its chaste isolation. Yet he still approaches it with the eye of an ideologue and welcomes it in the language that had voiced his "treason." "Obviously, only such suffering made sense, as was inevitable; that is, as was rooted in biological fatality." He has a vague glimpse of the eternal, but this too is cast in the abstract. Even his hope for the emergence of a "new movement" is expressed in predominantly mathematical terms; perhaps its members "will introduce a new kind of arithmetic based on multiplication." Rubashov's worthiest, most humane ideas are absorbed, pathetically altered, by a process of thought associated with cruelty.

The essential problem with *Darkness at Noon* is not aesthetic. The preparation for the confession is handled with great narrative skill. In his responses to prison and the past, Rubashov is one of the finest creations in modern political literature. But he is not a complete character. Out of a peculiar intellectual rigidity of his own, Koestler dooms Rubashov to an absolute dichotomy between historical belief and personal conscience.[20] He is not allowed to strive for their integration and reach a dead end. He is made to assume their eternal distinctness. There is no "middle ground of his experience," no change detailed within the narrative from Vassilij's Partisan commander to the betrayer of Richard and Arlova, because it seems that for Koestler purpose is instantly corrupted by method. What shapes the novel is not a conception of historical process, but an extraordinary ethical fatalism.

During the initial interrogation conducted by Ivanov, Rubashov says that his disillusionment with the course of the Revolution developed in "the last few years," at the time, that is, when he was driving dissident Party members to suicide or execution. But in the scene with Richard he is not shown to be conscious of any doubts about the Party's forging of historical change. Since the image of the *Pietà* and the paintings of human sensuality he sees in the gallery do not directly affect Rubashov's thinking, we must assume that he still believes the arguments he presents to his ideological victim with all the passion of the zealot.

The portrayal of his Belgian mission is similar. Listening to a dockworker who, like Richard, has arrived at the painful realization that "the Party is becoming more and more fossilized," Rubashov thinks: "I could tell you more about it." It would be understandable if he were merely unwilling to take the strike leader into his confidence. But Rubashov cannot sustain a *private* awareness of his uncertainties: "he was again fully convinced of the necessity and utility of his mission and could not understand why, in the noisy pub the night before, he had had that feeling of uneasiness." And again Rubashov completes his task with no further hesitation or reluctance.

The problem with these episodes is that Rubashov is not allowed to act in the interests of the Party and out of his years of commitment to the Revolution while also being aware of fundamental doubts about the validity of his actions. What would make sense of these fractured responses is the conception of "doublethink" Orwell was to dramatize in *Nineteen Eighty-Four*, the cementing of simultaneous, contradictory ideas by the totalitarian impulse. Unfortunately, Koestler is more interested in the constriction of the political mind, not in its elasticity.

Any knowledge of Bukharin and his colleagues adds a historical dimension to this literary difficulty and makes Koestler seem not only dogmatic but also strangely wilful in his paralyzing of Rubashov's consciousness. With the exception of the gloomy, short one, the Bolsheviks frequently made ambivalent decisions, choices that involved personal and ideological conflicts. For instance, despite private misgivings and his belief in *cultural* tolerance, Bukharin participated actively in the removal of Trotsky, Zinoviev, and Kamenev, thus allowing Stalin greater control of the Party bureaucracy.[21] In this case, fiction stumbles after biography. Koestler, by insisting on mental gaps and a configuration of psychological fragments, refuses his character such complex yet accessible individuality.

Although we come to understand and accept the confession, we are bound to question how ideological thinking could dominate any man to this extent. We are bound to wonder how, during the Richard and Arlova sequences, Rubashov's logic could be so self-contained as to preclude even a murmuring awareness of alternatives or contradictory feelings. It seems just as puzzling that this man who adores the past should have no memories of the Civil War and his own prominence in the battle for the future. If these issues were left unresolved, *Darkness at Noon* would still be a remarkable exercise in imaginative history. But at the end Koestler does provide an explanation for Rubashov's lack of ambivalence and apparent change.

After the trial Rubashov reflects on his successfully fought temptation to plead for his life, to declare the "subjective" truth and condemn the court itself, "to shout at his accusers like Danton":

> "You have laid hands on my whole life. May it rise and challenge you...." Oh, how well he knew Danton's speech before the Revolutionary Tribunal. He could repeat it word for word. He had as a boy learnt it by heart: "You want to stifle the Republic in blood. How long must the footsteps of freedom be gravestones? Tyranny is afoot; she has torn her veil, she carries her head high, she strides over our dead bodies."

Like most of the Bolshevik intellectuals, Rubashov was obsessed with the French Revolution, but instead of the ideologically pure speeches of Robespierre or Saint-Just's *Republican Institutions*, he memorized Danton's accusation. As a young revolutionary, Rubashov's mind was not stamped with visions of justice, with declarations of angry righteousness, but with an announcement of tyranny, betrayal, and decay. That the fascination with Danton's trial is more than a highlighted detail from the past is clear from another glimpse of Rubashov's political education.

"As a boy, he had believed that in working for the Party he would find an answer to all questions [of human suffering]. The work had lasted forty years, and right at the start he had forgotten the question for whose sake he had embarked on it. Now the forty years were over, and he returned to the boy's original perplexity." Koestler's bizarre and frightening suggestion is that "the question" is by nature incompatible with the empirical world, that it cannot survive even the first moments of contact with political choice and action.

These memories of his youth are not simply appropriate to Rubashov's state of mind after the trial; they account for his behavior, his sensibility, and they ultimately define the novel's ethical center. In a review of Koestler's autobiography, Stephen Spender remarks: "At moments one suspects that [he] thinks that a pattern of behavior is the same as an existence, just as he appears to think that the pursuit of a goal is the same as attaining one."[22] Out of a hidden metaphysic or mere impatience with intervening and irrelevant detail, Koestler asks us to believe in *Darkness at Noon* that the end of the Revolution is not just implicit in the beginning, but is *identical* with it, that vision and terror are indistinguishable twins. The "premises" of Rubashov's political career are the same as the conclusions. From this wholly terrifying, deeply antihistorical perspective, there is no linear process of change. The difference between Rubashov in the Civil War and Rubashov as a functionary of No. 1 is an illusion that belongs only to the porter, Vassilij. Rubashov need not be aware of doubts or of a more complex political understanding because as Koestler conceives him, Rubashov in the very act of commitment forfeited ordinary selfhood. Mind became ideology.

Inevitably, Koestler's metaphoric language reflects the stasis in Rubashov and in the novel's intellectual framework. Like the ocean, history is profound and disinterested; it absorbs all individual errors and feelings. The masses are its depths, its anonymous well. Other revolutionary parties understood only the surface changes of this vast ocean, but the Bolsheviks succeeded because they "descended into the depths" and "discovered the laws of her inertia." Clearly, the prevalent association of the sea is with the logic of history and the implementation of the Revolution.

But throughout the novel, the sea also symbolizes the contradiction of reason by the more elemental and subjective nature of man. Bogrov's terrible whimpering and the primeval ecstasy of the prisoners' drumming "smothered the thin voice of reason, covered it as the surf covers the gurgling of the drowning." The "silent partner" prompts the perception of infinity that Rubashov describes as the Freudian "oceanic sense." The tension between private and ideological attitudes to life is completely immobilized by these identical images.

The sense of distinct planes of experience—between which Koestler and Rubashov cannot allow any contact—is also produced by the novel's religious motifs. Through Vassilij, the image of the *Pietà*, and Rubashov's stunted vision of a new breed of monks, Koestler creates a firm association of religious feeling and biblical language with the affirmation of the personal. This kind of religion, like the "grammatical fiction," voices a gentle morality and compassion for mankind.

After the trial, Vassilij sees Rubashov as the suffering Christ, but Koestler also identifies Christ with No. 1, the creator of suffering, in order to extend the idea that closed systems like the Bolsheviks' militant philosophy develop a rigid hierarchical structure and become dogmatic: "The old man with the slanting Tartar eyes ... was revered as God-the-Father, and No. 1 as the Son.... From time to time No. 1 reached out for a new victim amongst them. Then they all beat their breasts and repented in chorus of their sins." Rubashov voices Koestler's most fundamental belief at this time—that revolutionary commitment is religious in origin. But by defining both poles of Rubashov's argument with himself, the religious allusions again suggest that public and private faiths are irreconcilable, that historical responsibility and personal conscience are implacable but static enemies.

Decades after the Moscow Trials and Stalinism, the debate over Rubashov's confession has lost some of its intensity, some of its threat to the vestiges of modern man's sense of innocence. Now we are prepared to believe virtually anything about the totalitarian mind. The essential fascination with *Darkness at Noon*, beneath the obvious narrative compulsions, lies in the curious bond between the author and the spirit of the Bolshevik intellectuals. The paradox is not that Koestler sees them as great men and as criminals, but that his judgment of what doomed the Revolution stems from the same quality in him—a corrosive rationalism which paralyzes choice, obliterates ambivalence, and pulls the novel away from history and the greatness of which it was genuinely capable.

NOTES

1. Koestler, *The Invisible Writing*, p. 478.

2. Ibid., p. 479.

3. Stephen F. Cohen, *Bukharin and the Bolshevik Revolution* (New York: Vintage, 1975), p. xv.

4. Koestler, *The Invisible Writing*, p. 190.

5. Sidney Hook, "Cold Warrior," *Encounter* LXI (July-August 1983): 12.

6. George Orwell, "Arthur Koestler," p. 239.

7. Koestler, *"Darkness at Noon* and *The Strangled Cry," Drinkers of Infinity: Essays 1955–1967* (London: Hutchinson, 1968), p. 281.

8. Raymond Aron, "A Writer's Greatness," *Encounter* LXI (July–August 1983): 10.

9. Koestler, *The Invisible Writing*, p. 490.

10. Ibid., p. 491.

11. See David Caute, *Communism and the French Intellectuals* (London: Andre Deutsch, 1964), pp. 132, 186.

12. Maurice Merleau-Ponty, *Humanism and Terror*, trans. John O'Neill (Boston: Beacon, 1969), p. 2.

13. Koestler, *The Invisible Writing*, p. 492.

14. Ibid., pp. 479–80.

15. Alexander Solzhenitsyn, *The Gulag Archipelago*, trans. Thomas P. Whitney (New York: Harper & Row, 1974), I–II, pp. 409, 412, 414.

16. Stephen F. Cohen, *Bukharin and the Bolshevik Revolution*, pp. 375, 378.

17. Irving Howe, *Politics and the Novel*, p. 229.

18. Ibid., p. 229.

19. Jenni Calder, *Chronicles of Conscience*, p. 129.

20. John O'Neill, the translator of Merleau-Ponty's *Humanism and Terror*, remarks that Koestler does not know "how to grasp the lived relation between the senses and ideology in a man's character" (ix-x). Merleau-Ponty's argument is that in believing that "either conscience is everything or else it is nothing," Rubashov is following "a sort of sociological scientism rather than anything in Marx," pp. 14–15.

21. Stephen F. Cohen, *Bukharin and the Bolshevik Revolution*, p. 240.

22. Stephen Spender, "In Search of Penitence," in *Arthur Koestler*, ed. Murray A. Sperber, p. 104.

W. MARSHALL

Viewpoints and Voices:
Serge and Koestler on the Great Terror

Both Victor Serge and Arthur Koestler have come to represent the
wandering *apatride* intellectual, engaged in, and victim of, the crises of the
first half of the twentieth century in Europe. Koestler is the Hungarian Jew,
the KPD member in Berlin before 1933, the intrepid journalist at work in
the USSR of the Five-Year Plan and a Spain ravaged by war. Victor Serge,
born in 1890 in Brussels to two exiled members of the Russian *intelligentsia*,
experiences imprisonment as an anarchist detained in France for five years
before and during World War I, activity in the syndicalist uprising in
Barcelona in 1917, war and militancy as a Communist in the defence of
Petrograd from 1919 and as an agent in Germany in the mid-1920s, and
finally victimization and exile as a Left Oppositionist under Stalinism in the
late 1920s and early 1930s, miraculously reaching the West in 1936. From
such a crude overview of the two men as *figures*, it is worth pointing out two
differences among many: a fifteen-year age gap, which means that Serge
experiences the events of the Russian Revolution at an adult age; and also the
irrefutable fact that Serge's life and activities are far less well known to
scholars and the general public today.

Indeed, this last remark is true of the two novels we are to investigate.
Darkness at Noon ultimately entered the mainstream of the canon of literary
studies. *L'Affaire Toulaév* did not. And yet analysis of both works reveals a rich

From *Journal of European Studies* 16, part 2, no. 62. (June 1986). © 1986 by Science History
Publications Ltd.

play of similarities and differences; it is in this sense that they are eminently *comparable*. Both were written at the close of the 1930s, with totalitarianism triumphant in Germany and the countries it was beginning to conquer, and in the USSR, where from 1936 to 1938 a Terror of monumental proportions had been unleashed, exterminating or banishing dissent; both were written by men who were by then on the margins of the international Communist movement, diagnosing totalitarianism as a historical phenomenon, and therefore inclined to investigate its origins. Thus the two novels are roughly contemporaneous in their composition: *Darkness at Noon* was written in 1938–40, during part of which time Koestler was interned in a French prison camp; *L'Affaire Toulaév* in 1940–42, with Serge on the run from the Nazis in France, the Caribbean, and finally Mexico. In addition, the two works seek to display, within 'literary' discourse, knowledge concerning the nature of totalitarianism and the fate of the Russian Revolution. This is achieved through a realist transposition of certain events occurring in the Soviet Union in the late 1930s, namely the Moscow Trials which, beginning in August 1936 with that of Zinoviev, Kamenev, Smirnov and others, had seen Old Bolsheviks confessing to incredible crimes of treason before being executed.

Parallels in subject-matter are reflected in intriguing resemblances of vocabulary and motifs. In *Darkness at Noon*, Rubashov's apprehension of "the oceanic sense" can come to crystallize around the "patch of blue sky" he can see from his cell.[1] In a network of vocabulary which has extended from Serge's first novel, *Les Hommes dans la prison* (1930), characters in *L'Affaire Toulaév* echo similar preoccupations. In *his* prison cell, for example, there is Roublev: "Maintenant, il se mettait dans l'angle droit de la cellule, tout contre la muraille, de trois quarts, levant vers la fenêtre son profil d'Ivan le Terrible, pour apercevoir un losange de ciel de dix centimètres carrés".[2] Motifs from other of Serge's post-1936 novels are echoed in the alternative titles of Koestler's work. That of the English version was suggested to him by the translator Daphne Hardy.[3] Taken from Milton's *Samson Agonistes* ("O dark, dark, dark, amid the blaze of noon"[4]), it seems to have two implications. Firstly, the hopes associated with the twentieth-century revolutionary movement have, once that revolution has been accomplished ("noon"), led to a new darkness. In addition, the reference to the physical blindness of Samson/Milton at this point could conceivably hint at Rubashov's moral blindness as he is imprisoned, not only physically, but within his own value-system. (Since Rubashov's "self-imprisonment" leads to his "self-execution", this particular interpretation is somewhat encouraged by Samson's declaration a few lines later in the poem: "Myself, my sepulchre, a moving grave."[5]) Serge's 1939 novel, *S'il est minuit dans le siècle*, plays on similar notions of the juxtaposition of light and dark, landscape and confinement, with a significant, but subtle, difference. Here it is light over dark, rather than dark obliterating light, that is stressed. In that passage which generates the title of the novel, the paradox of light co-existing with dark is applied to the phenomenon of thought: "un soleil de minuit. Glacial. Que faire s'il est minuit dans le siècle?" Rodion's reply to Elkine's question encapsulates the particularity of Serge's commitment to future-directed *praxis*: "Soyons les hommes de minuit, dit Rodion avec une sorte de joie."[6] A humanistic preoccupation with consciousness is implied by both titles, but already many of the differences between Koestler and Serge are adumbrated here. (The French title of Koestler's novel, *Le Zéro et l'infini*, is the one which, in an O.R.T.F. interview, he said he ended up preferring.[7] With this concept, that of the two mathematical symbols which upset all calculations, we are in typical Serge territory: that of the irreducibility of human consciousness to mechanistic or categorizing tendencies.)

This flux of similarities and differences seems to inform the attitudes of Koestler and Serge to each other. The occasions when they mention the other's name are dominated by the desire to stress the parallels, but in such a way that a certain misapprehension comes to the fore. (The two never met, of course, with Serge isolated in Mexico.) In 1946, Serge read *Le Zéro et l'infini*, which had been published in Paris the previous year. In August, he wrote to Antoine Borie: "Je vous signale le livre de Koestler, *Le Zéro et l'infini*, dont on m'assure qu'il s'est inspiré des miens; en tout cas, c'est un bon livre, rudement pensé. J'ai encore traité à *fond* le même sujet dans un roman que, pendant la guerre, on a généralement trouvé 'impossible', mais qui acquiert pour l'an prochain des possibilités de publication."[8] Serge sees the parallels and has (unecstatic) praise for Koestler's novel, but clearly believes that *L'Affaire Toulaév* is a more profound investigation of the subject. On the other hand, Koestler misunderstands Serge's position very badly. Writing in the second part of his autobiography about the non-Party fellow-travelling writers of the 1930s who maintained their creativity because they kept at a safe distance, he lumps Serge with three contributors to *The God that Failed*: "The few of us who actually took the plunge—such as Victor Serge, Richard Wright, Ignazio Silone—felt frustrated during their active Party career, and only found their true voice after the break."[9] This is in fact a nonsense. Serge was never a fellow-traveller *vis-à-vis* Stalinism, and never subordinated his artistic sincerity to a Party line. Significantly, Koestler refuses to acknowledge this.

It is the argument in the pages that follow that Koestler and Serge, *Darkness at Noon* and *L'Affaire Toulaév*, are in fact poles apart, both politically and in their attitude to literature and literary composition, and that their differing fates among the western intelligentsia since the 1940s are intimately bound up with political, rather than literary, judgements and evaluations. It is not our task simply to read off political differences between the two novels and to base our evaluation on the extent of our agreement with the ideological options they invite. It is not a question of ideology or ideologies, but of the *relationship* between the literary text and those ideological options and assumptions. In other words, when we read these two novels, is the relationship between ideology and the proclaimed specificity of literary composition oblique, subtle, contradictory, or can it be read off according to a preconceived schema?

It is necessary to begin with the very different basic structures of the two works. Both purport to investigate the Terror and its mechanisms. Both contain a quest for truth, for the authentic stance to be taken at this period in history. *Darkness at Noon* concentrates solely on one figure, Rubashov. In a sense, it is from this manoeuvre that all the contradictions of the text flow. Apart from a brief scene at the end (the first section of "The Grammatical Fiction", in which the porter and his daughter from the flat discuss Rubashov's trial and execution), it is Rubashov's point of view that dominates. In his quest for the truth of his situation, he explores the relationship between his present dilemma and his past, embodied in his relationship with others, who are thus subservient to him within the narrative. Having caused the deaths of Richard, Little Loewy and Arlova through his notion of the Party as the ends which justifies all means, having capitulated once before to a Party line with which he was in disagreement, he is in fact morally bankrupt, and cannot oppose Gletkin's demand for a confession and final sacrifice to the Party. Or rather, he could oppose Gletkin, but it would mean the invalidation of his whole life and commitment. For he had slowly, in prison, discovered the meaning of 'conscience', and half-realized his mistakes; he dies silently, believing there to be no goal left. Rubashov is in fact trapped in a vicious circle (*The Vicious Circle* was a draft title for the novel[10]), a moral as well as physical prison. The logic of revolutionary practice, as described in the novel, means that he has no choice other than to capitulate. The antinomies which emerge stare at each other across an unbridgeable chasm: ends/means, revolution/forgiveness, new/old, objective/subjective, we/'the grammatical fiction' ('I'). The first element is all, the second nothing, within the logic described.

In comparison, *L'Affaire Toulaév*, which is in fact one of the most tightly constructed of Serge's works, seems loose and sprawling. Serge's broad spectrum of protagonists produces a complex and pluralistic text which rings the changes on attitudes to the Terror according to the specificity of individuals and groups caught within the nexus of politics, society, psychology, struggle. At one extreme are the bureaucrats; at the other, those who die refusing to capitulate: Ryjik and Stefan Stern. Between them are Makéev and Erchov (who capitulate easily), Roublev (who agonizes but capitulates), Kondratiev (who develops from complicity in the Terror to resistance). It is thus a novel of *praxis* rather than fatalism, with resistance and renewal allowed to surface through Ryjik's hunger-strike, the figure of Kostia, and the youth festival at the end, muted by the ironies of Fleischmann, the uniform, the effigy of *le chef*.

Alan Swingewood is thus certainly wrong to liken *L'Affaire Toulaév* to *Darkness at Noon* because of its "fatalism" and "pessimism".[11] He underestimates the figure of Ryjik, the single most important, but not unique, anti-fatalistic element in the text. Ryjik is linked to a pattern of circle-imagery which goes beyond Koestler's philosophical vicious circle and its correlate, the miserable group of prisoners going round and round in the yard.[12] The whole of *L'Affaire Toulaév*, including a structure which examines one victim after another, can be read as a series of concentric circles, radiating outwards from the cataclysm of the shot that kills Toulaév. They are like the circles of Hell, or those of a pond when disturbed (the bureaucratic police-state disrupted by, first the murder, then Ryjik's suicide). The quest to escape the vicious circle is formulated thus: Roublev and his companions are "les hommes cernés";[13] "La pensée de Roublev ne cessait pas de tourner dans ce cercle de fer";[14] "comment sortir de ce cercle infernal, comment?".[15] The call is answered by the appearance of Ryjik which is deliberately delayed within the narration of events.

Indeed, throughout Serge's novel-cycle, the circle, from "la ronde" of *Les Hommes dans la prison* to the "vaste cercle tracé par la bassesse" which is Gobfin's universe in *Les Années sans pardon*,[16] evokes imprisonment and degradation. In a much more problematic way than Koestler's use of the word, Serge's circle-images can help to articulate *debate* concerning ends and means. It is Serge's preoccupation with the dilemma of power that is central here. Thus, in *Naissance de notre force* (1931) the revolutionary protagonists express confidence in the effectiveness of power in breaking the circle of oppression: "Ils ne sortiraient du cercle fermé de leur destinée que par la force."[17] However, it is the image of the concentric circle which a few pages later crystallizes the debates between the libertarians and the partisans of taking power:

> ... sa question tombait, ainsi qu'une pierre dans un flot profond, faisant courir autour d'elle des cercles innombrables:—Prendrons-nous le pouvoir, oui ou non?[18]

In *Les Années sans pardon*, the agonizing problematic implied by the circle image is expressed when D. realizes that "les justes" are now the oppressors, but that quietism and non-violence are untenable options as well: "Que, cherchant à briser le cercle du sang, nous y retombions. Conclure à la non-violence? Si seulement elle était possible!"[19] The form of *praxis* that Ryjik offers in *L'Affaire Toulaév* is one of powerless power, as his hunger-strike and death disrupt the machinations of the bureaucrats.

Clearly, the presence of a variety of protagonists does not automatically produce a novel of *praxis*, in the same way that a novel centring on one protagonist/victim of the Purges does not necessarily produce a work of fatalism and closure. The point is that various consequences ensue from the initial compositional strategy. In the case of *Darkness at Noon*, these take the form of distortions in two interrelated fields: historical representation, and narrative.

Koestler himself points out that Rubashov is an amalgam of a number of Old Bolsheviks: "L'idéologue c'est Boukharine, l'apparence physionomique c'est Radek. Et il y a des éléments de Trotsky aussi."[20] This combination is in itself outlandish: Radek the capitulator, Trotsky the leftist who never surrendered, Bukharin the rightist opponent of Trotsky in the 1920s. In the chapter on *Darkness at Noon* in *The Invisible Writing*, Koestler had attempted to meet objections concerning the artificially composite nature of the Rubashov figure by pointing out that he fully realized that some of the Old Bolsheviks had capitulated for other reasons: thus Rubashov was not Radek, who was trying to save his own neck, nor Kamenev, who was trying to save his family, nor the mentally broken Zinoviev. Rubashov is meant to represent the 'hard core' of capitulators such as Bukharin, Piatakov, Mrachkovsky, Smirnov. Koestler blames those who allege he was attempting to explain *all* the confessions through Rubashov for misreading the novel, and points out that he portrays the use of torture on Harelip, as well as Rubashov being denied sleep.

However, this is another sleight of hand on Koestler's part. The novel invites the identification with Rubashov, whose inner debate totally dominates. Harelip and the other characters are stimulants to that debate, rather than fully-fledged voices of their own. The conclusion is inevitable: there is no 'objectivity' to oppose to Gletkin's reasoning, no other political programme or *praxis*, merely the 'subjectivity' hinted at by the "oceanic sense", seen as a contradiction of revolutionary practice. With the single composite figure, cut off from specificities of psychology and history, there is nothing in the novel to suggest that another Old Bolshevik might reason differently. Koestler falls between two stools in wishing to portray quantity through one character. If he had featured different voices of roughly equal authority, then the ideological position invited by the novel would have been different: blame could not be laid against all revolutions, but against individuals and particular policies.[21]

Moreover, Koestler is historically incorrect in supposing that Rubashov's behaviour and intellectual conclusions could be modelled on those of Bukharin: "Men like Bukharin who shared their accusers' philosophy acted their role voluntarily in the conviction that this was the last service they could render to the Party after they had been politically defeated and had, according to the all-or-nothing law of totalitarian politics, forsaken their lives."[22] It is accepted by most commentators that Bukharin's testimony at his trial did not represent an intellectual capitulation to Stalinist logic. Victor Serge, in the heat of the event in 1938 and without much access to the developments behind the scenes, partially perceived this: "Boukharine, vivant ses dernières heures, le pistolet sur la nuque, a livré avec lucidité, avec humour, avec un courage sans bornes en tout cas, un étonnant combat. Pourquoi cette défense obstinée et victorieuse sur certains points, coïncidant avec, sur d'autres, des aveux insensés qui se réfutent eux-mêmes?"[23] The answers are provided by Stephen F. Cohen in his work *Bukharin and the Bolshevik Revolution*. After dismissing Koestler's theory of the confession as applying only to a tiny minority of the accused, he proceeds to explain that Bukharin, forced to stand trial because his wife and son were threatened, sought both to save his family and to undermine the myth of Stalinism as the rightful heir of the Revolution by making sweeping confessions to underline his symbolic guilty role, but denying or subtly disproving his complicity in any actual crime, making nonsense of the first element: "In a dazzling exhibition of doubletalk, evasion, code words, veiled allusions, exercises in logic, and stubborn denials, Bukharin regularly seized the initiative from an increasingly flustered Vyshinsky and left the case of the real prosecutor, Stalin, a shambles."[24]

Swingewood quotes a letter written by Bukharin shortly before his arrest, in which there is no trace of the dispirited Rubashov, as he bewails the "hellish machine" and "medieval methods" of the Terror, the "morbid suspiciousness" of Stalin, and describes the NKVD as a "degenerate organization of bureaucrats".[25] Even Manès Sperber, usually so close to Koestler, in that part of his autobiography which looks back at the 1930s, recognizes this point about the trial:

> … si je mentionne celui de Boukharine et de ses co-accusés, c'est uniquement qu'à divers points de vue il fut le plus honteux et qu'en même temps il apporta la preuve qu'il n'y a pas de limite à l'aveuglement de ceux qui se refusent à connaître la vérité.

Quiconque avait lu le procès-verbal des audiences publié en plusieurs langues à Moscou et répandu dans le monde entier, pouvait constater que Boukharine aussi bien que Rykov n'avaient fait aucun aveu, ou seulement d'une manière abstraite et générale, pour proclamer ensuite dans le détail et avec toute la clarté nécessaire la nullité de ces aveux.[26]

The historical distortions in *Darkness at Noon* also extend to the novel's portrayal of both Marxism and the revolutionary's relationship with the Party. Again, our argument here is not that there were never people who called themselves Marxist revolutionaries and who acted this way, but that the exclusivity created by the novel's narrow focus implies that all were like this, and lays down a single version of revolutionary theory, never contradicted in the text. In fact, there is very little that remotely resembles Marxism in *Darkness at Noon*. In his diary, Rubashov displays extreme idealism, seeing revolutionary conflict as a clash between two kinds of ethics, rather than the consequence of class division, which is not referred to all.[27] Indeed, Rubashov's inability to counter Gletkin's arguments is due to the poverty of his theory. 'History', for Rubashov and within Koestler's reading of Marxism, is a mechanism, a determinism: "We seem to be faced with a pendulum movement in history, swinging from absolutism to democracy, from democracy back to absolute dictatorship."[28] This is poles apart from the Marxist concept of man making his own history, the dialectical interaction of consciousness and the social and natural world. A quotation from *Capital* might suffice to illustrate this:

At the end of every labour process, a result emerges which had already been conceived by the worker at the beginning, hence already existed ideally. Man not only effects a change of form in the materials of nature; he also realizes his own purpose in those materials. And this is a purpose he is conscious of, it determines the mode of his activity with the rigidity of a law, and he must subordinate his will to it. This subordination is no mere momentary act. Apart from the exertion of the working organs, a purposeful will is required for the entire duration of the work.... Through this movement he acts upon external nature and changes it, and in this way he simultaneously changes his own nature. He develops the potentialities slumbering within nature, and subjects the play of its forces to his own sovereign power.[29]

As a consequence of this misapprehension, Rubashov has no answers to refute a mechanistic and dictatorial concept of the Party. Indeed, he had defended such a concept against the misgivings of Little Loewy:

> You and I can make a mistake. Not the Party. The Party, comrade, is more than you and I and a thousand others like you and I. The Party is the embodiment of the revolutionary idea in history. History knows no scruples and no hesitation. Inert and unerring, she flows towards her goal. At every bend in her course she leaves the mud which she carries and the corpses of the drowned. History knows her way. She makes no mistakes.[30]

This is the Stalinist point of view, in which the dialectic of Party and individual is replaced by a passive militant obeying an orthodoxy. Ivanov's resignation and acceptance ("we are in the hollow of a wave and must *wait* until we are lifted by the next"[31]) is thus not refuted by Rubashov. An inconsistency within the text betrays however the artificiality and falsity of the debate. Rubashov expresses nostalgia for the state of the Party at the time of the Civil War: the open discussion, the dialectic of theory and practice. The change that has taken place since is again placed on an abstract level: "the logic of history."[32] In other words, no reference is made to the concrete, lived historical and political struggles of the 1920s, the banishment of the Left Opposition and Trotsky, the victory of Stalin and the doctrine of "socialism in one country". The Opposition is of course mentioned in the novel,[33] but its origins are never explained. In fact, its very existence contradicts a basic premise. For if loyalty to the Party has its own relentless logic, then how do individuals exist who have renounced that logic? The answer must lie in the specificity of the organic experience of different groups and individuals. But since experiences other than those of Rubashov, along with his past compromises and lies, are not portrayed, then the monolithic structure of the tale survives.

The abstract nature of the argument means that 'history' in *Darkness at Noon* takes place in a vacuum. In fact, it is not recognisable as history at all. The country's leader, no. 1, is literally a cipher. Russia itself is never actually named, and thus the sense of its historical and cultural specificity is rather weak, apart from the references to Dostoevskii, whose work is nonetheless seen as part of a *general* moral argument.[34] Indeed, the most frequent reference to tradition is to Judaism and the Old Testament, with their a-historical notions of Messianism and fatalism: the Belgian Communists inquire about Soviet industry like children asking about the grapes of

Canaan;[35] the historical development of man must be sluggish like the forty years the Israelites spent in the desert;[36] like Moses, Rubashov had not been able to enter the Promised Land, but unlike Moses he had not succeeded in even getting a glimpse of it.[37]

As for the masses, the working-class, they are not a presence in the novel; if anything, they are a function via which ideological points are scored, from the taxi-driver who becomes another symbolic reference point for Rubashov's guilt,[38] or Vasily the porter and his daughter, who provide the contrast between the old humanism and the new amoral 'objectivity'.[39] Ivanov's view of the people, shared ultimately by Rubashov, is that of an anonymous, abstract, mechanistic force: "It bears you, dumb and resigned, as it bears others in other countries, but there is no response in its depths. The masses have become deaf and dumb again, the great silence X of history, indifferent as the sea carrying the ships.... A long time ago we stirred up the depths, but that is over."[40] Consistent with this argument, the new 'objective' leaders justify the lies about scapegoats and sabotage.[41] Rubashov merely utters a vague call for truth, but has no alternative to offer. Our objection here is not that this is an untrue portrait of the Stalinist leadership of the USSR in the late 1930s, but that this is presented as the only view compatible with revolution and Marxism.

L'Affaire Toulaév presents and represents history not as an abstract chess game, but as an organic process of lived contradictions occurring in a specific time and place among specific individuals. There can be no single representative of the Old Bolsheviks, for there is no single reading of history. The choices men and women make are bound up with a host of social and psychological phenomena, of which the concept of "loyalty to the Party" is just one element. The spectrum of characters included in the novel provides opportunities for exploring motivations and struggles that *Darkness at Noon* does not even address. The oscillations of Roublev, who eventually capitulates, represent a genuine flux of compromise and assertion, in which the just position sought is perceived not in terms of all or nothing, but of a play of greater or lesser emphasis on one of the antinomies in the dialectical relationship between conscience and Party loyalty. Roublev is caught in a contradiction that is untenable, as his hesitant, interrogative discourse testifies.[42] He believes that this contradiction can be overcome by both acceding to the Party's demands and composing the diary of his true thoughts for future generations. However, his stance, erroneous or not, acquires meaning only in relation to that of the other characters: the contrast with Ryjik is emphasized in the transition between Chapters 6 and 7. There also exists the contrast with Kondratiev, who develops from being an agent of Stalinism in Spain to a position of (relatively unspectacular) dissent. In

Darkness at Noon, references to the Civil War emerge in a rather arbitrary division between the golden age of the Party at war, and the present terror methods beginning only at the time of forced collectivization.[43] In *L'Affaire Toulaév*, interpretations of the brutalities of the Civil War, which Serge himself saw as a crucial factor in the subsequent development of the Revolution, *differ* according to the position the protagonist is adopting at that point within the flux of his psychological and ideological dilemma. Thus, within the flashback relating Roublev's Civil War experience, a relationship of guilt is established between past and present,[44] a factor which presumably influences his final decision to capitulate. On the other hand, Kondratiev interprets *his* execution of a hostage in the opposite manner, asserting that it throws a negative light on the price human life has reached twenty years later.[45]

Roublev also contrasts with Erchov and Makéev, whose past activities as hatchet-men make their capitulation almost automatic: having lied and killed for their *unquestioned* concept of the Party, when it was not a matter of their individual advancement, they can offer no counter-arguments when these values are evoked.[46] To that extent, Rubashov can be read as a composite of Roublev, Erchov, and Makéev, if such a hybrid ever existed historically.

There are historical elements at play in *L'Affaire Toulaév* which are absent from *Darkness at Noon*: the sense of Russia and the problems posed by its history, as evoked in the panorama provided by the plane journeys made by Kondratiev and Xénia, as well as the disquisition on the history of Makéev's remote region;[47] the sections on Spain and France which illustrate the ramifications of the Terror in the concrete struggles of other countries, as well as the repercussions on the bureaucratic regime of 'socialism in one country' of revolutions in the West; the presence of the masses, in the depiction of the material conditions under which they live (the poverty of Kostia and Romachkine, the food queues in Barcelona) and the psychological and ideological *contradictions* those conditions produce (the complex interplay at the beginning of *L'Affaire Toulaév* between Kostia's material and emotional needs, as he purchases the cameo rather than the shoes; the dawning of revolt in Romachkine; and the murder itself).[48]

Perhaps the most striking difference of all in the portrayal of history is the treatment of Stalin. In *Darkness at Noon*, he is the cipher "no. 1", either a melodramatic figure of menace, looking at Rubashov with a "strangely knowing irony" from behind clouds of smoke,[49] or the unseen and feared leader, in a *non-problematic* relationship with his "Party" and "Revolution", with whom Rubashov must come to terms. This is consistent, of course, with the introspective structure of the novel: no. 1 and the problem of revolution thus posed are seen through the eyes of Rubashov, and of Rubashov alone.

The multiplicity of characters in *L'Affaire Toulaév* offers different perspectives. In the confrontations with Erchov, *le chef* is the figure of menace, implicated in the network of power. Erchov is not portrayed in a manichean way, and when *le chef* is perceived from his point of view, insights are permitted into *le chef*'s psychology: "Les hautes portes s'ouvrirent à la fin devant lui, il apercut le chef à sa table de travail, devant ses téléphones, seul, grisonnant, la tête baissée, une tête lourde—et sombre, vue à contre-jour."[50]

It is this aspect of *le chef*—the victim of the processes surrounding him—that emerges in the scene with Kondratiev. The latter not only has a kind of friendship with him, but is in a more authoritative position, both politically and within the narrative, to challenge *le chef*'s positions. (This is why there are two scenes of dialogue between them, to emphasize Kondratiev's development.) At the first meeting, he emerges from the solitude of a corner of a vast, bare, white room. He confesses that he is suffocating, in lies and isolation ("Je vis au sommet d'un édifice du mensonge"[51]), and Kondratiev diagnoses his situation: "Cette étincelle au fond des prunelles, ce visage ramassé, vieillissement d'homme fort vivant sans confiance, sans bonheur, sans contacts humains, dans une solitude de laboratoire."[52] Kondratiev eventually plays on his understanding of *le chef*'s isolation to save his own life.

Le chef is therefore not a special case. A frequent device in Serge's prose is to construct vignette portraits of individuals; thus here *le chef*'s physical and psychological *specificity* is evoked, and placed in the context of the dynamics of history. Serge's *portrait de Staline* of 1940 is part of the renewed project of understanding psychology as part of revolutionary knowledge, as he attempts to trace the interrelation between specific personalities (Stalin's inferiority complex and fear, his immense will and energy) and historical developments (the rise of the bureaucracy in and after the Russian Civil War) that produce phenomena such as Stalinism. The cursory nature of Koestler's portrayal of "no. 1" thus fits in with his neglect of this problem in favour of a monolithic view of revolution: if he had gone further in describing a specific leader, a subjectivity at odds with specific emotional flaws, his fatalistic view of revolution would have been undermined.

In his 1951 review of the American translation of *L'Affaire Toulaév*, Irving Howe is rather too ready to assure us that Rubashov and Roublev capitulate for the same reason, "that it is necessary to subordinate opposition because of the threat of external capitalism". This is correct in the sense that neither of the two men has an alternative *praxis*, an oppositional programme or activity to offer. But there is an important difference between a blinkered loyalty to the Party and Rubashov's mental drama. Rubashov decides that no opposition (or pluralism) is possible within the Party; any opposition must throw the oppositionist out of the "swing of history", and invalidate all his past revolutionary activity. Howe goes on: "If it be replied that Serge is superior, not because Rublev [*sic*] is different from Rubashov, but because he also shows Old Bolsheviks who do not capitulate, then one has moved to the preposterous position of attacking a novelist for not having written about something. This may be a valid criterion for an encyclopedia, but not for a novel."[53] But it is surely the case that literary discourse, while being irreducible to 'knowledge' of historical events as such, does not transcend such facts. A realist and polemical work such as *Darkness at Noon* must, among other criteria, be judged according to historical veracity. It is the absences and silences of the novel that produce such contradictory pressures: Rubashov as single figure but composite of irreconcilable stances; the absence of the masses, concrete struggles, psychological specificity; the ghostly presence of an 'opposition' which, by the novel's own logic, cannot exist. These absences distort the intellectual argument that take place. The game is rigged, the reader crudely manipulated. The passage relating the execution of Bogrov, perceived, as ever, from Rubashov's point of view, owes its considerable power largely to the contradiction produced by the fact that it has been suggested to both protagonist and reader that pity and concern for human life are secondary considerations for a Party member. To be emotionally affected by the account of the execution, as is inevitable, means that the option of political quietism must be embraced. No stance exists in the text between Yogi or Commissar. The conflict is a manichean one, because the antinomies involved are frozen rigid.

The preceding pages relating the importance of historical considerations when evaluating these two works have frequently hinted at their artistic consequence: the narrative and structural organization of the two novels. The distinction to be made here is that between texts which are open, that is to say in which no stable or fixed (ideological) reading is possible, and texts which are closed, that is in which one (ideological) position dominates. Clearly, in a 'political' novel, which dramatizes political loyalties and identifications as they have penetrated the consciousness of the characters, the *direct* exposition of political issues must be deemed a failure, especially if the author's own ideological position is dominant instead of being one of many within a play of opposing viewpoints: the result would be propagandistic, rather than something recognizable in our culture as literary discourse.

It seems to us that there exist two main criteria for assessing the extent of authoritarianism or pluralism, closure or openness, within such texts. These involve certain questions of 'point of view' and of voice, which indicate the degree of perceptibility of the narrator. 'Point of view' (or 'focalization', to avoid stressing the exclusively visual aspect of the concept) indicates the authorial position or positions from which narration or descriptions are conducted. The 'focalizer', the centre of consciousness within the narrative act, can be either external or internal to the text, an objective/omniscient narrator or itself a part of the represented world observing and *evaluating* that world. It can, in turn, focalize from without (an observation of the external aspects or manifestations of a scene or character), or from within (the external or internal focalizer penetrates the consciousness of a character, or else the focalized becomes his or her own focalizer: the interior monologue is the main technique in this latter case). Focalization can be discussed in the contexts of perception (who is seeing the represented scene or event, the narrator, or protagonist?), psychology and cognition (who is feeling or knowing?), and ideology (who is evaluating or judging this event, action or utterance?). Clearly, these categories will overlap and inform each other. In Boris Uspensky's *A Poetics of Composition*,[54] there emerges a spectrum of possibilities of the ways in which ideology, in the sense of textual norms or the authorial belief-system, can enter a compositional structure. At one extreme would be the presence in the text of a single dominating point of view, that of narrator-focalizer. A character in a non-concurrent relation with this point of view would therefore be transformed from an evaluating subject into an object of evaluation. The extensive use of external focalization of a character from within, in that case, would be a prime example of this, as would the privileging of one internal focalizer. On the other hand, a multiplicity of judgements and evaluations might be discerned in the text, in which different points of view acquired more or less equal ideological weight. Here, internal focalizations, and shifts between them, would play a key role. This is what Uspensky observes in Mikhail Bakhtin's reading of *Crime and Punishment*,[55] in which a non-unitary, polyphonic reading of the text is produced by the interplay of a variety of ideological positions which either concur or are opposed to each other and which have no absolute hegemony. This is despite Dostoevskii's own ideological predilections and prejudices.

Questions of focalization inevitably come to embrace questions of voice, and Bakhtin's ideas on dialogics and the novel can contribute further to our analytical armoury. For Bakhtin, the novel as a genre is dialogical, developing, self-critical, in process, inconclusive, containing a diversity of social speech types and individual voices interpenetrating each other. There is no unifying, unanimous, unquestioned ideology (unlike the epic), but rather clashes of language and individuals who are themselves 'ideologues'. Debates on language are apt to forget that language is social and therefore dialogic. When we speak, we do not speak in a vacuum. Our words come up against all the other things that could be said, and against the anticipated argument(s) of our interlocutor(s). In the genuine novel, then, the point of view of the author is elusive within the outflow of 'heteroglossia':

> The author utilizes now one language, now another, in order to avoid giving himself up wholly to either of them; he makes use of this verbal give-and-take, this dialogue of languages at every point in his work, in order that he himself might remain as it were neutral with regard to language, a third party in a quarrel between two people (although he might be a *biased* third party).[56]

This polyphony can be achieved in different ways. Each time a discourse alien to the authorial position is permitted to sound, another ideological position is unveiled. Characters present different languages in the form of pure dialogues, different genres such as firstperson diaries may intrude, or else different languages may be dispersed beyond the boundaries of direct discourse itself, since all utterances interrelate and are dialogic. As with focalization, we might suggest a spectrum of manners of representing voice, from the bare report that a speech act has occurred ("he started telling stories"), through free indirect discourse and direct discourse to potentially the most polyphonous and pluralistic of all: free direct discourse, that is, direct speech devoid of its conventional cues. In a novel in which ideological clashes are foregrounded, the extensive use of free direct discourse would have considerable advantages, not the least because it might be difficult to assess the author's attitude toward the character involved: one of ironic distance, empathy, or an ambiguous combination of the two.

We may say, then, that *Darkness at Noon* is an authoritarian text of ideological closure created through the clash of two monologues rather than of polyphonous and dialogic interpenetration. It gags, whereas *L'Affaire Toulaév* attempts to let the gagged speak. The most blatant example of this authoritarianism is to be found when Ivanov proclaims to Rubashov: "'I don't approve of mixing ideologies.... There are only two conceptions of human ethics, and hey are at opposite poles. One of them is Christian and humane.... The other starts from the basic principle that a collective aim justifies all means'."[57] Not once is this highly arbitrary *and eminently debatable* statement questioned in the text, and obviously not by Rubashov here.

L'Affaire Toulaév provides instability in its spectrum of stances and psychologies. Despite a certain degree of ideological steering, it is certainly true that there is no single reading of this novel. Indeed, this is the point. It is the bureaucrats who are seeking to impose a monolithic reading of events on the irreducible and multifarious. Let us examine two analogous sections from *L'Affaire Toulaév* and *Darkness at Noon*, in order to assess the degree of narrative pluralism in each. These sections are: the discussion between Roublev, Philippov and Wladek in the snow-filled wood, from "Philippov, d'une longue foulée, passa devant", to "La peur vient tout à fait comme la nuit";[58] the discussion between Rubashov and Ivanov that takes up most of Chapter 7 of "The Second Hearing", from "He groaned in his sleep", to "Who could call it betrayal if, instead of the dead, one held faith with the living?".[59]

Other analogous passages might have been deemed more appropriate for analysis, such as the confrontation which takes place in the cell (as with Rubashov and Ivanov here) between Roublev and Popov in Chapter 6. However, that scene does not take place between protagonists of remotely equal narrative and ideological stature: Popov's stance is undermined by Roublev, but not completely, for an ironic gap begins to appear within Roublev's discourse as the text prepares us for the appearance of the ideologically consistent Ryjik. The scene with Philippov and Wladek is a genuine discussion; the equivalent scene in *Darkness at Noon* is the nearest that novel gets to a discussion.

For our purposes, the Serge passage can be divided into three subsections. Each sub-section contains an exchange in direct discourse, ending, not in closure and a sense of ideological completion, but in an emotional tone which postpones that closure indefinitely: "—Merveilleuse Sibérie, murmura Roublev que le paysage rasserénait"; Wladek's desire for hot tea, followed by the snowball fight; the farewells and Roublev's interpretation of the crescent moon as a premonition of death. The ideological stances (Wladek contemplating suicide if captured and describing current events as counter-revolution, Philippov pledging no deals with the bureaucrats, Roublev already contemplating the *possibility* of capitulation) are less important in themselves than the narrative weight they command. But, in fact, they are of more or less equal weight; there is little narrative intervention to support one over another. In the first subsection, the characters are all externally focalized from without by the omniscient narrator, and are given their sections of direct discourse to present their views. Verbs of perception do not privilege one point of view: "Les deux autres regardaient au loin", coming after an intervention by Wladek, is a continuation of the external focalization from without, rather than Roublev and Philippov internally focalizing a scene. It is true that on two occasions Roublev is privileged by being externally focalized from within ("Différent d'eux en son âme aussi", and "que le paysage rassérénait"), but this is partly counteracted by the phrase: "Roublev, en le répétant d'un ton embarrassé, avait sa mine de pédagogue préoccupé. Wladek s'emporta...." The description of his *appearance* (to whom?) could be read as his being focalized internally by Wladek and Philippov, just as much as his being externally focalized in the normal manner.

In the second subsection, the slight privileging of Roublev, internally focalizing his hands, and his reaction externally focalized from within ("il regarda ses mains qui étaient fortes et longues, un peu velues au-dessus des articulations—'des mains encore chargées d'une grande vitalité' pensa-t-il"), is balanced by the internal focalization of Wladek by *both* Roublev and Philippov ("Ils virent que ses grosses lèvres tremblaient"; "Ça se voyait en vérité à son visage bouffi"), and by the external focalization from within of Wladek, coupled with a snatch of free direct discourse (something not allowed even Roublev in this section): "Il découvrait le paysage désert, triste et lumineux. Des idées lentes comme le vol des corbeaux dans le ciel lui traversaient l'esprit: toutes nos paroles ne servent plus à rien,—je voudrais bien un verre de thé chaud...." In the third subsection, the focus on Roublev at the end, internally focalizing the moon and externally focalized from within, is again partially counteracted by another effect: the reader is left with an evocation of Roublev's emotional state, but it is Wladek who wins the ideological argument as he effectively caps Roublev's closing remark. Throughout the scene, then, genuine pluralism and polyphony have been at work: one character's perspective has been only partly privileged, and the omniscient narrator has not intervened in an obtrusive manner through, say, the use of irony.

For our purposes, the corresponding section of *Darkness at Noon* can be divided into four sections. The first lasts from the beginning of the chapter to Rubashov allowing Ivanov five minutes to speak (that is, down to "He stood leaning against the wall opposite Ivanov and glanced at his watch"). The next three subsections follow the pattern of Ivanov making his points at length, Rubashov then offering an objection, which is subsequently easily countered: that is, from "'In the first place', said Ivanov" to "... the message given him by the barber"; from "'What of it?' repeated Ivanov" to "... showed it in a very dubious light"; and from "'I don't approve of mixing ideologies'" to the end.

In the first section, Rubashov, typically for the novel, is externally focalized both from without and within by the omniscient narrator; it is he whose voice is dominant, with the long speech in direct discourse rebuking

Ivanov for the *mise en scène* of Bogrov's execution. However, this does not automatically mean, as we might expect, that it is Rubashov whose ideology is privileged and dominant. Unusual things are happening with focalization on the perceptual level, and in the use of verbs of perception. It is Rubashov who internally focalizes the scene and Ivanov. But only twice do the verbs of perception suggest that psychological and ideological dominance are associated with him: "…blinked at him ironically through his pincenez"; "Rubashov leaned his back against the wall of No. 406 and looked down at Ivanov." (Even this is undermined by Ivanov's *show* of equanimity: if Rubashov is doing the focalizing, it is Ivanov who is manipulating what is focalized.) All the other verbs of seeing imply that Rubashov is not in control: "Rubashov blinked at him, blinded by the light"; "Rubashov's eyes followed him, blinking"; "He was awake, but he saw, heard and thought in a mist." When things clear, the verbs are no more than neutral ("glanced at his watch"), and Ivanov keeps control of what is focalized ("showed his gold teeth"). Indeed, any dominance that might have been suggested by this pattern of focalization is partially undermined by a brief moment when, for the only time in this whole section, Ivanov focalizes Rubashov: "'Would you like some brandy?' Ivanov asked." This prepares the reader for the rigged game of ideological and narrative power that is to follow.

In the second subsection, the pattern is initiated of Ivanov being given complete dominance in voice, while the omniscient narrator's external focalization of Rubashov from both without and within is used to manipulate the explanation of why Rubashov is not answering. (For example: "He felt helpless and incapable of clear argument. His consciousness of guilt, which Ivanov called 'moral exaltation', could not be expressed in logical formulae— it lay in the realm of the 'grammatical fiction'".) Rubashov is unable, and is not allowed, to speak. It is the externally focalizing omniscient narrator that is visibly laying down the parameters and terminology of the debate. This has to be done for the reader to understand that Rubashov's one intervention, concerning pity for Bogrov, is irrelevant to the debate as such. Pity and revolutionary politics do not mix, and that is the end of the matter: "It was no use to try and explain it. The whimpering and the muffled drumming again penetrated his ears, like an echo. One could not express that. Nor the curve of Arlova's breast with its warm steep point. One could express nothing." Or rather, Rubashov is not allowed to express this view. In the process of this manipulation, Rubashov's narrative role as focalizer of Ivanov is played down, emerging only in terms of his ideological powerlessness: "He took off his pince-nez and looked at Ivanov out of redrimmed, hunted eyes."

In the third section, Rubashov is well and truly defeated, in his own and, it is supposed, the reader's mind. This is not a case of ideological steering, but bulldozing. Rubashov's repeated silences, and the representation of them, produce irony and débâcle. To Ivanov's total rejection of pity, Rubashov produces no counter-argument. This absence is, of course, devastating: all he can do is have a drink. But it is totally arbitrary: through external focalization from within, the reader learns that Rubashov himself had defended this view; any change which might have taken place must therefore mean he has to reject his whole past in order just to contradict Ivanov. It is unintentionally ironic that Ivanov declares: "'A pity that the opposite party is not represented. But that is part of its tricks, that it never lets itself be drawn into a rational discussion.'" There exists therefore a veritable *diktat* on the part of the narrator: no voice is allowed to irrupt into the text which might contradict the view that, say, no dialectical relationship exists between ends and means. When Rubashov rallies and attempts to contradict Ivanov, *within the terms laid out*, he in fact puts forward weak arguments that are easily beaten, both generally (Raskolnikov's crime is, indeed, not a political crime; a war situation is not radically different from that facing the Soviet regime) and within the narrative: yet another repetition of "Rubashov did not answer".

This process of discussion *appearing* to take place but automatically capped by an ideological closure, or sense of completion, leading inevitably to total rejection or total acceptance of Ivanov's view, continues in the fourth section. This begins with Ivanov's outrageous statement about "mixing ideologies", which is followed, not by an objective reply, but by Rubashov's withdrawal into "the oceanic sense" as he contemplates the stars. Rubashov's final effort is a powerful one: the promised end is not in sight. Ivanov's joyous acceptance of the bloody sacrifices made leaves him open to attack on objective grounds. But instead of invoking the Opposition, an alternative *praxis*, Rubashov's reaction is the product of another blatant example of external focalization from within: "Rubashov wanted to answer: 'Since then I have heard Bogrov call out my name'. But he knew that this answer did not make sense." The word "blatant" is appropriate: the account of what a character did *not* say renders the narrator and his manipulations glaringly visible. From that point, Ivanov is allowed his powerful arguments (the forces of counter-revolution have no moral scruples, so why should they?—this is not the point of course, it all depends on the context and aim of the "unscrupulousness", not the lack of scruples as an absolute in itself). Rubashov does not answer. More external focalization from within tells the reader that his resistance has gone.

The combination of narrative strategies here produces a very authoritarian text. By having Rubashov focalize Ivanov but giving Ivanov the lion's share of voice, Rubashov is bound to be affected by, and even drawn into, Ivanov's discourse. By such extensive use of external focalization from within, any *velléités* of resistance on Rubashov's part are undermined, and the ironic gap between his silence and his thoughts exploited. The discussion is in fact a monologue, with the terms laid down by the narrator who is seeking closure rather than openness and plurality. Ivanov's arguments are often powerful and this has its own significance (Koestler knew the Stalinist arguments well). But although the scene and the structure of the 'discussion' can be read as a mimesis of the relationship between jailed and jailor, it is in fact a representation of Rubashov's ideological *self*-imprisonment, and, at one level above that, the prison-guard attitude of Koestler himself toward his literary text.

As we have seen, lyricism, the contemplation of nature, the so-called "oceanic sense", are seen in *Darkness at Noon* as incompatible with revolutionary *praxis*. Any such passages thus participate in the process of ideological closure within the text, since they represent one element of the rigid opposition it proposes. In *L'Affaire Toulaév*, pluralism permits the interaction of Serge's lyrical interludes with political practice. In the passage just quoted, Wladek's fear of the Terror is overcome by the liberating experience of the snowball fight. The best example of this process in the novel is the account of Ryjik's journey with Pakhomov through the snow-filled Siberian night.[60] There is no equivalent of this passage in *Darkness at Noon*.

It takes place in transit. Ryjik is poised in *time* before a future which can only be death. On the previous page, his discouragement is stressed. The first paragraph of this section ("Ses déterminations prises depuis longtemps") refers to his outburst in *S'il est minuit dans le siècle* and his intentions of killing himself in order to let "Koba"/Stalin have his "dernier crachat".[61] The section ends with Ryjik refreshed, his consciousness and determination bolstered, and ready to face death with equanimity.

After the first paragraph, rationally appraising and describing the situation, there follow four others describing the natural scene and its effects on the men's consciousness, punctuated by four snatches of dialogue. The joy and liberation that the night brings engulf the two men, sweeping away the guard/prisoner relationship that actually prevails here, despite their friendship. The transition from rational appraisal to another state entirely is clearly delineated by Ryjik imbibing alcohol and dropping off to sleep ("il s'abandonna à la torpeur").

When he wakes up and sees the starlit night, it is a kind of rebirth. There is no gradual transition that might palliate the effect: "Il ne se réveilla qu'à la nuit haute." The phrase "le néant terrestre" stresses the kind of no-man's-land Ryjik is now inhabiting. In the description of the stars, the vocabulary of light and intelligence is to the fore ("scintillement", "éclair", "infime et souveraine lumière", the reference to his eyes), as well as connotations of sensuality ("on les sentait convulser", the stars caressing the shifting sea-like horizon). The stars are both mobile and immobile, full of energy ready to manifest itself in the world of men. They interact with the crystalline snow, in a reference to Kostia's experience in Chapter 1. And they point out the unity of man with the cosmos, as the movement of Pakhomov's body hides and then uncovers the constellations. The paragraph is unified semantically ("régnaient/souveraine", "enchantement/magique"), and at the same time covers a progression within Ryjik's consciousness, imitating his gradual awakening: his evaluating "*doux* vert glacial" becomes a statement on the stars' "unique vérité", and then Ryjik's focussing on his companion, eyes now wide open as never before.

The snatch of dialogue introduces the theme of communion and human fraternity ("chaleur commune", and the connotations contained in "berçait" of childhood and innocence). The sentences in this paragraph have the following structure: *plural* pronouns, past participle, verb. The stars, both multitudinous and individual, summarize the nature of the communion of Ryjik and Pakhomov: neither loses his individual identity in this moment of peace, in which the categories and structures of terror, and moreover even civilization (reason and unreason, time, material and immaterial) are surpassed. Again the word "rayonnant" emphasizes the links between the stars, and between man and the firmament. Such is the identification of Ryjik and Pakhomov that in the next snatch of dialogue, the origin of the utterances is not named, simply "l'un" and "l'autre".

The fourth paragraph is the transition from the state of reverie to the real world. Joy ("allègrement", "élan pareil à un chant") gives way to sleep again, or rather, the boundary between joy in the wakened or sleeping state is broken down. However, the awakening from the state of *assoupissement* coincides with the first light of dawn. The experience under the stars is now part of Ryjik's past, open to the organizing processes of memory ("Ryjik se souvint"), and thus of consciousness and *action*. Ryjik has learned that death does not ultimately mean loss. Both men are aware of the end of this state of grace, as the sun rises (from "colonnes de lumière nacrée", through "des couleurs inconnues qui envahirent le ciel", to "une blancheur totale"). The existence of the cities, and the executioner, is a contradiction of the indefinable lyrical experience. Reality, conflict, return with the slight tension between the two men, Ryjik's determined proclamation of "la vérité", and Pakhomov's tears. Ryjik's mental admonition to Pakhomov to bare his soul to his grief and the cold contains the seeds of what is to come. Pakhomov is "pauvre Pakhomov"; the (power) roles of guard and prisoner are overturned, as will happen between Ryjik and the bureaucrats, and his question ("qu'as-tu à perdre?"), echoing his conclusions about death in the fourth paragraph of the section, anticipates this death, which is described in terms of stars, *éclairs*, the substance of the universe.[62]

The parallels between Koestler and Serge hinted at at the beginning of this article are in reality rather superficial. Unlike Koestler, who had joined the German Communist Party at the beginning of the 1930s, Serge had never had any truck with Stalinism. Unlike *Darkness at Noon*, *L'Affaire Toulaév* could never be appropriated by Cold War propagandists. On another point which provides a telling contrast, their respective interests in later life in developments in psychology testify to their wildly differing concepts of humanism: Serge wished to integrate psychology into revolutionary practice, Koestler eventually drifted into a-historical notions of man, and even into an interest in the paranormal.

Koestler's political and ideological positions in the years that follow the publication of *Darkness at Noon* shed light on the logic of that novel, and it is easy to point out the contradictions. Thus the man who castigated the logic of the ends justifying the means supported Jewish terrorism in Palestine after World War II. It could be argued that Koestler was allowing, as a Jew, emotional prejudices to dictate his political stance. In the writings which look back on the fellow-travelling period, he of course strives to use this point to his own advantage. His explanations in *The God that Failed* are loaded with such references to his *personal* needs at the time of joining the Party in Berlin in 1931: "A faith is not acquired by reasoning. One does not fall in love with a woman, or enter the womb of a church, as a result of logical persuasion. Reason may defend an act of faith—but only after the act has been committed, and the man committed to the act."[63] These twin, non-rational themes of sex and religious faith are encapsulated in his comparison of Communist Party membership to Jacob waking to find he has slept with the ugly Leah and not Rachel, in other words, with an illusion.[64] The other psychological aspect of his 'conversion' was to do with his sense of *guilt*; as a child he suffered pangs of guilt whenever his impoverished middle-class parents bought him books or toys, and later as an adult when a suit he would buy for himself would mean less money to send home; he thus disliked the rich because they could afford to buy without a guilty conscience: "Thus I projected a personal predicament onto the structure of society at large."[65]

Koestler is describing his past commitment deliberately in this way, in order, by his "frankness", to denigrate the Communist mentality ("le système clos de la pensée") as a whole: "Je me plais à les appeler des 'sots intelligents', expression que je ne considère pas comme injurieuse, puisque j'ai été du nombre."[66] While it would be easy to point out the contrast of the lucid consistency and unity of Serge's life (Koestler's qualms about the disastrous 'social-fascist' policy with regard to the German Social Democrats are dispelled in five minutes[67]), Koestler lacking the critical faculty from the beginning but Serge never abandoning it, these admissions he makes not only risk backfiring, they shed light on his portrayal of Marxism in *Darkness at Noon*, where Rubashov is a bad Marxist racked by guilt.

Moreover, Koestler's position is itself influenced by an emotional problem: the need for an *absolute*, as Manès Sperber points out: "[Koestler] continue infatigablement la recherche d'un premier amour éternel, d'une cause inaltérable par les événements, d'une Rachel qui jamais ne deviendrait une Leah."[68] Koestler himself insists in an interview on this idea of an absolute, of all or nothing: "l'homme [i.e. Koestler] n'aime pas vivre avec un pis aller et se construit une utopie à laquelle il veut croire, et qui est l'absolu. Pas un relatif mais un absolu."[69]

As well as being a singularly non-Marxist approach, this may also explain why Koestler felt unable to be a dissident-within-the-revolution like Victor Serge; he had either to be virulently pro- or anti-Communist. After he resigns from the Party in 1938, with the arrest in Russia of his brother-in-law and friends Eva and Alex Weissberg, and before his complete intellectual break at the time of the Hitler-Stalin pact, he describes the discomfort of the political limbo of Trotskyists and crypto-communists: "We were all hellishly uncomfortable, suspended in no-man's-land...."[70] It may be for this reason that, as well as presenting just one version of Bolshevism in *Darkness at Noon*, he studiously avoids examining the political struggles of the 1920s in the sections on the USSR in *The Yogi and the Commissar*. Thus, when he explains away his Communist commitment in terms of blind emotion or neurosis (for example, "nos perceptions sont toujours filtrées par nos partis pris sentimentaux"[71]), he forgets that his virulent anti-Communism is as much a political stance as any other, and is just as open to analysis from the point of view of his neuroses. By refusing to embrace the importance of Trotsky, the Left Oppositionists, indeed all anti-Stalinist revolutionaries, he is simply continuing the monolithic, absolutist, "système clos" mentality of his fellow-travelling days. In this way, *Darkness at Noon* is the classically predictable product of an ex-Stalinist. Indeed, it shares certain characteristics with the products of the aesthetic prescriptions of Zhdanov. In an essay written by Bakhtin in 1934–35, it is possible to discern, as well as wider preoccupations, a critique of this current literature, dictated by an official Party form of ideological discourse:

authoritative discourse permits no play with the context framing it, no play with its borders, no gradual and flexible transitions, no spontaneously creative stylizing variants on it. It enters our verbal consciousness as a compact and indivisible mass; one must either totally affirm it, or totally reject it. It is indissolubly fused with its authority—with political power, an institution, a person—and it stands and falls together with that authority.[72]

NOTES

1. Arthur Koestler, *Darkness at Noon* (Harmondsworth, 1964), 203. Henceforth referred to as *DAN*. First published by Jonathan Cape, 1940.

2. Victor Serge, *Les Révolutionnaires* (Paris, 1967), 826. Henceforth referred to as *LR*.

3. P. Debray-Ritzen, "Un croisé sans croix: Communisme 1930–50", in Cahiers de l'Herne, *Arthur Koestler* (Paris, 1975), 188.

4. J. Milton, *Complete Shorter Poems*, ed. by John Carey (London, 1971), 347 (line 80).

5. *Ibid.*, 348 (line 102).

6. *LR*, 576. From a private communication, dated 20 October 1981, between Koestler and the author of this article there is an indication that Koestler, at an early stage, read and was influenced by *S'il est minuit dans le siècle*. Such an assertion must, however, remain speculative.

7. Cahiers de l'Herne, *op. cit.* (ref. 3), 188.

8. Victor Serge, *Témoins*, xxi (février 1959), 11. The emphasis is Serge's own.

9. Arthur Koestler, *The Invisible Writing* (London, 1954), 29; idem, *The God that Failed*, ed. by Richard Crossman (London, 1950).

10. Koestler, "Darkness at Noon", in *The Invisible Writing*, 393–405.

11. Alan Swingewood, "The Revolution Betrayed: Koestler and Serge", in *The Novel and Revolution* (London, 1975), 169–89.

12. *DAN*, 89.

13. *LR*, 710.

14. *Ibid.*, 731.

15. *Ibid.*, 832.

16. Victor Serge, *Les Années sans pardon* (Paris, 1971), 59. Henceforth referred to as *LASP*.

17. *LR*, 190.

18. *Ibid.*, 196–7.

19. *LASP*, 80.

20. Cahiers de l'Herne, *op. cit.* (ref. 3), 188.

21. This was seen by George Orwell in his essay "Arthur Koestler", *Collected Essays* (London, 1946). See also S. de Beauvoir, *La Force des choses* (Paris, 1963), 85.

22. Arthur Koestler, *The Yogi and the Commissar* (London, 1945), 148.

23. Victor Serge, *La Révolution prolétarienne*, no. 267 (25 mars 1938), 12.

24. Stephen F. Cohen, *Bukharin and the Bolshevik Revolution* (New York, 1973), 377.

25. Swingewood, *op. cit.* (ref. 11), 188.

26. Manès Sperber, *Au-delà de l'oubli* (Paris, 1979), 144.

27. *DAN*, 81.

28. *Ibid.*, 135.

29. Marx, *Capital*, i (Harmondsworth, 1976), 284 and 283.

30. *DAN*, 40–41.

31. *Ibid.*, 123 (my emphasis).

32. *Ibid.*, 142.

33. *Ibid.*, 168, for example.

34. *Ibid.*, 126.

35. *Ibid.*, 55.

36. *Ibid.*, 82.

37. *Ibid.*, 211.

38. *Ibid.*, 44–45.

39. *Ibid.*, 193–8.

40. *Ibid.*, 72.

41. *Ibid.*, 181.

42. *LR*, 729, 733, 832.

43. *DAN*, 86–88.

44. *LR*, 721.

45. *Ibid.*, 879.

46. *Ibid.*, 809–10 and 814 for Erchov; 832–4 for Makéev.

47. *Ibid.*, 740–1.

48. Erchov wonders at the masses as he drives through the streets, in terms which evoke the irreducible as opposed to the mechanistic, as well as the problematic *and therefore contradictory* relationship between leaders and led: "Et moi, que sais-je d'eux, sinon qu'ils sont des millions d'inconnus, classables par catégories dans les fichiers, dans les dossiers, tous différemment inconnus pourtant et tous indéchiffrables de quelque manière…", *LR*, 698. Anonymity does not imply abstraction, as in *Darkness at Noon*.

49. *DAN*, 54.

50. *LR*, 689.

51. *Ibid.*, 794.

52. *Ibid.*, 798.

53. Irving Howe, *New International*, xvii, no. 1 (January-February 1951), 58.

54. Boris Uspensky, *A Poetics of Composition* (Berkeley, 1983).

55. Mikhail Bakhtin, *Problems of Dostoevsky's Poetics* (Ann Arbor, 1973).

56. Mikhail Bakhtin, *The Dialogic Imagination*, ed. by Michael Holquist (Austin, 1981), 263 (author's emphasis).

57. *DAN*, 128.

58. *LR*, 721–5.

59. *DAN*, 117–32.

60. *LR*, 843–4, from "Ryjik songeait que les gens de Dyra", to "qu'as-tu à perdre?"

61. *Ibid.*, 617.

62. *Ibid.*, 861.

63. Koestler, *The God that Failed* (ref. 9), 25.

64. *Ibid.*, 82.

65. *Ibid.*, 27.

66. Cahiers de l'Herne (ref. 3), 146.

67. Koestler, *The God that Failed* (ref. 9), 39.

68. Cahiers de l'Herne (ref. 3), 11.

69. *Ibid.*, 141.

70. Koestler, *The God that Failed* (ref. 9), 81.

71. Cahiers de l'Herne (ref. 3), 150.

72. Bakhtin, *The Dialogic Imagination* (ref. 56), 343.

HOWARD FINK

Orwell versus Koestler:
Nineteen Eighty-Four *as Optimistic Satire*

T he intellectual relations between Orwell and his friend Arthur Koestler were complex and ambiguous. The two writers, both veterans of the Spanish Civil War and political rebels, were drawn together when Koestler came to Britain in 1940. Orwell was already familiar with Koestler's writings; he admiringly reviewed Koestler's *Spanish Testament* in 1938. In a 1943 review of Koestler's fictional autobiography, *Arrival And Departure*, Orwell claims that "for the past dozen years we in England have received our political education chiefly from foreigners; ... none, except perhaps Silone, cried more effectively than Arthur Koestler." And in discussing Koestler's *The Yogi and the Commissar* in "What Is Socialism?" (1946), Orwell calls this book simply the best discussion of the problems of twentieth-century socialism.[1] In their novels as in their essays, Koestler and Orwell deal with many of the same concerns, especially the conflict between personal and political vision. Orwell much admires Koestler's solutions to the aesthetic problems of political content in fiction.

Yet despite the personal, political, and literary sympathy between the two writers, Orwell clearly has irreconcileable differences with Koestler and objects to the ultimate philosophical implications in Koestler's later novels. In his 1944 essay, "Arthur Koestler" Orwell attacks Koestler's political perfectionism, his utopianism, because, he feels, the failure of Koestler's

From *George Orwell*, eds. Courtney T. Wemyss and Alexej Ugrinsky. © 1987 by Courtney T. Wemyss and Alexej Ugrinsky.

political dreams have led him to a dangerous political quietism.[2] Orwell sees a root problem in Koestler's loss of faith in the common man, the backbone and hope of the Marxist revolution, and in Koestler's related failure of hope in the political intellectual, whose basic motivation Koestler believes to be, inevitably, individual neurosis.

All of these themes find their way into *Nineteen Eighty-Four*, where they have special importance in our understanding of the hero and of the final message. Orwell's attitude toward Koestler's political limitations clarifies the distance between the failure of Winston Smith's political rebellion and Orwell's own relatively optimistic position. Winston's fate must not be confused with Orwell's ultimate vision. Winston is a figure patterned after Koestler's ficitional heroes: political intellectuals whose failures illustrate the limitations of contemporary political attitudes. Orwell clearly identifies the influence of Koestler on *Nineteen Eighty-Four* by a number of echoes and parodies of themes and images from Koestler's works, especially *Darkness at Noon*. Before looking more closely at *Nineteen Eighty-Four*, however, let us see what Orwell's essays on Koestler reveal of these connections.

One of the themes that draws Orwell to Koestler's writings is the latter's treatment of the concept of power in revolutions. But although Orwell accepts much of Koestler's analysis, he cannot agree with Koestler's negative conclusions on this subject. In his "Koestler" essay Orwell argues that "Koestler's published work really centres about the Moscow trials. His main theme is the decadence of revolutions owing to the corrupting effect of power." (III: 235) In elaborating on the presence of this theme in Koestler's *Darkness at Noon*, Orwell goes on to reveal the quarrel he has on this subject:

> If one writes about the Moscow trials one must answer the question, "Why did the accused confess?" and which answer one makes is a political decision. Koestler answers, in effect, "Because these people had been rotted by the Revolution which they served," and in doing so he comes near to claiming that revolutions are of their nature bad.... Revolution, Koestler seems to say, is a corrupting process.... It is not merely that "power corrupts": so also do the ways of attaining power. (III: 240)

Orwell makes a more optimistic political deduction from these trials:

> If one assumes that the accused in the Moscow trials were made to confess by means of some kind of terrorism, one is only saying that one particular set of revolutionary leaders has gone astray. Individuals, and not the situation, are to blame. (III: 240)

In a 1945 essay entitled "Catastrophic Gradualism"[3] Orwell discusses Koestler's attempt in *The Yogi and the Commissar* to deal constructively with this problem of power in revolutions:

> Throughout history, one revolution after another has simply led to a change of masters, because no serious effort has been made to eliminate the power instinct.... Koestler calls for a "new fraternity in a new spiritual climate, whose leaders are tied by a vow of poverty to share the life of the masses, and debarred by the laws of fraternity from attaining unchecked power." (IV: 18-19)

Orwell is skeptical, however, of how closely Koestler's own convictions correspond to his new ideal:

> Koestler is generally assumed to have come down on the side of the Yogi. Actually ... Koestler is somewhat nearer to the Commissar's end. He believes in action, in violence where necessary, and consequently in the shifts and compromises that are inseparable from government. (IV: 17)

Orwell suggests in his "Koestler" essay several specific sources for Koestler's pessimism about the possibility of successful revolution. These sources are Koestler's lack of faith in the masses, his belief that revolutionary political action issues from individual neurosis, and his overidealism or perfectionism. Orwell has, of course, already discussed the intellectual's lack of admiration for the common man in *The Road to Wigan Pier*.[4] In that book he speaks mainly to the English middle classes in an attempt to get their support for an alliance with the working classes, which he sees as the only way to carry out a successful revolution. The greatest obstacle to this alliance, Orwell argues is bourgeois prejudice and lack of information about the proletariat. In the "Koestler" essay, Orwell identifies exactly this prejudice in Koestler; he refers to Koestler's confession in *Scum of the Earth* that "he had never made contact with real proletarians, only with the educated minority," and he goes on to quote what he calls Koestler's "pessimistic conclusion: 'Without education of the masses, no social progress; without social progress, no education of the masses.' *In Scum of the Earth* Koestler ceases to idealize the common people." (III: 241) This position of Koestler is far from the traditional Marxist idealization of the masses, a necessary corollary of the belief that they will inherit the earth.

A related attack in the "Koestler" essay is Orwell's criticism of Koestler's cynicism concerning the psychological limitations of the political idealist. Orwell defines *Arrival and Departure*[5] as "a tract purporting to show that revolutionary creeds are rationalizations of neurotic impulses." (III: 242) What Orwell objects to in this autobiographical novel is the pessimistic conclusion that Koestler arrives at by imposing, on a Marxist utopian political vision, the Freudian view of man as determined by his unconscious: the title of Orwell's 1943 review of *Arrival and Departure* is, as we have seen, "Freud or Marx?" In this novel Koestler describes the protagonist as a "clinical, textbook case" of neurotic guilt. As Orwell points out in his "Koestler" essay "the psycho-analyst drags out of [Slavek] him the fact that his revolutionary enthusiasm is not founded on any real belief in historical necessity, but on a morbid guilt complex.... By the time that he gets an opportunity of serving the Allies he has lost all reason for wanting to do so." (III: 242) Despite Orwell's agreement with Koestler that "it may be true in all cases that revolutionary activity is the result of personal maladjustment," (III: 242) Orwell finds Peter Slavek's final irrational urge to action as unsatisfactory from a philosophical or political point of view as his earlier neurotic motivations. Orwell comes to the more optimistic conclusion that despite personal flaws the ideals of socialism are objectively valid motivations: "With such a history as [Slavek] has behind him, he would be able to see that certain things have to be done.... History has to move in a certain direction, even if it has to be pushed that way by neurotics." (III: 243) For Orwell the fact of individual neurotic motivation to political action, however universal, can never be allowed to gainsay the moral vision leading to political action.

The final charge that Orwell brings in his "Koestler" essay is that Koestler's pessimism stems in an essential way from his idealism, which is unrealistic and "hedonistic." Koestler's ultimate objective, as Orwell points out, is a pure utopian ideal: it is "the Earthly paradise, the Sun State," of which Koestler writes so clearly in his *Spartacus*. As a result of the inevitable failure of this unrealistic utopian ideal, Orwell charges that Koestler has retreated to the opposite extreme, to "short-term pessimism, ... the quasi-mystical belief that for the present there is no remedy, all political action is useless, but that somehow, somewhere in space and time, human life will cease to be the miserable brutish thing it now is." (III: 243) This pessimism of Koestler's is tantamount to the paralysis of all political action, and Orwell objects in a central passage, which indeed is the polemic conclusion to his "Koestler" essay:

At the basis of this [pessimism] lies his hedonism, which leads him to think of the Earthly Paradise as desirable. Perhaps, however, whether desirable or not, it is impossible. Perhaps some degree of suffering is ineradicable from human life, perhaps the choice before man is always a choice of evils, perhaps even the aim of Socialism is not to make the world perfect but to make it better. All revolutions are failures, but they are not all the same failure. It is his unwillingness to admit this that has led Koestler's mind temporarily into a blind alley. (III: 244)

Orwell rejects the practical—psychological, class, political—objections of Koestler to the possibility of revolution. And Orwell goes beyond, to a more positive belief in the possibility of revolution, based on an ultimately spiritual solution to the problem: a new, normative spiritual vision to replace Koestler's extreme Yogi idealism, its corollary, hedonism and Koestler's ultimate pessimistic reaction. These themes are central to Orwell's intentions in *Nineteen Eighty-Four*; the evidence is the many echoes and parodies found there of Koestler's beliefs and his fictional strategies.

Nineteen Eighty-Four[6] reflects the world created by Koestler in his novels, especially *Darkness at Noon*:[7] life in a totalitarian country in general, and in particular the scene, atmosphere, and processes of political arrest, torture, confession, and liquidation. The number of echoes of Koestler's work in *Nineteen Eighty-Four*, including frequent verbal equivalents, precludes mere coincidence. At the head of the Party in *Darkness at Noon* stands the figure of Stalin, the high priest celebrating the mass of his cult. The portrait of Stalin "hung over every bed or side-board in the country and stared at people with frozen eyes." This image is faithfully parodied in *Nineteen Eighty-Four*; everywhere in Oceania, on the signboards, on the landings of every building "the poster with the enormous face gazed from the wall.... BIG BROTHER IS WATCHING YOU, the caption said, while the dark eyes looked deep into Winston's own" (*Nineteen Eighty-Four*, pp. 5–6).

The political religions of both Koestler's Russia and Orwell's Oceania have been simplfed to absolute good and evil. Rubashov writes in his diary, "What is presented as right must shine like gold; what is presented as wrong must be as black as pitch" (*DN*, p. 224). Orwell echoes this archetypal opposition:

White always mates, he thought with a sort of cloudy mysticism. Always, without exception, it is so arranged. In no chess problem since the beginning of the world has black ever won. Did it not symbolize the eternal, unvarying triumph of Good over Evil? (*Nineteen Eighty-Four*, p. 25)

There is further opportunity for parody in the infallible correctness of the party line in *Darkness at Noon*, which is controlled by a periodic updating of written materials. Such a revision takes place while Rubashov is head of the trade delegation;

> The classics of social science appeared with new footnotes and commentaries, the old histories were replaced by new histories, the old memoires of dead revolutionary leaders were replaced by new memoires of the same defunct. Rubashov remarked jokingly to Arlova that the only thing left to be done was to publish a new and revised edition of the back numbers of all newspapers. (*DN*, p. 117)

Orwell takes up this obvious challenge to his parodic gifts; Rubashov's joke becomes a reality in the world of *Nineteen Eighty-Four*. Winston Smith himself is one of the hundreds of people in the Ministry of Truth who are necessary for the task of transforming the printed documents of Oceania; it is clearer now why *his* specific task is to update the back numbers of the *Times*. Orwell goes even further, from parody to satiric exaggeration:

> This process of continuous alteration was applied not only to newspapers, but to books, periodicals, pamphlets, posters, leaflets, films, sound-tracks, cartoons, photographs—to every kind of literature or documentation which might conceivably hold any political or ideological significance. Day by day and almost minute by minute the past was brought up to date. (*Nineteen Eighty-Four*, p. 43)

The form and function of this effective satire of information control, exaggeration to the point of self-ridicule, is as obvious as the kernel of the parody in *Darkness at Noon*.

The impossibility of unorthodoxy in Russia is described in *Darkness at Noon*. It is not only the conscious rebel who is destroyed by the Soviet party; anyone who is aware enough to be able consciously to articulate the party's philosophy is theoretically dangerous, no matter how loyal. When Ivanov, Rubashov's old friend and his first inquisitor, is himself liquidated, Rubashov speculates on the reason: "perhaps because he was mentally superior and too witty, and because his loyalty to No. 1 was based on logical considerations and not on blind faith. He was too clever" (*DN*, p. 178). Orwell creates an icy echo of Rubashov's speculation in Winston's thoughts about Syme:

> One of these days, thought Winston with sudden deep conviction, Syme will be vaporized. He is too intelligent. He sees too clearly and speaks too plainly.... Unquestionably Syme will be vaporized, Winston thought again.... There was something he lacked: discretion, aloofness, a sort of saving stupidity.... Orthodoxy was unconsciousness. (*Nineteen Eighty-Four*, pp. 56–58)

When Winston is finally arrested, the prison atmosphere is very much like that described in *Darkness at Noon*: the complete impersonality of Rubashov's captors, the destruction of time, the unending surveillance, the threat of certain death, and especially the constant artificial light in the prison where Rubashov finds himself. This light is the central philosophical symbol of Koestler's novel and, appropriately, the ironic symbol of its title, *Darkness at Noon*. It is echoed in *Nineteen Eighty-Four* by the phrase "the place of no darkness." At first this image is a positive symbol of Winston's utopian ideal; after his arrest it becomes an ironically reversed comment on that ideal: the constant light in the Ministry of Love where he is held prisoner. "In this place, he knew instinctively, the lights would never be turned out. It was the place with no darkness" (*Nineteen Eighty-Four*, p. 235).

The cycle through which Rubashov passes is a well-worn Soviet 1930s ritual of arrest, torture, interrogation, confession, release, employment in a useless sinecure, rearrest, a second confession, repentance, conversion to orthodoxy, and death. This pattern, the fruit of Koestler's own experience, is closely followed by Orwell in the fates both of the trio of Jones, Aaronson, and Rutherford and later of Winston himself. During the ritual each ruling party insists on controlling its victims' minds as well as their bodies; Rubashov writes, "We persecuted the seeds of evil not only in men's deeds but in their thoughts. We admitted no private sphere, not even inside a man's skull" (*DN*, p. 101). In *Nineteen Eighty-Four* Winston's faith before his arrest that you control at least "the few cubic centimeters inside your skull" is proved false; he must surrender to O'Brien especially his conscious internal reality.

At the end of this ritual of purification in Koestler's novel is the bullet in the back of Rubashov's neck which he accepts as the inevitable fate of the rebel (*DN*, pp. 21, 254). In *Nineteen Eighty-Four* from the moment Winston Smith admits his rebellion, even privately in his diary, he also knows that his is the same fate: "*theyll shoot me i dont care theyll shoot me in the back of the neck i dont care down with big brother they always shoot you in the back of the neck*" (*Nineteen Eighty-Four*, p. 23). Winston's fate is an echo of Koestler's pessimistic political vision. If it is asked how Winston knows he will receive a bullet precisely in the back of the neck, or how he knows that the lights will never be turned out in the Minstry of Love, the answer is that his creator is making a precise, ironic reference to the world of *Darkness at Noon*. By Winston's final failure Orwell emphasizes the inevitable failure of the utopian vision and the methods of the political intelligentsia described by Koestler.

It is on this point that Orwell's novel diverges from Koestler's. For in *Nineteen Eighty-Four* Orwell does not cancel the possibility of freedom and equality or the perfectibility of society. To understand this, however, it is necessary for the reader to recognize Orwell's attitude toward his protagonist and to withdraw from Winston. For, despite Winston's intense desire for escape from the rigid constructs of Oceania, he rejects the ultimate value of the individual in favor of a substitute orthodoxy demanding, like the party's, a ruthless exploitation of individuals for the sake of the group. Winston has no faith in the Proles, ability for revolution. Furthermore Winston's political faith is seen to be an excessive and unrealistic idealism. Finally, like the hero of *Arrival and Departure*, Winston's primary motive for political action is a neurotic trauma from his childhood, though he understands this only after his Freudian dreams in the secret bedroom with Julia.

To begin with Winston's compulsive orthodoxy: though rebelling against the party hierarchy and its symbols, Winston is not satisfied with his recreation of the past in isolation with Julia. Like the correct political intellectual that he is, he must find a new mass faith and a new political power base with which to identify. When Winston contacts the Brotherhood (as he believes) through O'Brien, he willingly accepts a new political religion, with the same antihuman moral flaws as that of the party he has rejected.

The Marxist faith in the ability of the masses to carry out the revolution, which Orwell says Koestler lost before *Arrival and Departure*, is impossible for Winston to believe or act on. Koestler's pessimistic epigram (attacked by Orwell in his "Koestler" essay), "Without education of the masses, no social progress; without social progress, no education of the masses," (III: 241) is closely echoed by Winston's pessimistic belief that "until they become conscious they will never rebel, and until after they have rebelled they cannot become conscious" (*Nineteen Eighty-Four*, p. 74). Perhaps the most bitterly ironic attack on Winston's lack of faith in the Proles is the early scene in which Winston acts out the role of a political intellectual in confrontation with the old Prole in the pub. Winston questions him in an attempt to discover whether the history books tell the truth about the past. But the two of them speak at cross-purposes, although this is not immediately apparent because the confrontation is reported from

Winston's point of view. Studied closely, however, the scene turns out to mean exactly the reverse of Winston's reported impression. His questions are on a completely theoretical, "historical" level, while the Prole offers in answer a series of authentic personal reminiscences, which function as quite satisfactory replies to Winston's questions. Winston cannot understand these replies, first because they contradict the accepted versions of the Brotherhood orthodoxy, but more seriously because he cannot accept the authority of the Prole's, real memories, because of his class prejudice against him (*Nineteen Eighty-Four*, pp. 92–96). It is clear even at this point that Winston's position is not to be confused with that of Orwell, who has condemned the class prejudice of his fellow left-intellectuals as early as *Wigan Pier*.

It will take a long apprenticeship with Julia, and the resurrection of his repressed memories of his family, to enable Winston to replace his abstract, intellectual approach and his middle-class prejudice by an appreciation of the human value of the Proles, near the end he can say

> the people of only two generations ago…were governed by private loyalties which they did not question. What mattered were individual relationships and a completely helpless gesture, an embrace, a tear … could have value in itself. The Proles, it suddenly occurred to him, had remained in this condition…. For the first time in his life he did not despise the Proles…. The Proles had stayed human. (*Nineteen Eighty-Four*, pp. 169–170)

A new faith in validity of the ordinary people leads both Rubashov and Winston Smith in their respective novels to a new social vision, a mystical utopian vision of the individual-as-unique and *at the same time* identified with mankind as a whole. In *Darkness at Noon* this vision is seen by Rubashov as a mysterious spiritual revelation of what is significantly called the "oceanic sense" (*DN*, p. 244). From his "oceanic sense" grows Rubashov's social vision of the future:

> Perhaps later … the new movement would arise…. Perhaps the members of the new party will … [achieve] the joining of a million individuals to form a new entity which, no longer an amorphous mass, will develop a consciousness and an individuality of its own, with an oceanic feeling increased a millionfold. (*DN*, p. 244)

In *Nineteen Eighty-Four* Winston has a similar vision just before his arrest. The Prole grandmother-washerwoman which he and Julia contemplate from their secret room becomes the symbol of the vitality and indestructibility of mankind and its potential in the future:

> The mysterious reverence he felt for her was somehow mixed up with the aspect of the pale, cloudless sky, stretching away behind the chimney pots into interminable distance. It was curious to think that the sky was the same for everybody.... And the people under the sky were also very much the same—everywhere, all over the world, hundreds of thousands of millions of people just like this ... who were storing up in their hearts and bellies and muscles the power that would one day overturn the world.... Sooner or later it would happen, strength would change into consciousness. (*Nineteen Eighty Four*, p. 226)

The new vision of the future articulated by the figure of the washerwoman is further symbolized here by Orwell through the image of the sky; this pale blue sky is precisely Koestler's own symbol for his "oceanic sense":

Over the machine-gun tower one could see a patch of blue. It was pale, and reminded him of that particular blue which he had seen overhead when as a boy he lay on the grass.... Apparently even a patch of blue sky was enough to cause the "oceanic state." (*DN*, p. 245)

For Rubashov, as for Winston, the human vision results from the reestablishment of contact with one's childhood roots. But beyond this optimistic vision, both protagonists fall into the short-term pessimism for which, Orwell has criticized Koestler in his essays. As Rubashov says, "Perhaps later, much later, the new movement would arise;" and further, "History had a slow pulse; man counted in years, history in generations. Perhaps it was still only the second day of creation" (*DN*, pp. 248–249). As for Winston, his faith in the Proles cannot overcome his conviction that Utopia can be conceived only in the far future: "Our only true life is in the future.... But how far away that future may be there is no knowing. It may be a thousand years" (*Nineteen Eighty-Four* p. 181). And Again:

> The proles were immortal.... In the end their awakening would come. And until that happened, though it might be a thousand years, they would stay alive. (*Nineteen Eighty-Four*, p. 226)

It should be clear by now that Orwell separates Winston from our sympathy at this point. As we have seen, he has criticized Koestler's vision of a long-delayed future utopia as political quietism. Indeed, he parodies Koestler's visionary "oceanic state" of mind most cruelly in *Nineteen Eighty-*

Four by calling the despotic political state—which has swallowed up England and which victimizes Winston Smith—by the very name of Koestler's ideal (mental) state: "Oceania." Winston, by echoing Rubashov's long-term optimism but short-term pessimism, is being distanced from the reader. The future, Orwell argues, will no longer belong to the Rubashovs and Winstons; not to the Koestlers but to a newer, more conscious and saner generation, which resides in the fertile loins of the proletariat:

> And could he be sure that when their time came the world they constructed would not be just as alien to him, Winston Smith, as the world of the Party? Yes, because at least it would be a world of sanity. (*Nineteen Eighty-Four*, p. 226)

Orwell here unmistakably separates the dehumanized and neurotic political intellectual from the human hope of the future, and from the new society mankind will surely create.[8]

This is the clearest indication that the final ritual and failure of Winston Smith, so much like Rubashov's and Koestler's own experience, is not to be generalized to the final message of the novel itself, or to be confused with Orwell's own position. *Nineteen Eighty-Four* is best understood as a satiric parody of *Darkness at Noon*, its pessimism and over-idealism. The novel, concludes then, with Orwell's rejection of Marxist communal and state utopianism, in favor of his positive belief in the possibility of a more reasonable program of melioration of society, based on a more human and rational ideal, once the errors of the bourgeois intellectual are left behind. And this is just how Orwell concludes his "Koestler" essay: "Perhaps some degree of suffering is ineradicable from human life, perhaps … even the aim of Socialism is not to make the world perfect but to make it better."

The writings of Arthur Koestler provide Orwell with details of totalitarian methods and life in an oligarchical regime, which Orwell projects into the imagined Britain of *Nineteen Eighty-Four*. More important for Orwell, Koestler provides a model for the hero of *Nineteen Eighty-Four*: Rubushov is an epitome of the political intellectual with his rationalization of cruel methods, his political religion (or "Nationalism" as Orwell terms it), his neurosis, and his final "short-term" despair of social revolution; and Winston Smith is patterned after Koestler's hero. Orwell's *attitude* toward the material he uses from, Koestler is indicated in *Nineteen Eighty-Four* through ironic reversal, exaggeration, and other forms of parody. By these techniques Orwell communicates his criticism of the overidealism and materialism of contemporary political ideology. The parody quality of Winston Smith and of the events of the novel preclude accepting literally the pessimism suggested by Winston's fate. The reversal of all hope is part of the parody-exaggeration itself; and the final message is an optimistic vision of a strong and sane mankind.[9]

NOTES

1. George Orwell's review of *Spanish Testament* appeared in *Time and Tide*, February 5, 1938; in *Collected Essays, Journalism and Letters of George Orwell*, ed. Sonia Orwell and Ian Angus 4 Vols. (London: Secker and Warburg. 1968), I: 295–296; cited subsequently as *CEJL*. Orwell's review of *Arrival and Departure*, "Freud or Marx?" appeared in *Manchester Evening News*, December 9, 1943. His article "What Is Socialism?" appeared in *Manchester Evening News* January 31, 1946.

2. George Orwell, "Arthur Koestler," written in 1944 and first published in *Critical Essays* 1946, *CEJL*, III: 234–244.

3. George Orwell, "Catastrophic Gradualism," *Common Wealth Review*, November 1945; *CEJL*, IV: 15–19.

4. George Orwell, *The Road to Wigan Pier* (London: Gollancz, 1937).

5. Arthur Koestler, *Arrival and Departure* (London: Cape, 1943); cited subsequently in the text as *AD*.

6. George Orwell, *Nineteen Eighty-Four* (London: Secker and Warburg, 1949).

7. Arthur Kostler, *Darkness at Noon*, trans. D Hardy (London: Cape, 1940); cited subsequently in the text as *DN*.

8. Kostler's theme of the political activist's neurosis and its effects on his political decisions is clearly reflected in the pardoy of Winston Smith's childhood traumas and his "sexual" cure through his relation with Julia, as well as his rat-induced neurosis at the climax of *Nineteen Eighty-Four*. The subject is to extensive for ths paper, but it is clear that Koestler's Freudian pessimism is one of the main objects of Orwell's criticism.

9. There is clear evidence in *Nineteen Eighty-Four* for this optimistic interpretation, especially the whole tenor the "Appendix Newspeak"; see my article, "Newspeak: The Epitome of Parody Technique in *Nineteen Eighty-Four*," *Critical Survey* V, no. 2 (Summer 1971).

REED B. MERRILL

Darkness at Noon *and the Political Novel*

> The attempt to escape ideological and utopian distortions is, in the last
> analysis, a quest for reality.   —Karl Mannheim

> Faith is a wonderful thing; it is not only capable of moving mountains,
> but also of making you believe that a herring is a race horse.
>   —Arthur Koestler

The usefulness of the term "political novel" remains somewhat controversial. In what continues to be the most useful, if problematical, study of the subject, Irving Howe's *Politics and the Novel* (1957), Howe maintains that it is *not* a genre since the term does not designate any "fundamental distinctions of literary form". Nevertheless, throughout his book he uses the term to make generic distinctions. Howe's assessment of the generic validity of the political novel echoes that of Wellek and Warren, who define "genre" as a "grouping of literary works based, theoretically, upon both outer form (specific meter or structure) and also upon inner form (attitude, tone, purpose—more crudely, subject and audience)".[1] And they find little difference between social or political novels (an opinion shared by Howe), a proof, they maintain, that the generic term is too murky and lacking in precise substance to be of theoretical use. Howe reduces the term "political novel" *ad absurdum* when he says: "I meant by political novel any novel I

From *Neohelicon* 14, no. 2. © 1987 by Akadémiai Kaidó, Budapest.

wished to treat as if it were a political novel, though clearly one would not wish to treat most novels that way. There was no reason to".[2]

The fact remains that the term clearly meets generic requirements as well as Wellek's and Warren's definition; that it contains distinctive elements which set it apart from other novelistic types; that rather than being an unclassifiable socio-political amalgam—in the drawing room sense of the early novels of Disraeli or Henry Adams, as suggested by M. E. Speare,[3] or in the theoretical sense of *Theory of Literature*—its inner form consistently concerns the inherent conflict between the individual and political ideology or, as Arthur Koestler puts it, the ethical problems of ends versus means. It would be difficult to find a better example of a political novel that personifies the genre at its best than Arthur Koestler's *Darkness at Noon*, a work which Howe finds to be more a propaganda piece and didactic tract than a viable novel. Howe believes that the political novel is necessarily a lesser form because its ideological biases overwhelm the novel's most profound purpose —to combine life experiences and ideas into synthesis (cf. Howe, 22).

Of course, an ideologue can turn what should be the dialectical tension of ideas in conflict with ideologies into a tract, but that is certainly not to say that a successful dialectic cannot be displayed by an author who has no ideological axe to grind. Such is the case in *Darkness at Noon*. The subject matter of any political novel will obviously concern this critical problem of narrative point of view, and certainly, because of their authors' obvious ideological biases, many novels (Sholokov's *Don saga*, Gladkov's *Cement*) do not contain the necessary tension and openness, conflict, and dialectical complexity of such masterworks of the genre as Conrad's *The Secret Agent* Dostoevsky's *The Devils*, or *Darkness at Noon*. For that matter, an author can choose the novel form for other didactic or "moral" purposes than political ones, as E. M. Forster demonstrates in regard to the novels of Thomas Hardy and their all too predictable pre-patterned plots.[4] And any kind of novel can be manipulated by an author into a platform for his own world view in such a heavy-handed way as to distort the freedom, reality, and credibility of its characters' choices and actions. It is all too tempting to want to play with causality, to assume the function of puppetmaster or "cosmoteer." It seems more writers do it than not.

A political novel will negate the requirement of the world's pluralism whenever it propagates a monistic thesis at the cost of depicting lived experience. But that is not to say that this genre cannot exist on the highest level with other kinds of novels, even though it is given to a specific subject: the inherent incompatability of political ideology and individual freedom. Howe singles out *Darkness at Noon* as the novel which illustrates all the negative attributes of the ideological novel, but I will attempt to prove that this novel personifies the genre at its best, that essentially Howe misunderstands Koestler's real intention in the novel, and that the novel pretty clearly meets all of Howe's own standards for the "ideal" political novel.

The thesis of Howe's book is that "the political novelist, even as he remains fascinated by politics, urges his claim for a moral order beyond ideology; [and] that the receptive reader, even as he perseveres in his own commitment, assents to the novelist's order" (26). In respect of the political novel in the twentieth century, Howe maintains that it "moves along a line of descent, an increasingly precipitous fall into despair" (230), and he condemns *Darkness at Noon* because of what he calls Koestler's "often crude theorizing about the moral premises which, he claims were the basis of the Old Bolshevik capitulation to Stalin" (231). Howe's evaluation of *Darkness at Noon* is inaccurate and insensitive to the text and Koestler's relationship to its point of view. To say that the novel illustrates "prefabricated themes" is to deny its ambivalence and enigmatic consequences.

Darkness at Noon was completed in 1940 and published in 1941 (Koestler read the galleys for the novel in Pentonville Prison). In his "Postcript" to the Danube edition of his collected works, which was published in 1973, he describes the purpose of this novel as part of a trilogy of political novels; at the same time he defines the genre itself:

> *Darkness at Noon* is the second novel of a trilogy—the other two are *The Gladiators* and *Arrival and Departure*—which revolves around the central theme of revolutionary ethics, and of political ethics in general: the problem whether, or to what extent, a noble end justifies ignoble means, and the related conflict between morality and expediency. This may sound like an abstract conundrum, yet every politician is confronted with it at some stage of his career, and for the leaders of a revolutionary movement, from the slave revolt in the first century B. C. (the theme of *The Gladiators*) to the old Bolsheviks in the nineteen-thirties and the radical New Left of the nineteen-seventies, the problem assumes a stark reality, which is both immediate and timeless. It was the realisation of this timeless aspect to Stalin's regime of terror which made me write *Darkness at Noon* in the form of a parable—albeit thinly disguised—without naming persons or countries; and which made Orwell, in writing *Nineteen Eighty-Four*, adopt a similar technique.[5]

This conflict between morality and expediency troubled Koestler to the end of his life in 1982. He had originally intended to entitle the novel *The Vicious Circle*. However, his friend and translator Daphne Hardy paraphrased a line from *Paradise Regained* for the English title ("Oh! dark, dark, dark, amid the blaze of noon"). Koestler himself chose the title for the French edition *Le Zéro et l'infini*. It is of some value to examine the implications—ontological, historical, political, and cosmological—of the three titles, since each represents one of the three points of view in the novel itself. *The Vicious Circle* suggests an all-too predictable cyclical view of history as deterministic, reductivistic, and causal, this being the ideologically orthodox position of the main character Rubashov's interrogators, especially Gletkin; *Darkness at Noon* indicates apocalypse and chaos in a world torn apart, notably from the perspective of Rubashov, whose own belief in historical inevitability and his destined role has been eclipsed by the brutality and fundamentalism of Stalinism, and who will be exterminated for having strayed from the ideological "order of things"; *Le Zéro et l'infini*, on the other hand, might represent Koestler's own perspective, the Zeno-like paradox of attempting to find meaning and order in a world of intellectual, historical, and cosmic randomness and relativity. There is little doubt that Koestler intended the novel to depict the tragic irony of good intentions turned to dust by the machine of historical necessity—an intentional mixed metaphor illustrating the grotesqueness of any abortive attempt to synthesize the unsynthesizable. However, it is not surprising that many of Koestler's critics, above all Howe, insist that *Darkness at Noon* is a thesis novel, among other reasons because ideologues and positivists are more often than not bewildered and confused by open-ended ironies, unresolvable dilemmas, and the absence of authorial didactic "moral guidelines" within the text.

Darkness at Noon is the story of the final days of former Commissar Rubashov, an old-guard Bolshevik intellectual and hero of the Revolution, who ironically finds himself arrested and imprisoned during the horror of the Stalin purge trials of the thirties. The events of the novel concern his imprisonment as an enemy of the people, interrogations, public confession, and execution as a traitor to his country. As Koestler has stated in several places, Rubashov is meant to be a composite stylized, of course, not biographical of Bukharin, Radek, and Trotsky.

The conflict in the novel is between the old Rubashov, who represents the composite ideologue-intellectual who rose in the Revolution to become a powerful force for Russian Communism, but who suddenly finds that he no longer fits the utilitarian purposes of the Party. Before his arrest it seems Rubashov has had little time for second thoughts, but after his incarceration he begins a series of reflections about the ethics of expediency as contrasted to a new-found sense of Christian humanism. Perhaps the knowledge of his hopeless situation has driven him to this revaluation. The paradoxical essence of this conflict unfolds and is accentuated by a series of three interrogations during which Rubashov is initially questioned by a former comrade in arms, Ivanov, a man whose own doubts about the veracity of the Party's new mission under Stalin reflect those of Rubashov, and a young zealot, Gletkin, whose vision of the Party's inexorable ends is unblemished by reflection or doubt about the scientific truth of Marxist–Stalinist dialectical materialism. Ivanov is a reflection of the present Rubashov who is filled with ambivalence and guilt; Gletkin is an image of the earlier Rubashov in his messianic fervor and cynical dedication. The novel itself is headed by quotations from Dostoevsky and Machiavelli, and the four sections are headed by quotations from Saint-Just, Dietrich von Nieheim, Machiavelli and the Book of Matthew, finally Ferdinand Lassalle—each meant to illustrate the antithesis of Christian humanism and its relativism, and unbending, manipulative political expedience.

The plot is as inevitable and inexorable as the ideology it is meant to reflect specifically; and as a parable, the plot describes the consequences of any ideology bent toward ends at whatever cost to freedom and ethical values. The "necessary" execution of Rubashov serves the kind of absolutistic "logic" of ideologies driven by blind faith and "scientific truth". Rubashov now looks on his past with regret and guilt; his present situation is one wherein he must decide to serve the purposes of the cause through a confession of guilt, or reject all he has thought and worked for in his adult life; he knows that his destiny is now wholly in the hand of the Party and history, that he is a non-person. The body of the novel is largely concerned with whether or not Rubashov will capitulate to historical inevitability and the unfathomable demands of the Party by signing a public confession. His ambivalence is constantly tested by scenes from his past reminding him of his cynical dedication to the cause at the expense of the human factor and ethical responsibility. They are countered by the image of Michelangelo's *Pietà*, which frequently appears in his mind as a symbol of pity and compassion for human suffering and sacrifice. His brutal dedication has caused many deaths, and now his mind is filled with regrets, sorrow and pity, feelings and emotions that refute his previous dedication and ironically mark his personal as well as his political guilt and punishment.

Although he gives himself to the Revolution by confessing to 'crimes' against the state, it is obvious that Rubashov's confession comes more from his fatalism and scepticism about mankind's ability to accept Christian humanism than his belief in historical destiny. And though he is dubious in the extreme that destiny will validate the dialectical process and vindicate him for his part in it, he finds his choice to be a Hobson's choice. He gives himself to historical possibility and to ideological necessity, and in so doing he dedicates his life to a concept of blind faith, to the irrationalism of a "higher power", and to a future utopia. At the same time he rejects the humanistic alternative of man-made values and ethical choices in a world of love and benevolence. The difference between one kind of absolutistic faith and another is only a matter of degree to Rubashov. For the ideologue, one comes to faith in a higher destiny than that of the individual by rejecting freedom and individuality and submitting to a collective myth. Rubashov's final thoughts before his execution clearly mirror the paradox of ideological faith and the nihilism that is its consequence:

> But where was the Promised Land?
>   Did there really exist any such goal for this wandering mankind? That was question to which we would have liked an answer before it was too late. Moses had not been allowed to enter the land of promise either. But he had been allowed to see it, from the top of the mountain, spread at his feet. Thus, it was easy to die, with the visible certainty of one's goal before one's eyes. He, Nicolai Salmanovich Rubashov, had not been taken to the top of a mountain; and wherever his eyes looked, he saw nothing but desert and the darkness of night.[6]

If there is any single guiding idea in *Darkness at Noon*, it is that there can be no possible conciliation of Christian humanism and absolutism of any kind. Although there are other kinds of humanism which might have greater intellectual appeal, I refer to "Christian" humanism since it is that sort of humanism that obsesses Rubashov, that he (not Koestler as some suppose) finds to be the only alternative to dialectical materialism. Rubashov is in no sense Koestler's spokesman. One must allow a character his choice and views. Rubashov's choice is the kind of either/or dilemma which Kierkegaard recognized when he differentiated between Christendom (ideological, nihilistic "Christianity") as being the antithesis of the humanistic Christianity of Christ himself. In the Marxist sense, ideology is the "deliberate creation of false images by the dominant class to manipulate and control the masses, and to perpetuate its own rule."[7] The concept of ideology has evolved in meaning from its being a science of ideas, to ideal or visionary speculation, to false social or political systems, to the present idea that ideologies have negative connotation or even that they are simply belief systems of a neutral nature. However complex the term might be to define, it seems clear that Koestler intended *Darkness at Noon* as an attack on those ideologies that corrupt and debase ethical values. In *The God That Failed*, a collection of essays on Marxist Communism by former members and fellow travellers such as Koestler, Spender, Gide, Silone, and others, Koestler suggests that there is little to choose between a revolutionary ideology and a traditionalist's religious faith, in that both are uncompromising, radical, absolutistic, and dangerously utopian in their idealism and irrationality: "All utopias are fed from the sources of mythology; the social engineer's blueprints are merely revised editions of the ancient text."[8] Ideologies are distortions of reality meant to provide final answers and ends which can never be discovered in the real world, as Karl Mannheim suggests:

> We have a case of ideological distortion, therefore, when we try to resolve conflicts and anxieties by having recourse to absolutes, according to which it is no longer possible to live. This is the case when we create "myths", worship "greatness in itself", avow allegiance to "ideals", while in our actual conduct we are following other interests which we try to mask by simulating an unconscious righteousness, which is only too easily transparent.[9]

Using Howe's terms, it would be impossible to find an imposition of "moral order" on the part of Arthur Koestler in *Darkness at Noon*. It is true that Rubashov's capitulation to the Party in essence at least says that ideology is preferable to a vague Christian mysticism. Yet there is no indication that Koestler condones his character's choice or adopts Christian humanism as a system of "moral order beyond ideology" as Howe suggests. The historical fact is that shortly after the completion of this novel Koestler himself became totally disaffected from politics and ideologies, that he was a life-long agnostic at best, and that his life was dedicated to the broad study of unifying the schism which separates irrational from rational man. That disaffection with ideological or religious solutions to the complex questions seems relatively obvious if one reads *Darkness at Noon* without a bias of one's own. Even a work such as Dostoevsky's *The Devils*, which Howe considers to the be masterpiece of the genre, is marred by Dostoevsky's particular kind of Slavophile Christianity and his lack of understanding of the value of the tragic humanistic tradition. But *Darkness at Noon* contains no authorial bias, no moral system which lies like a silver cloud over the text. It is amusing that all his life Koestler confessed to having the "disease of absolutitis", whereas his works demonstrate over and over his acceptance of the necessary pluralism of things, his realization of the pervasive and dehumanizing nature of monistic theories—ideological or otherwise.

In all his works Koestler has displayed a consistent kind of dualistic structuring of his theories, and this tendency has often over-simplified some of his ideas which might better have been spread accross a spectrum instead of being polarized by antithesis. In *Darkness at Noon*, Rubashov does find himself in an either/or position of accepting the passivity of the Christian view or the amoralism of the Party, and it would seem that a man of his intellectual capacity might find other alternatives to this dualism. The fact remains that under the given conditions Rubashov really *had no choice* at all.

Koestler's novels are hypothetical in that they are generated by a single intellectual dilemma, in virtually every instance by a protagonist who is confronted by some kind of ideological menace to his freedom. Such is the case in *The Gladiators*, which concerns the revolt of the slaves against Roman tyranny; in *Arrival and Departure*, whose subject is commitment to fighting Hitler's fascism; in *Darkness at Noon*, which concerns an ideologue caught in his own snare and suffering the consequences; in *The Age of Longing*, which concerns the devastating results of Pavlovian behaviourism turned toward the confrontation of East and West; (*The Call Girls*, which parodies international academic congresses, is his only work of fiction which belies his tendency to use the novel to test a theory.) Howe refers to this method as a "rigid fascination with absolutes and an equally rigid elimination of any possible choices of action lying between these absolutes, [which] lends his novels the appearance of intellectual clarity, of getting down to 'fundamentals'; but the fundamentals prove to be little more than a dazzling phrase and the clarity that of an overfocused and thereby untrustworthy picture" (233). Koestler wrote his novels as a scientist would carry out an experiment, but Howe misses the essential value of the novels, which are invariably attacks upon reductivistic thinking, and not platforms for the presentation of Koestler's own ideology, whatever that could possibly be.

Howe concludes his discussion of *Darkness at Noon* by restating his concern about the validity of the genre because of its tendency to become a moral tract when he says that the novel is "an example of how the modern appetite for ideology can harm a novelist when he turns to public themes" (235).

Darkness at Noon has survived a number of political novels by Silone, Malraux, and other contemporaries, because it serves a more universal purpose by transcending ideology with the kind of humanistic enlightenment that dominates Koestler's writings. He was too much a realist to accept panaceas and universal belief systems, and too much the sceptic to be called an ideologue (particularly after his rejection of politics in the late forties), and he was too much the humanist to allow himself to fall into the error of polarity or insularity in any of his ideas. Although he sought unity in a world of diversity, he was aware of the impossibility of trying to isolate that complexity into a single principle; he knew that to do so would be incongruous with reality. Whatever else one might say about Arthur Koestler, he tried to be realist as much as any man of our time and never a peremptory "moral puppeteer" guiding the fate of his characters or his readers.

NOTES

1. René Wellek and Austin Warren, *Theory of Literature* (New York: Harcourt Brace, 1947), p. 221.

2. Irving Howe, *Politics and the Novel* (New York: Fawcett Books, 1967), p. 18. (Further references to this work will be made by page number only.)

3. Morris Edmund Speare, *The Political Novel: Its Development in England and in America* (New York: Oxford University Press, 1924). Although Speare's work is outdated, it is of historical value because it illustrates the radical changes in political process from the early nineteenth-century novel to the late nineteenth-century novel.

4. E. M. Forster, *Aspects of the Novel* (New York: Harcourt, Brace and Company, 1927), pp. 140–41.

5. Arthur Koestler, *Darkness at Noon*, transl. by Daphne Hardy (London: Hutchinson of London, Danube Edition, 1973), p. 257.

6. *Darkness at Noon*, pp. 253–54.

7. Mostafa Rejai, "Ideology", in *The Dictionary of the History of Ideas* (New York: Scribners, 1973), p. 554. Rejai's article on ideology contains a useful, carefully delineated definition of the term, cf. p. 556.

8. Artur Koestler, in *The God That Failed* (New York: Harper Bros., 1950), p. 16.

9. Karl Mannheim, *Ideology and Utopia: An Introduction to the Sociology of Knowledge*, transl. by Louis Wirth and Edward Shils (New York: Harcourt, Brace & World, 1955), p. 96, cf. also pp. 97, 98. Mannheim's book remains perhaps the most important study of ideology as a system of ideas, particularly in regard to his discussion of utopianism and positivism as concepts with similar teleological purposes to those of ideologies.

WILLIAM PIETZ

The "Post-Colonialism" of Cold War Discourse

The idea of totalitarianism and the discourse of the cold war would seem to bear at most a negative relation to colonial discourse. By translating all political events and social struggle anywhere in the world into the master code of U.S./Soviet confrontation, there remains neither room nor need for the sort of colonial discourse so heavily relied on by Western states during the nineteenth and early twentieth centuries. While I am overstating the case—obviously colonial discourse did not vanish after 1940—the function of cold war language as a substitute for the language of colonialism raises the question of the comparability and actual continuity of colonial and cold war discursive structures. Can the almost immediate recognition and acceptance of cold war discourse after the war be explained in part by its appropriation of ideologically familiar elements from the earlier discourse of Western colonialism? An examination of four of the most important contributors to the intellectual legitimacy of cold war thinking—George Kennan, George Orwell, Arthur Koestler, and Hannah Arendt—suggests that this is the case.

The idea of totalitarianism is the theoretical anchor of cold war discourse. As such, its abstract conceptual core—that of a society in which all arrangements are directly administered through state institutions—becomes secondary to its expression of the concrete, historical idea that communism and fascism are the same thing, and that they—or rather it—represent a

From *Social Text* 19–20 (Fall 1988). © 1988 by Coda Press.

fundamentally new political phenomenon. While the word as the signifier of this equation and assertion already had currency in the 1930s, culminating in this country in the 1939 symposium on "The Totalitarian State" held by the American Philosophical Society,[1] it was in the years during and just after the Second World War that it achieved its full development and became the keystone of the dominant ideology of the period—an ideology which could declare the "end of ideology" and yet have no trouble distinguishing a true totalitarian like Mussolini or Tito from a mere authoritarian like Franco or Somoza. Grounded in history and fact through the equation of Stalin with Hitler and Soviet Russia with Nazi Germany, the general idea of totalitarianism could equate any form of total (hence "totalitarian") social or economic planning with the project of the total political domination of a society. But the supposed specificity, the unprecedented novelty, of totalitarianism lay neither in its political nor in its economic totalizations, but rather in its use of new communications and weapons technology to enforce a total control over language, the expression of ideas, and even, ideally, over thoughts. It was this latter dimension of totalitarian government—what Orwell named the "Thought Police"—that, for the promoters of the discourse of totalitarianism, revealed its true historical significance.

Totalitarianism was understood to reveal for the first time in history the essence of ideology, because under totalitarian governments ideological language and thought found its proper and definitive supplement: technologically sophisticated police terror. In thus connecting with police terror as the necessary supplement for its social actualization, ideology revealed its essence to be the will of the political state to dominate the very processes of thought and subjectivity. When the will to power (to power for the sheer sake of power) is embodied in the political state, ideology is at last revealed as the sheer will to will: the will to will will, to will belief, opinion, consciousness, forgetfulness, desire or absence of desire—the will to control at will all that is most private and personal, all that is most essentially human. And yet it was this ultimate revelation of the essence of ideology that made it possible for intellectuals for the first time to stand beyond ideology. By recognizing the truth of totalitarianism and embracing an enlightened anti-communism, the intellectual arrived at the end of ideology as such, there by perfecting his or her vocation as an intellectual, that is, as a critic of the ideological corruption of the intellect. Thus the essence of being an intellectual was actualized in the theory of totalitarianism and the praxis of the cold war struggle against socialism.

And yet the evidence for the historical object of this grand discourse was tenuous at best. Indeed, at least one of the thinkers I am considering,

George Kennan, came close to asserting about totalitarianism what Claude Levi-Strauss said about totemism: that it was the name for a social institution which never actually existed, but which was perceived to exist by the inventors of the term in order "to mark off certain human phenomena ... which scholars preferred to regard as alien to their own moral universe, thus protecting the attachment they felt toward the latter."[2] While we are still trapped within the totalitarian illusion in a way Levi-Strauss was not trapped within the totemic illusion—unlike him, we cannot say that it is a "problem which today seems unreal"[3]—we can see some obvious parallels between totemism as Levi-Strauss characterized it and totalitarianism. Proponents of both ideas perceived themselves to be true representatives of Western civilization, while the object of their study—an institution generating a social order characteristic of a number of alien and otherwise very different societies—was proper to a state of savagery completely excluded from authentically civilized societies and minds. Levi-Strauss characterized the theory of totemism as an act of exorcism and denial, and the same may be said of the cold war theory of totalitarianism: construed as an unprecedented, radically novel phenomenon, it could be regarded as alien to the truly civilized heritage of the West, as not only a monstrous but an illegitimate birth.

It was George Kennan, in his contribution to the 1953 American Academy of Arts and Sciences symposium on totalitarianism, who voiced a doubt about its historical reality. Kennan noted the absence of any satisfactory definition of totalitarianism; and, while there was general agreement that the two best historical examples of totalitarianism were Nazi Germany and Soviet Russia, these two states were so disparate in nature and origin that totalitarianism's two paradigmatic examples themselves cast doubt on the coherence of the concept. Indeed, Kennan found the real unifying ground of this historical concept not in "objective" historical fact, but in a kind of collective historical delirium, in the social power of a public dream expressed by certain writers:

> When I try to picture totalitarianism to myself as a general phenomenon, what comes to my mind most prominently is neither the Soviet picture nor the Nazi picture as I have known them in the flesh, but rather the fictional and symbolic images created by such people as Orwell or Kafka or Koestler or the early Soviet satirists. The purest expression of the phenomenon, in other words, seems to me to have been rendered not in its physical reality but in its power as a dream, or a nightmare. Not that it lacks the physical reality, or that this reality is lacking in

power; but it is precisely in the way it appears to people, in the impact it has on the subconscious, in the state of mind it creates in its victims, that totalitarianism reveals most deeply its meaning and nature. Here, then, we seem to have a phenomenon of which it can be said that its deepest reality lies, strangely enough in its manifestation as a dream, and that it is by this manifestation as a dream that it can best be known and judged and discussed.[4]

Totalitarianism, then, despite the fact that it denotes certain desperately important historical facts whose reality must never be doubted, finds its ultimate ground of meaning and authority in the dream or social delirium made accessible to intelligent comprehension in the literary works of certain writers. Although I believe the category of "totalitarianism" blocks rather than helps our understanding of the concrete phenomena it is intended to characterize, at the end of this essay I will argue in favor of Kennan's view that "literature" may be a privileged ground for interpreting (that is, for understanding what is true about) "totalitarianism." Before examining the two contemporaries whom Kennan names as definitive dreamers of the totalitarian dream, I wish to consider the "post-colonialism" in the cold war writings of George Kennan himself.[5]

American cold war discourse about totalitarianism served a double function: in regard to the Soviets, it justified a policy of global anti-communism by reinterpreting all struggles for national self-determination in terms of the geopolitical contest for zones of power against totalitarian Russia (thereby also rejecting the case for a continuation of the British colonial empire made by Churchill in his famous "Iron Curtain" speech in favor of a non-colonial "Pax Americana"); in regard to Nazi Germany, it saved the traditional pre-war faith concerning "the values of Western civilization" held by post-war foreign-policy "wise men"[6] by displacing the human essence of fascism into the non-Western world. Such a recovery of traditional ideals was especially important for old-style diplomats in the context of the new post-war world of electronic and aerospace military high technology and the new logics modeled on them, especially because what was most distinctive about the Nazis was their use of new police technology to further social terror. Here was an issue requiring a distinction. The necessary conscience-soothing exorcism was achieved by affirming the equation of Nazi Germany and Soviet Russia, combined with an historical interpretation of the essential Orientalness of the Russian mentality. The basic argument is that "totalitarianism" is nothing other than traditional Oriental despotism plus modern police technology. The appearance of the first truly totalitarian state in the heart of Europe was thus an accident, explainable by the fact that the technology permitting totalitarianism was invented by Western science and was thus first accessible in the West. Moreover, Germany's totalitarian moment is characterized by Kennan as a "relapse" into barbarism; far from showing a flaw in Western culture, it proved the need for constant alertness in preserving our distinctly Western values.

These interpretive moves are evident in Kennan's two key tests of the time his famous secret cable from Moscow in February, 1946, in which he formulated the policy of containment which within the next year became the basis of official U.S. policy as expressed in the Truman Doctrine[7]; and his anonymous 1947 article in *Foreign Affairs*, which was the most articulate justification of the new commitment to a cold war policy, a policy which programmatically ruled out the very possibility of dialogue and negotiation with the Soviets. In both the cable and his essay, Kennan supported his argument by pointing to what he called "the natural outlook of the Russian people." "At [the] bottom of [the] Kremlin's neurotic view of world affairs," Kennan's cable states, "is [the] traditional and instinctive Russian sense of insecurity."[8] Kennan goes on to characterize Russian psychology (which he views as the basis of Russian policy) in terms Edward Said has taught us recognize as the colonialist language of Orientalist. "The natural and instinctive urges of the Russian rulers," argues Kennan, cause the Russian government to be pervaded by an "atmosphere of oriental secretiveness and conspiracy."[9] The Russians' Oriental "mental world" is explicitly contrasted with that proper to the "Western" mind:

> Their particular brand of fanaticism, unmodified by any of the Anglo-Saxon traditions of compromise, was too fierce and too jealous to envisage any permanent sharing of power. From the Russian-Asiatic world out of which they had emerged they carried with them a skepticism as to the possibilities of permanent and peaceful coexistence of rival forces.... Here caution, circumspection, flexibility and deception are the valuable qualities; and their value finds natural appreciation in the Russian or the oriental mind.[10]

History—specifically the pre-modern geopolitics of the Eurasian "ecumene" which produced the "Russian-Asiatic world"—explains the Oriental essence of the Russian mind.[11] This mentality is distinguished by its ability, after centuries of direct contact with Europe, to *appear* civilized and to use this facade of civility for its own barbaric ends.

For Kennan and the cold war thinkers, communist Russia and totalitarian governments in general were nothing other than "ancient oriental despotisms" plus modern police technology.[12] The presence of such technology, Kennan argues, opened up Western nations (such as Germany) to the possibility of totalitarianism—which he characterizes as a "relapse" for what he calls "Western man had risen above Oriental despotism by his faith in "the dignity of the human spirit." Kennan makes it clear that he is not willing to attribute such faith to non-Western peoples:

> [Totalitarianism] is a condition made possible by modern police weapons, a state into which any great national entity *can* relapse, if it doesn't watch its step. Whether it might be considered a natural state for peoples of other climes and eras, I do not know. But for Western man, taught as he has been to look for hope and solace in the dignity of the human spirit, it is surely a pathological, abnormal state.[13]

It is the notion of ideology that permits Kennan to link modern totalitarianism with the traditional Oriental psyche, with its alleged neurotic sense of insecurity and lack of faith in human dignity. Kennan explains that in "Marxist dogma" the Russians had found "a perfect vehicle for the sense of insecurity"[14] which he earlier proposed as the central characteristic of the Russian-Asiatic mind. Kennan, and cold war ideologues in general, justified a policy based on the rejection of the very possibility of communication, negotiation, and compromise with communist totalitarians by presenting a double picture of the way the Russian-Oriental mind corrupts the very process of truthful language and reason by embracing an ideology which panders to their neurotic insecurity. On the one hand, Kennan writes that Russian communists are completely hypocritical, using Marxism merely as "the fig leaf of their moral and intellectual respectability."[15] Any use of rational thought or principled justification is merely the cover for an irrationally paranoid and immoral pragmatism which has no allegiance to reason and honesty. But at the same time, according to Kennan, they follow absolutely the logic and dictates of Marxist dogma. "Like the white dog before the phonograph," Kennan writes, "they hear only the 'master's voice.'"[16]

Thus communist totalitarians are doubly irrational and untrustworthy: they are irrational in their hypocritical, nihilistic pragmatism, which makes rational speech a mere vehicle for hidden, irrational motives; and they are irrational in their blind obedience to the logic of Marxist ideology, which makes rational speech the vehicle of overrationalistic motives detached from pragmatic reality. Totalitarian irrationality is thus simultaneously subrational and hyper-rational. Kennan explains the possibility of this paradox by appealing to the Russian-Oriental capacity for denial and detachment from the real world, which permits a kind of "self-hypnotism":[17]

> The very disrespect of Russians for objective truth—indeed their disbelief in its existence—leads them to view all stated facts as instruments for furtherance of one ulterior purpose or another.[18]

This ultimate explanation of the psychological ground of totalitarianism and ultimate justification of cold war policy by appealing to an apparently unprecedented (and yet all too familiar) capacity for irrationality and contradiction in the communist-Oriental mind based on a lack of all sense of the truth of objective reality is not peculiar to Kennan, but rather is characteristic of the other great forgers of the cold war discourse about totalitarianism.

Consider George Orwell's *1984*, the definitive novelistic vision of totalitarianism (published in 1949). As Jacobo Timerman said during a PEN speech in the actual year of 1984, what is striking about *1984* as a historical prophecy is how completely wrong it has turned out to be. The power of the book, as Kennan pointed out, lay in its ability to render an authoritative nightmare rather than an accurate historical picture. Where in this nightmare do we find colonialist elements?

For Orwell, of course, British colonialism was not only a national but also a familial inheritance. Born in Bengal to a father in the British imperial service, Orwell himself went into the family business as an imperial policeman in Burma after his unhappy years in English boarding schools. Orwell's disgust with British colonialism is familiar to all of us who read his "Shooting an Elephant" in high school (a favorite assignment in high school and college composition courses, along with the classic cold war essay "Politics and the English Language"). I am concerned here only with *1984*, a novel in which one might think all colonialist images have vanished in the vision of a warring world divided into three equally totalitarian empires. (Orwell was explicit in his letters of the time that the division of the post-war world into zones of power was a fundamental concern of *1984*.) There is, indeed, a fourth global area (roughly encompassing sub-Saharan Africa, India, and Southeast Asia, over which the totalitarian superpowers contend for control of cheap labor power; but, like the area of Winston Smith's city inhabited by the "proles," it is of no political significance in itself. In Orwell's totalitarian empires, colonialism and racism, like anti-Semitism, are nothing in themselves and exist only as minor ideological instruments used in mass media propaganda. Indeed, Orwell writes that,

> In no part of Oceania [the empire of the protagonist Smith] do
> the inhabitants have the feeling that they are a colonial
> population ruled from a distant capital.... Nor is there any
> discrimination, or any marked domination of one province by
> another. Jews, Negroes, South Americans of pure Indian blood
> are to be found in the highest ranks of the Party, and the
> administrators of any area are always drawn from the inhabitants
> of that area.[19]

Colonial racism exists only as an image in propaganda, in the form of the
Oriental faces of the hostile Eurasian army: "row after row of solid-looking
men with expressionless Asiatic faces." (Orwell, p. 7) So that, on the last page
of the novel, when the broken hero Winston Smith thinks lovingly of Big
Brother as "the rock against which the hordes of Asia dashed themselves in
vain,"[20] it is meant to be clear to the reader that behind the racist image is
not the truth of colonialism, but a fraud, a displacement from the truth of
totalitarianism.

Nevertheless, as in the case of Kennan, the persuasiveness of the vision
of totalitarianism is due in part to its adoption of Orientalist stereotypes.
This is especially evident in the philosophies Orwell attributes to the three
totalitarian powers. While Oceania and Eurasia both adopt modern socialist
political philosophies (English Socialism, or "Ingsoc," for Oceania, and
"Neo-Bolshevism" for Eurasia), the state of Eastasia simply promotes
traditional Oriental philosophy, which Orwell calls "Death-worship" or
"Obliteration of the self."[21] This equation of socialism with Oriental
philosophy to produce a convincing night-mare of totalitarian ideology is a
key to the theoretical heart of Orwell's book: his conception of
"doublethink." It is the mentality of "doublethink" that Orwell presents as
the psychological ground that makes totalitarianism possible. According to
Orwell,

> Doublethink means the power of holding two contradictory beliefs
> in one's mind simultaneously, and accepting both of them ... to tell
> deliberate lies while genuinely believing them, to forget any fact
> that has become inconvenient, and then, when it becomes
> necessary again, to draw it back from oblivion for just so long as it
> is needed, to deny the existence of objective reality and all the while
> to take account of the reality which one denies... [22]

Doublethink is the ultimate violation of the principle of non-contradiction
as the law guiding honest, rational, conscious thought. It is precisely what

Sartre had already analyzed in his notion of "bad faith" and which, earlier still, Freud had studied within the phenomenon of sexual fetishism in terms of "disavowal" (*Verleugnung*). But around the time he was writing *1984*, Orwell was characterizing Sartre as "a bag of wind."[23] What for Freud, Sartre, and many other thinkers was a crucial theoretical problem touching on a fundamental truth about the human psyche, Orwell and the inventors of totalitarianism rejected as alien to the human (or, at least, to the civilized Western) mind. This denial was, ironically, made possible by a contradictory pair of propositions: on the one hand, that totalitarianism was a radically novel, historically unprecedented phenomenon (O'Brien, the incarnation of the totalitarian spirit, explains that earlier despotisms were crude and ineffective by comparison because they did not seek to control subjectivity itself); and, on the other hand, that totalitarianism is simply the political expression of the traditional Oriental mentality. O'Brien is a new kind of man, a totalitarian superman, but his servant, Martin, has an "expressionless" "Mongolian face."[24] O'Brien and his "little yellow-faced servant"[25] are a pair embodying the paradox of the complete novelty and the traditional Orientalness of totalitarianism. The *expressionlessness* of Martin's Oriental face is the very capacity for doublethink (realized by O'Brien) made visible. That is, inscrutable expressionlessness represents the achievement of complete power in suppressing and concealing from others one's true thoughts and reactions—hence behind the expressionless face *anything is possible*. This traditional "Oriental" power is the necessary ground for the final refinement of modern totalitarianism, the capacity for "doublethink," the ability to conceal true thoughts and knowledge even from oneself, while at the same time one's behavior takes them into account.[26]

While the Orientalist ground of totalitarianism is mostly implicit in Orwell, it is perfectly explicit in the other great popularizer of the totalitarian idea: Arthur Koestler. In 1942, Koestler published an essay in *Horizon* magazine entitled "The Yogi and the Commissar," which later became the title for a popular collection of his essays published in 1947.[27] It was Koestler's constant thesis that the non-Western, non-civilized, non-democratic part of the world could be viewed along a single "sociological spectrum" whose extreme policies of social behavior were represented by the communist Commissar (an activist who believes that his revolutionary end justifies even the most immoral means) and the mystical Yogi (a totally passive type who doubts all ends and thinks that means alone count). Koestler's discourse, even more than Kennan's and Orwell's, demonstrates that redistribution and blending of discursive structures from older colonialist and anti-communist discourses characteristic of cold war language.

Lacking both Kennan's grasp of political history and Orwell's literary talent, Koestler authorized himself as a cold war sage through his stature as an ex-communist, his ability to construct popular essays around simplistic dualisms as "The Yogi and the Commissar," and his enthusiastic use of the apocalyptic discourse of totalitarianism. In his 1950 "Berlin Manifesto," Koestler wrote that "The theory and practice of totalitarianism are the greatest threat which humanity has faced in all its recorded history."[28] It is unprecedented among past "despotisms" because "the citizen of the totalitarian state must not only refrain from breaking the law, but must also adapt his thoughts and actions to the prescribed pattern."[29]

While the Hindu Yogi was Koestler's favorite "Oriental" figure, the whole repertoire of colonialist stereotypes—rendered with an almost classical purity—can be found in Koestler's essays and autobiographical writings, as when one reads of:

> ...the surly fanaticism of Islam—that harsh faith, born in the desert, which has never been reformed and liberalized, which became petrified at the stage of development that Christianity had left behind in the days of the Inquisition.[30]

The constant thrust of such passages is to dissociate "the West" and its authentic values from historical phenomena—such as the Inquisition or the slave trade—which might demonstrate totalitarianism's roots in European culture.

Like Kennan, but speaking with the authority of one who has experienced it from the inside, Koestler views Russian communism as shot through with the fanaticism, corruption, inefficiency, and small-minded irrationality of the Oriental despotic mentality. Describing his first meeting after joining the Party with his contact, "Herr Schneller," Koestler writes:

> It was my first experience of that unpunctuality which was *de rigueur* in the higher strata of the Party. The Russians, as semi-Orientals, are congenitally unpunctual; and as, consciously or unconsciously, every Party bureaucrat tried to live up to the Russian style, the habit gradually filtered down from the top Comintern bureaucracy into every national CP in Europe.[31]

This anecdote functions in Koestler's text as a sort of synecdoche for the corruption of the legitimate aspirations and moral integrity of European national communist parties by the "semi-Oriental" mentality and behavior of the Russians. European radicals in the 1930s became totalitarian, we are to believe, to the extent that they modeled themselves on the semi-Oriental Russians.

As for Kennan and Orwell, so for Koestler, the temptation and realization of totalitarianism is made possible by the double incapacity of the non-Western mind to be at the same time rational (guided by the principle of non-contradiction) and empirical (guided by objective facts). Either the Yogi abandons logical, non-contradictory thought in favor of direct mystical experience and irrational poetic language, or the Commissar becomes a hyper-rationalistic puppet of ideology, abandoning his capacity for reality-testing. Either way there is a loss of connection with what Koestler is pleased to call "objective reality." Like Kennan, Koestler finds at the root of non-Western psychology "the feeling of insecurity."

In some essays, Koestler makes his point about the self-contradicting, "ideologized" nature of all non-Western thought by proclaiming the uniqueness of the Western "scientific" mentality. Here he appeals to the anthropologist, who is to the colonialist discourse about "primitives" what the Orientalist is to the discourse about "Orientals." In "Anatomy of a Myth," Koestler seeks to explain "the magic aura of the Soviet myth."[33] Koestler (appealing also to the science of psychology) posits that "the human mind is basically schizophrenic.... The hot stream of belief and the ice block of reason are packed together inside our skulls."[34] Koestler's primary example of the "socially approved split mind patterns" characteristic of all non-Western cultures is the fetishism of "the Primitive":

> The Primitive knows that his idol is a piece of carved wood, and yet believes in its power to make rain; and though our beliefs underwent a gradual refinement, the dualistic pattern of our minds remained basically unchanged.[35]

Koestler proceeds to establish the scientificity of this fundamental dualism—the basis of that capacity Orwell termed "doublethink"—by citing "recent progress in neurology" distinguishing the thalamus ("seat of feeling and emotion") from the cortex ("the rind of the relatively new brain hemispheres")[36]: "Thalamic behavior is dominated by emotion, cortical behavior by formal reasoning."[37] Speaking now with the authority of "science," Koestler proceeds to argue that there is an essential continuity between the pre-logical mentality of the primitive fetishist and the ideologized mentality of those who believe in the "myths" of totalitarian movements. In totalitarianism, "fetishism" is simply displaced from material reality to language: what the magic-working idol is to the primitive, his system of ideology is to the totalitarian.

Both anthropology and psychology have during the last fifty years led to convergent results. Levy-Bruhl proved that the mentality of the primitives is pre-logical; the Kantian categories of (homogeneous) space, time, and causality do not exist in the primitive mind; it is controlled not by formal reasoning but by ready-made beliefs (*pré-liaisons collectives*). Freud demonstrated the affective roots of thought and traced them down to totem and tabu; Jung showed that certain archaic or archetypal images and beliefs are the collective property of our race. Even modern philology came more and more to the same results; Ogden and Richards proved the emotional fetish-character of words and tautological statements. Science has at last reached a stage sufficiently rational to be able to see the irrationality of the mind's normal functioning.[38]

The disjunction between the argument Koestler makes and the manner in which he argues is breathtaking. His invocation of authorities is completely uncritical: Levy-Bruhl "proved," Freud "demonstrated," Jung "showed," Ogden and Richards "proved." Yet he invokes them in this way to establish the fact of the irrational credulity of all minds that have not yet reached the "stage" of "science." Western science, Koestler argues, puts us for the first time beyond the split-mindedness normal to humans (though even for us, a relapse into pre-scientific "schizophrenia" is always possible, since this is an organic condition overcome only by the intellectual discipline unique to Western science). His innovation here is to map the familiar "magic versus science" argument of the human sciences, which functioned to distinguish Westerners from primitives, onto current political arguments seeking to distinguish "ideology" from the mode of political reasoning proper to those cold war intellectuals who had arrived at "the end of ideology."[39]

I have thus far tried to support my argument that very similar uses of colonialist rhetoric and of a complementary theory about the nature of the ideologized "totalitarian" mentality can be found in the seminal cold war discourses of Kennan, Orwell, and Koestler. The same structure of argument appears in the 1951 book which lent an academic respectability to the new theoretical discourse about totalitarianism. This was *The Origins of Totalitarianism* by the reactionary political philosopher Hannah Arendt. Her theory of totalitarianism must be understood in the context of Arendt's lifelong Heideggerian project of destroying every category basic to leftist political thought (above all, the concept of labor) according to a reactionary nostalgia for the political life of the Greek city-state (at least, as the world of the *polis* was conceived in the fantasies of thinkers such as herself and Leo Strauss).

For Arendt, the rise of "totalitarianism" means that "the essential structure of all civilizations is at the breaking point," that it threatens to destroy the essence of man," that for the first time in history "absolute evil appears," that "history itself is destroyed."[40] For Arendt, totalitarianism's novelty resides in the functional interdependence of ideology (whether Nazi or communist—she even equates the Nazi vision of a master race with the communist ideal of a classless society) with arbitrary, total terror. The coupling of absolute ideology with arbitrary terror, that is, of blindly hyper-rationalistic conformance to the logic of an idea (whose true appeal is its appeasement of one's sense of insecurity) with the release of a sub-rational power of pure caprice in the form of arbitrary police terror, is another version of the double-structured discourse about ideology embraced by anticommunist intellectuals wishing to deny any responsibility for fascism on the part of "Western civilization."

Arendt's particular contribution was to argue that totalitarianism was, in fact, the historical product of colonialism, an argument she developed in order to locate the true side of arbitrary social terror, and of racism as well, outside Europe, in "tribal" Africa. Arendt's argument only makes sense in the context of her general political philosophy (most clearly articulated in the *The Human Condition*), which is at bottom a reaction against Marxist theory. Arendt's philosophy is based on her distinction between "labor" and "work": "labor" is the never-ending process of satisfying our organic, bodily needs; it is contemptible, though—like sex—necessary, because it relates only to our animal species being. There is nothing essentially human about labor. "Work," on the other hand, involves the production of objects which endure and which build a specifically human environment (the city), which for the first time in history clears a space of appearance for action revealing the essence of what it is to be human, that is, political action. But the modern world is characterized by the intrusion of properly private, biological concerns into the public space of politics; with the French Revolution, a new actor steps onto the public stage of politics, "the mob," a rootless deterritorialized mass of proletarians.

Arendt argues that "the political principles of the mob [are to be] encountered in imperialist ideologies and totalitarian movement."[41] To understand Arendt's oracular pronouncement that "the organization of the mob will inevitably take the form of the transformation of nations into races,"[42] one must follow her argument about the corruption of the European mentality by contact with the primitive societies of black Africa.

Arendt argues that imperialist adventures in uncivilized parts of the world provided an outlet for the decivilized mob of Europe. Arendt's conception of "savages" is somewhere between those of Joseph Conrad and Edgar Rice Burroughs:

The world of native savages was a perfect setting for men who had escaped the reality of civilization. Under a merciless sun, surrounded by an entirely hostile nature, they were confronted with human beings who, living without the future of a purpose and the past of an accomplishment, were as incomprehensible as the inmates of a madhouse.[43]

"Prehistoric men," as Arendt calls them, only begin to influence Western man during the scramble for Africa in the late nineteenth century. Specifically, it is with the Boers in South Africa that the "post-historic" mob-man meets the pre-historic "tribal" man ("the accidentally surviving specimens of the first forms of human life on earth"[44] Such savages lack the work-built artificial environment necessary for truly human life to exist:

What made them different from other human beings was not at all the color of their skin but the fact that they behaved like a part of nature, that they treated nature as their undisputed master, that they had not created a human world, a human reality, and that therefore nature had remained, in all its majesty, the only overwhelming reality [Arendt was a literal-minded reader of the descriptions of the jungle in *Heart of Darkness*]—compared to which they appeared to be phantoms, unreal and ghostlike. They were, as it were, 'natural' human beings who lacked the specifically human character, the specifically human reality, so that when European men massacred them they somehow were not aware that they had committed murder. Moreover, the senseless massacre of native tribes on the Dark Continent was quite in keeping with the traditions of these tribes themselves. Extermination of hostile tribes had been the rule in all African native wars....[45]

Not only genocidal massacres, but institutionalized slavery as well, are not essentially European, but rather are ways Europeans "adjust" to the non-Western cultures to which such practices are proper.[46] We should remember that is was only with the political de-colonization of Africa beginning in 1955 that Western scholars "discovered" that primitive "peoples without history" did, in fact, have histories. Fortunately, there is now more than enough scholarly writing to discredit the historical accuracy of Arendt's obscene characterization of African societies. (However, Arendt's argument about the "tribal" politics of Africans is still a factor shaping actual American policy toward Africa.) I am here concerned only with tracing the logic of Arendt's argument about the colonial roots of totalitarianism.

The lack of a built environment (and, thus, of a human culture) leaves Africans determined by the mere animalistic principle proper to "labor." This finds its social form in the biologically kin-oriented "tribe," whose logic is essentially that of race. Indeed, Arendt argues, racism is nothing other than the mode of thought proper to primitives; racism entered Europe by way of the Boers, who learned it from the Africans:

> The Boers were the first European group to become completely alienated from the pride which Western man felt in living in a world created and fabricated by himself.... The Boers lived on their slaves exactly the way natives lived on an unprepared and unchanged nature. When the Boers, in their fright and misery, decided to use these savages as though they were just another form of animal life, they embarked upon a process which could only end with their own degeneration into a white race living beside and together with black races from whom in the end they would differ only in the color of their skin.... [The Boers] had transformed themselves into a tribe and had lost the European's feeling for a territory, a *patria* of his own. They behaved exactly like the black tribes who had also roamed the Dark Continent for centuries.[47]

Arendt's vision of the nomadism of African "tribes" is meant to indicate such cultures' ceaseless movement (allowing no space—literally—for philosophical reflection or human [i.e., political] action) as determined by the ceaseless flow of biological need and physical labor. Western man is susceptible to such nomadism, and the racist politics proper to it, only when he has been reduced to the rootless, deterritorialized mob:

> Rootlessness is the characteristic of all race organizations...the rootlessness of the Boers was a natural result of early emancipation from work and the complete lack of a human-built world.[48]

Arendt is here also adapting Hegel's master-slave dialectic, with its argument about the stagnant fate of the master, to her distinction between work and labor. Ruling over a merely natural world of labor, lacking entirely a human world built by work, "the Boers had sunk back to the level of savage tribes.... They were perfectly willing to pay the price, to recede to the level of a race organization...."[49]

The racism with which tribal Africa infected Europe by way of the Boers initiated a new form of politics, "tribal nationalism," which is to be distinguished from the good nationalism proper to the liberal European nation-state. "Tribalism [was] the nationalism of those peoples who had not participated in national emancipation and had not achieved the sovereignty of a nation-state."[50] It is tribal nationalism, "the driving force behind continental imperialism,"[51] which was responsible for the emergence of anti-Semitic politics in Europe:

> The clue to the sudden emergence of anti-Semitism as the center
> of a whole outlook on life and the world...lies in the nature of
> tribalism rather than in political facts and circumstances.[52]

It was Arendt's signal achievement to frame a set of historically grounded political concepts capable of locating the origin of "totalitarianism" in general and modern European anti-Semitism in particular—and by implication, the responsibility for the Nazi holocaust—outside Europe, in the savage "tribalism" of "the Dark Continent."

The principal concern of this essay has been to demonstrate the use of colonialist discourse by those writers most responsible for the construction of cold war rhetoric during and after World War II, that is, at the moment when America and the geopolitical logic of zones of power dividing the world between the "superpowers" replaced the colonialist vision of the world proper to the epoch of the British Empire.[53] Specifically, cold war discourse mapped certain traditional Orientalist stereotypes onto the Russians (not only did this justify the practical policy of containment, but it contributed to a new theory of the neurotic psychological basis of all "ideology," that is, of all left political argument); in addition, primitivist stereotypes were used to explain the component of state-backed social terror so prominent in twentieth-century European history. Cold war discourse was grounded in the theory of totalitarianism, which in this essay I have sought to debunk. The truth of "totalitarianism," I would argue, is to be found precisely in the use of technologically-marked state terror in a radical assault on human subjectivity (more radical in its attempted dehumanization than that degradation inflicted on the nineteenth-century industrial proletariat, to whose contrary assertion of basic humanity and right to power Marx looked for the impulse toward that condition of radical human liberation called communism.) If the technologically-assisted assault on subjectivity by the state in secret prisons and detention centers is the truth of "totalitarianism"—a truth erasing the conceptual boundaries between capitalist, socialist, and "Third World" states—how does this help us understand the use of colonialist elements in the discourse of the cold war?

Use of torture and sadistic technique in interrogation is not new: what is new is the context of what Donna Haraway calls "the informatics of domination."[54] In a number of recent essays, Haraway has pointed out the general intellectual paradigm shift in the conception of power which occurred during and just after World War Two. The application of the new electronics and computer technology to fulfill the essential state functions of surveillance and accountability, along with the military centrality of related new acrospace technologies, gave rise in those years to new models and habits of political thought based on cybernetics and information systems theory, and ultimately, on the general category of C[3]I—"command-control-communication-intelligence."[55] This mode of thought, novel in the 1940s, is all too familiar to us today: newspaper reports of the international "intelligence community" are full of such phrases as "backchannel communications" and who was or was not "in the loop." It is only natural that in his rewrite of *1984* (in his film *Brazil*), Terry Gilliam renames Orwell's "Ministry of Love" with the title "Information Retrieval Services." The emergence of this new intellectual paradigm caused a fundamental ideological problem in the immediate post-war years: "technology," as the physical sign of "Progress," was essential to the myth of the West through which politicians and intellectuals alike understood themselves and their role in world history. Yet the unprecedented evil of the Nazi concentration camps, and of the Gestapo and the S.S. as police institutions, was characterized by the rational application of sophisticated Western technology. How to save the myth of the West, with its essential ideological component of "technology," in the face of Nazi Germany? The theory of totalitarianism, with its adoption of accepted colonialist "ideology" was the answer. Fascism and Nazism could be identified as examples of totalitarianism, whose Russian version revealed the unprecedented use of technologically sophisticated police terror by twentieth-century European states to be, in essence (that is, in its social and human truth) nothing but traditional Oriental despotism. In a complementary fashion, the new component in state terror of the radical and violent assault on subjectivity could be attributed to the savagery of "pre-historic" primitives. In this way, the ideology of "Western civilization" was preserved among cold war intellectuals.

Surely the most striking aspect of the cold war discourse about totalitarianism was its proclamation of the "end of ideology." Ironically, this anti-theoretical position was based on a quite specific theory of the psychological basis of the ideologized consciousness, whose *locus classicus* is Orwell's theory of "doublethink." This theory is understood to explain the human reality underlying the horrifying image of Winston Smith at his job, rewriting history in a manner determined by the standards of totalitarian ideology rather than empirical truth. The fact of such practices is not to be denied: I recall the account of a friend's son who recently spent time in Russia describing his inability to convince his scandalized Russian friends that there had been such a thing as the "Nazi-Soviet Non-Aggression Pact." The ideological distortion of historical truth by American and European textbooks and by the mass media—which was, after all, the primary referent of Orwell's satire—is hardly superior. (Agreement or disagreement with this last statement is surely some sort of cold war shibboleth.)

It is not the historical fact but the explanatory theory which deserves to be challenged. The theory of "doublethink" is an updated version of British empiricist argumentation: the totalitarian mentality is said to involve the disregard of "objective truth" in perception and the abandonment of the principle of non-contradiction in thought. While proclaiming itself as the champion of honest scepticism and tolerance, this discourse was ever at the service of colonialist ideology, going back to the racist tirades of David Hume. The cold war attack on "theory"—most recently in the denunciation of "textual leftism"—denies the presence of "non-logical" mediations (i.e., mediations structured by productive contradictions) and hence of their status as legitimate objects of study. According to empiricist ideology, those of us who would employ a model of the text, rather than a narrowly analytic model of logical argument, to study political and cultural history would also deny that there is any such thing as objective truth. Relativists and nihilists, it is we who leave the door open for the totalitarian ideologue, because we, the "yogis," do not raise the banner of "objective truth" and "logical argument" which alone can resist the abuse of language by the "commissar" of ideology.

Perhaps for those who teach the humanities, one useful response to the current unproductive and abstract disputes about the political and ethical status of "theory" and "deconstruction" is to try to change the conversation, to turn with a fresh eye to literature which presents to us the reality and meaning of the radical attach on human subjectivity enacted by the agencies of modern state terror. If such works are no longer viewed as exemplifications of the politics of "totalitarianism," then they must be confronted afresh. In the PEN speech I referred to earlier, the Argentine journalist Jacobo Timerman, whose *Prisoner without a Name, Cell without a Number* reflects on his experience as one of "the disappeared" during the state terror of 1976–82, denied the historical accuracy of Orwell's view that rationally administered torture could successfully extinguish the singular subjectivity of the victim. To examine the literature of Timerman and others as it reveals to us the politics of subjectivity might be one way to escape the cold war ideology which still stifles our political culture in general and the academic humanities in particular.

NOTES

This essay is a slightly expanded version of a paper for a panel devoted to "Post-Colonial Discourse" organized by Gayatri Chakravorty Spivak for the 1984 MLA. I wish here to apologize to those people who were kind enough on that occasion to ask for a copy of the talk, and who received my promise but never my paper.

1. The symposium papers were published in *Proceedings of the American Philosophical Society*, vol. 82 (1940). The principal paper, Carlton J.H. Hayes' "The Novelty of Totalitarianism in the History of Western Civilization," concludes: "In sum, the dictatorial totalitarianism of today is a reaction—nay more, a revolt [he refers approvingly to Ortega elsewhere in the essay]—against the whole historic civilization of the West." (p. 101)

2. Claude Levi-Strauss, *Totemism*, tr. Rodney Needham (Boston: Beacon Press, 1963), p. 1.

3. Levi-Strauss, *Totemism*, p.15

4. Kennan, George F., "Totalitarianism in the Modern World," in *Totalitarianism: Proceedings of a Conference held at the American Academy of Arts and Sciences, March, 1953*, ed. Carl J. Friedrich, (Cambridge: Harvard University Press, 1954), p. 101.

5. It is perhaps worth remarking that I choose Kennan and Orwell, not in order to discredit them, but precisely because they are both thinkers of exceptional intellectual and moral integrity. If such men of good will and extensive experience could lead the way in forging a cold war discourse whose practical use could only have appalled them, then it is important for us to understand what elements were present in their discourse to allow this abuse—elements which they themselves did not reflect on.

6. For the cultural presuppositions of Kennan, Acheson, Harriman, and other key proponents of containment policy—whose clean Eurocentric spheres-of-power logic ultimately bogged down and disintegrated in the Third World mire of Vietnam—see the early chapters of Walter Isaacson and Evan Thomas, *The Wise Men: Six Friends and the World They Made*, (New York: Simon and Schuster, 1986).

7. See Barton J. Bernstein, "American Foreign Policy and the Origins of the Cold War," in *Politics and Policies of the Truman Administration*, ed. Barton J. Bernstein) Chicago: Quadrangle Books, 1970), pp. 53-55.

8. "Kennan's Cable on Containment," in *The Truman Administration: A Documentary History*, eds. Barton J. Bernstein and Allen J. Matusow, (New York: Harper and Row, 1966), pp. 200, 202.

9. Kennan's Cable on Containment," p. 203

10. [George Kennan], "The Sources of Soviet Conduct," *Foreign Affairs*, vol. 25, no. 4 (July 1947): 568, 574.

11. From the perspective of cold war history, whose definitive textbook is William McNeil's 1963 *The Rise of the West: A History of the Human Community* (Chicago: University of Chicago Press, naturally), Russians could be viewed as victims of the millennium-long "steppe gradient" in which barbarian Oriental nomads were pushed westward across the great Eurasian steppe by even more barbaric hordes further to the east. Positioned in the northern forest at the western edge of the steppe, yet receiving Western influences from the Christianity of Byzantium and from the military-economic challenge of the Baltic Knights Templar, the non-nomadic Russians suffered a centuries' long choice between the civilizing process offered by Western influences and the brutal barbarian modes of life and thought which had to be embraced to fight the successive waves of Huns, Tartars, and Mongols sweeping west from the Orient. In good cold war fashion, McNeill attributes the

end of the Eurasian nomads as a historical force to the rise of modern European weapons technology: firearms end the competitiveness of horse nomads with agrarian states because these new, superior weapons require an industrialized factory production system beyond the organizational capacity of stateless hordes. The ultimate decision of Russia to embrace the West is viewed not as a turn to "Western values" but as continuation of the Oriental power-logic: specifically, with the rise of Sweden as a military competitor in Lithuania through its use of the new cannons and firearms, Russia is forced to turn to the West in order to acquire the new weapons technology. Thus Russian society is nothing other than the adaptation of Oriental barbarism to the new world of industrialized military power which has made the traditional form of barbarism, Asiatic horse nomadry, obsolete. From their geopolitical position in world history, the modern Russians are thus viewed as the passive product of two alien cultures—Oriental barbarism and Western civilization—whose irreconcilable principles cannot be synthesized, thus leaving the Russian mentality as a sort of Manichean internalization in which the irrational but cunning, power-worshipping Oriental side suppresses, or worse, displays as a deceptive façade (as a "human face"), the authentic humanity internalized through centuries of contact with Western civilization. This line of thought denies any distinctiveness or transformative capacity to Russian culture in itself; this erasure of substantial difference by imposing the "West versus Orient" grid on Russia itself enables the subsequent denial of difference to all "Third World" cultures through imposition of the "West versus Soviets" framework of argumentation.

12. Kennan himself can be more circumspect, but he still accepts the basic categories that define the discussion: totalitarianism is the combination of traditional non-Western Oriental despotism with the novel surveillance and enforcement technologies produced by Western science. "I have heard it said by well informed people [hence Kennan authorizes the interpretation but defers to professional Orientalists] that all the essential features of Soviet Communism could be observed in certain ancient oriental despotisms. I cannot be a good judge of this, for I know nothing about oriental history. I would be inclined to doubt that this could be wholly true, precisely because of the importance of the technological component in the totalitarian system as we know it today. In any case, so far as the West is concerned, totalitarianism does seem to have been something made possible only by the technological developments of the past century and a half, which have operated to enhance enormously the potential scope and intensity of absolute power." (George Kennan, "Totalitarianism in the Modern World," p. 21)

The component of Western-produced modern police technology explains the historical novelty of totalitarianism, as well as its emergence in Europe, that is, in the very heart of the West. The attribution of the mentality proper to the political abuse of this technology to Oriental despotism locates the historical ground and proper sphere of the human essence of totalitarianism in the non-Western world. In his 1947 *Foreign Affairs* article on "The Sources of Soviet Conduct," Kennan simply assumes the correctness of the argument that totalitarianism is Oriental despotism plus modern technology: "The Soviet leaders, taking advantage of the contributions of modern technique to the arts of despotism...." (p. 576)

13. Kennan, "Sources of Soviet Conduct," p. 576.

14. "Kennan's Cable on Containment," p. 202.

15. *Ibid.*, p. 202.

16. Kennan, "Sources of Soviet Conduct," p. 574.

17. "Kennan's Cable on Containment," p. 203. In "The Sources of Soviet Conduct," Kennan speaks of the "Russian capacity for self-delusion." (p. 580)

18. *Ibid.*, p. 202.

19. *Orwell's Nineteen Eighty-Four: Text, Sources, Criticism*, ed. Irving Howe (New York: Harcourt, Brace, Jovanovich, 1963), p. 92.

20. *Ibid.*, p. 131; see also p. 8.

21. *Ibid.*, p. 87.

22. *Ibid.*, p. 95.

23. Orwell uses this phrase twice in letters of October, 1948, to characterize Sartre; at the time he was preparing a hostile review of Sartre's *Portrait of an Anti-Semite*. See *The Collected Essays, Journalism and Letters of George Orwell*, eds. Sonia Orwell and Ian Angus, vol. IV, (New York: Harcourt, Brace and World, 1968), pp. 448, 450.

24. *Ibid.*, pp. 74, 77.

25. *Ibid.*, p. 75.

26. In colonial discourse, the great companion of Orientalism is primitivism. While I will argue that Arendt, and in general the discourse about totalitarian terror, adopt discursive structures from earlier language about primitive savagery, Orwell makes little use of it, although at one point early in *1984*, during the "Two Minutes of Hate" when the people are chanting "B. B." (for "Big Brother"), we read that the chant became "a heavy, murmurous sound, somehow curiously savage, in the background of which one seemed to hear the stamp of naked feet and the throbbing of tom-toms...an act of self-hypnosis [a notion employed by both Kennan and Koestler], a deliberate drowning of consciousness by means of rhythmic noise.... The general delirium [was caused by] this subhuman chanting...." (p. 9)

27. Arthur Koestler, *The Yogi and the Commissar, and Other Essays*, (New York: MacMillan, 1947).

28. "The Berlin Manifesto" [written primarily by Arthur Koestler] in *The New Leader* (July 8, 1950), p. 8.

29. "The Berlin Manifesto," p. 8.

30. Arthur Koestler, *The Invisible Writing*, p. 109.

31. Arthur Koestler, in *The God that Failed*, ed. Richard Crossman (New York: Harper and Brothers, 1949), p. 26. In recounting his experience in Russia, Koestler remarks upon "The Asiatic backwardness of life" in that country.

32. *Ibid.*, p. 219.

33. *Ibid.*, p. 129.

34. *Ibid.*, p. 117.

35. *Ibid.*, p. 117.

36. *Ibid.*, p. 117.

37. *Ibid.*, p. 118.

38. *Ibid.*, p. 118.

39. In 1960 Koestler turned his dualizing analytic grid onto non-communist Asia alone; his book entitled The Lotus and the Robot (New York: Harper and Row, 1960), now finds the same polar extremes expressed in India (the lotus) and Japan (the robot), the sub-rational Yogi or the hyperrational technocratic potential commissar. Writes Koestler: "Common to both [cultures] is a type of reasoning indifferent to the 'laws' of contradiction and excluded middle, to the distinction between subject and object, between the act of perception and the thing perceived ... an approach to Reality which is intuitive and a prioristic rather than rational and empirical, and relies on fluid analogies rather than well-defined concepts." (p. 227.)

40. Hannah Arendt, The Origins of Totalitarianism (New York: World Publishing, 1958), pp. vii, viii–ix, 9.

41. *Ibid.*, p. 156.

42. *Ibid.*, p. 157.

43. *Ibid.*, p. 190.

44. *Ibid.*, p. 192.

45. *Ibid.*, p. 192.

46. "Slavery in the case of the Boers was a form of adjustment of a European people to a black race, and only superficially resembled those historical instances when it had been a result of conquest or slave trade.... Ruling over tribes and living parasitically from their labor, they came to occupy a position very similar to that of the natural tribal leaders whose domination they had liquidated. The natives, at any rate, recognized them as a higher form of tribal leadership, a kind of natural diety to which one has to submit; so that the divine role of the Boers was as much imposed by their black slaves as assumed freely by themselves." *Ibid.*, p. 193. This is standard nineteenth-century colonialist argument, given an extra philosophical charge from Arendt's reading of Conrad (the Boers are essentially "Mr. Kurtz").

47. *Ibid.*, pp. 194, 196.

48. *Ibid.*, pp. 196–97.

49. *Ibid.*, p. 207.

50. *Ibid.*, p. 227.

51. *Ibid.*, p. 229.

52. *Ibid.*, p. 229.

53. Certainly the U.S. (and Germany) had established dominance over Britain in heavy industrial production by the turn of the century, and had emerged out of World War I as the dominant power in world finance, but only with World War II did the United States displace Britain as the dominant political power in the world.

54. Donna Haraway, "A Manifesto for Cyborgs: Science, Technology, and Socialist Feminism in the 1980s," Socialist Review (March-April 1985), no. 80, pp. 65–107.

55. Haraway, "A Manifesto for Cyborgs," p. 66.

ANDERS STEPHANSON

Comment on an Aspect of Pietz's Argument

If one accepts the vast Saidian totalization known as "orientalism," it is true that there were elements of this in the postwar western conceptualization of totalitarianism in general and the Soviet Union in particular. That much is right about William Pietz's argument, but it amounts to less than he thinks and the rest is on the whole wrong.

The question posed is whether the instant success of cold war discourse came about as a result of the inclusion of "ideologically familiar elements from the earlier discourse of Western colonialism." Pietz finds this to be so: "the colonialist vision of the world proper to the epoch of the British Empire [demarcated by Pietz as the nineteenth and twentieth century]" was replaced by one whose core concept, totalitarianism, was actually an adaptation of pre-war colonialist precepts.

Pietz appears to have forgotten that a world war had just been fought against a constellation of powers which legitimated *themselves* as totalitarian. The term, after all, had begun as the self-justification of Italian fascism in the 1920s. An immense war effort, then, had recently been undertaken against these powers. A central theme of this monumental mobilization, *from the beginning*, had been the conviction, emanating from the Munich experience, that appeasement of dictators-fascists-totalitarians was as morally repugnant as it was useless. Squash them in their infancy and, if that's not possible, put

From *Social Text* 19–20 (Fall 1988). © 1988 by Coda Press.

an early stop by whatever means necessary to their innate desire for territorial expansion, for they will never rest until they have conquered everything and obliterated freedom everywhere: such was the historical lesson of the war. A lot of people had died in making sure that it would never be forgotten.

We are dealing here with, to use language comprehensible to the lit-crit industry, quite a powerful narrative sanctioned by ample experience. It did not need to be accepted. *It was already in place.* The fact that it was in place had little or nothing to do with the plausibility of any traces of "colonialist discourse." It had to do with war and sacrifice.

What is to be explained, therefore, is not the dissemination of the totalitarian narrative but the insertion of the Soviet Union into all this. Moscow's extraordinary emphasis on nationalism and complete elimination of references to socialist and anti-colonial liberation—witness the dissolution of the Comintern in 1943—coupled with the grand alliance itself, bringing in its train profuse Soviet accolades to the progressive nature of the western leadership, created an impression in the United States among official and public alike that the Stalinist dictatorship had somehow been transformed into a more ordinary kind of state, a reversal to a recognizable Russia the Great Power. The USSR, in short, *having once in some blurry way been part of the totalitarian configuration*, was now an honored and courageous member, personified by Uncle Joe, of the all-out effort to crush it. When the war ended and the internal conflicts began to surface, first over the regime in Poland, then on a whole series of issues, it was natural that one would also begin to question whether the notion of a Russia transformed had actually been right. A debate ensued, against the backdrop of ever-increasing tension, until the Greek civil war and the enunciation of the Truman Doctrine in the spring of 1947 settled the problem once and for all. The Soviet Union was henceforth a totalitarian state, first of all because it was a dictatorship but, more immediately, *because it was expansionist.* Concessions to its territorial and political aims was thus tantamount to another Munich treachery and would lead to World War III. This, then, is the determining logic behind the success of "cold war discourse." People accepted it because to do otherwise seemed to run counter to an overwhelming recent experience and would result in an even more devastating tragedy. They did not accept it because it had elements of "the colonialist vision of the world proper to the epoch of the British Empire." That would have been absurd.

Actually, I doubt that a "colonialist vision" ever dominated the western states of the nineteenth and early twentieth century. Did Bismarck, for instance, think coloniall? He certainly thought about a German empire and was indeed instrumtal in its formation; and towards the end of the nineteenth century this empire engaged in the acquisition of colonies. Yet his was chiefly an empire of contiguous, European kind, monolingual but otherwise similar to its Austro-Hungarian and Russian counterparts. Bismarck worried a great deal about other European states. So did they, and with very good reason. At any rate, to characterize the period of European history between the Congress of Vienna and World War I (or II?) in terms of a "colonialist vision" seems to me largely false.

*

For the exponents of cold war discourse, opines Pietz, totalitarianism was "nothing other than traditional Oriental despotism plus modern police technology." The concept came to justify "a policy of global anti-communism by reinterpreting all struggles for national self-determination in terms of the geopolitical contest for zones of power against totalitarian Russia"; and "to preserve the traditional pre-war faith concerning 'the values of Western civilization' held by post-war foreign-policy 'wise men' by displacing the human essence into the non-Western world."

Were these really the chief two functions of the concept? The cold war was preeminently conceived and executed within the European theater, where, after all, the two main antagonists stood face to face and had a series of sticky things to resolve. The effect of the initial western moves, Marshall Aid (1947) and NATO (1949), models for ensuing maneuvers on a global scale, was indeed *the division of Europe*. That, first and foremost, was the "function" of "totalitarianism," not the need to classify struggles of national liberation. I mention this mainly to point to a certain, so to speak, colonialist bias in Pietz. For Kennan, to take the one policy maker he cites, wars of national liberation outside the industrial formations of "the northern temperate zone" were actually supremely uninteresting. The third world, in his view, was incomprehensible to the western mind and best left to its own no doubt tragic fate. Nothing would have been further from Kennan's mind than to interpret the struggles there as one between totalitarianism and the free world.

In fact, contrary to the impression one might get from Pietz's account, totalitarianism was of little conceptual importance to Kennan. He attached it intermittently to ideas and arguments he had mostly worked out already; in itself, it yielded few explanatory benefits. He did not counterpose it to any "free world" and really did not think terribly much and often about it in general. When he did think about it, he had the ethical problem of means and ends primarily in mind, not "oriental despotism plus police technology." With regard to the "non-western," on balance, he was more inclined to stress the Byzantine element than the Asiatic. Nor did he, as Pietz believes, posit any "insecure" oriental essence. When Kennan spoke of insecurity, he was referring to the psychological effects of the historical absence of secure borders on the Russian plains, an absence which in fact had facilitated endless invasions from both east and west. Said insecurity was thus not without historical foundation; more to the point, it was not in any way alleged to be essentially "oriental." Kennan thought of the Soviet Union rather as I think Sartre did, as "a gigantic mediation between East and West." That mediation, however, was not the sum total of oriental despotism and modern technology.

I bring this minor point up because it leads to the question of empirical evidence. Pietz offers a smattering of readings from what he considers four central contributors to the cold war discourse of totalitarianism: Kennan, Orwell, Koestler, and Arendt. These readings strike me as problematic, and as an illustration of Pietz's simplifications I wish to offer an alternative account of Kennan's relationship to the concept of totalitarianism.

Kennan was unusual among American policy makers in that he was a organicist conservative with strong attachments to the virtues of hierarchy and authority. He was in fact on the whole outside the normal liberal purview of American politics as such. Before the war, having experienced "expert rule" under Austro-fascism, he had become an advocate of "benevolent authoritarianism"; and during the war, while stationed in Portugal, he had established friendly relations with Salazar, whom he admired copiously. For our purposes, what is essential about this is that he rejected, very explicitly, the given dictatorship/democracy couplet within which the American conception of the war tended to be thought. Not to put too fine a point on it, he had little to say in favor of democracy and much to say against it. On the other hand, he abhorred Hitler and Stalin as a pair of gangsters, untraditional and uncivil.

How did the concept of totalitarianism enter into this? A sporadic presence in his writings before the end of the war, it became a part, if not really an integrated one, of his outlook as it developed after the return from Moscow in 1946. What mainly attracted him to it was the ethico-political aspect (and here he was influenced, I think, by Koestler's important *Darkness at Noon*, inexplicably ignored in Pietz's account). For it was precisely on ethical grounds that Kennan himself had earlier put Hitler and Stalin conceptually together. The concept thus allowed him to put a name on a previous thesis of his. Denying that the basic conflict in world politics had anything to do with questions of collectivism, socialism, or capitalism, indeed with any aspect of economic conditions, he now insisted that it revolved around the ethical pivot: on one side (the totalitarian) were those who adhered to the adage that the ends justify the means; on other other, those who thought unethical means ruin the end no matter how intrinsically worthwhile the latter happens to be:

> We have on the one hand the familiar pattern of totalitarianism. This is the philosophy which holds that a single man or group of men, who have come into the monopolistic possession of the instruments of internal power, are qualified and entitled to decide what constitutes the interests of the peoples under their immediate control (and often peoples elsewhere as well), to draw up programs ostensibly for the promotion of what they have defined as public interests, and to require unquestioning acceptance of these programs by the people at large and total collaboration in their realization. No independent values are recognized here, which might take precedence over the execution of these programs. No individual rights or liberties are allowed to impede it. Since it is predicated that the goal is a beneficial one, it is also assumed that all means which this goal are automatically permissable. The means are invariably justified by the prescribed end. Thus the selection and employment of method is governed by no ethical principles whatsoever. Expediency becomes supreme. Values which men have accepted for centuries are cheerfully tossed overboard and replaced by a simple mechanical scale of efficacy in the realization of the desired goal, against which all methods and all actions are measured. In this concept, there can be no deed too black, no duplicity too profound, no punishment too cruel, no sacrifices too great, if it is interpreted by those who hold power as serving the goal which they have indicated. Where this outlook comes to prevail, the machinery of human society loses its balance-wheel; the balance-wheel of the ethics common to the great religions of the world, and the engine of political power begins to race in a furious and uncontrolled orgy of acceleration which the protagonists of the system define as progress and in which others see only a horrifying plunge toward the failure and disaster of human society. (May 1947)

Kennan would also describe this instability of Soviet totalitarianism metaphorically as a crust atop an underlying mass of uncertain qualities: break the crust and the whole thing might well disintegrate and self-destruct. In other words, without the thin ruling stratum, the result might be complete collapse. What ought to be remembered here is probably the impression of something essentially unrestrained, something extreme possibly on the verge of exploding or imploding.

With regard to Soviet policy specifically, the totalitarian theme signified little in Kennan's analysis but a reaffirmation of an old idea of his, namely that Moscow would use any skullduggery in the attempt to eliminate forces beyond its control.

*

The concept, then, never became an organic part of his thinking. There are several reasons. There was his nominalist dislike for generic concepts, typical of traditional conservatism and bound to make him reticent about any promiscuous use of "abstractions" such as totalitarianism. There was the problem of internal coherence to consider. He had argued that totalitarians recognize no "rules of the game." Yet he had also found realism an outstanding characteristic of Soviet foreign policy, and if this realism was not to become sheer contingency it would certainly have to observe some "rules." The Long Telegram of 1946 (referred to by Pietz) had established that Stalin was outwardly cautious, disinclined to adventurism of any kind. Only with some difficulty could this be squared with the image of overspilling totalitarian delirium.

Nor could he easily accept the Munich lesson attached to the concept. In part, this was simply because his own attitude in 1938 had been largely favorable to the agreements; but it was also to argue oneself into substantial trouble to say that, yes, here is a totalitarian regime similar in all essentials to the Nazis which ought not to be appeased, while simultaneously maintaining that said regime was not adventuristic or interested in war. Indeed, Kennan soon found reason to warn against "the danger" of "thinking of Russia as just a larger and improved 1948 version of Hitler's Germany," but such words of wisdom fell on unfertile ground. The American outlook was becoming captive to the lesson of the 1930s and thus commensurately militarized. (Always a sign of the times, the lesson reemerged farcically in the early 1980s as a justification for actions to obliterate "totalitarian" Nicaragua before it had expanded to San Antonio.)

There was finally the aspect of political outlook. Having earlier rejected the dichotomy of dictatorships and democracy, he was now unable to accept whole-heartedly the dichotomy of totalitarianism and the free world. Occasionally, he would employ it himself in a simple binary way, but then not without clear reservations. He was in fact reluctant to push the opposition even for propaganda purposes.

His predicament is perhaps best understood if it is rewritten in classical

Greek terms—which in any case might have been his immediate source of inspiration. A multitude of political "forms" were set forth by Greek thinkers, but the central issue for them seems to have been the contrast between the stable and orderly (traditional for short) on the one hand, and the arbitrary, capricious, and criminal on the other. From this perspective, Kennan's "totalitarianism" may be grasped as a fairly straightforward translation of the Greek notion of "tyranny," implying as it did arbitrary despotism, immoderation, lack of respect for the law, and insatiable desires on the part of the tyrant, all in all an unstable compound teleologically destined for destruction. Among the positive counterparts to tyranny (since this was not a dichotomy), Kennan would then have been more inclined to "aristocracy" than "democracy," though again, the form was less important than the question of order and stability. Such an implicit typology would for him have had the virtue of making a "traditional" regime like Salazar's eligible for favorable classification.

When, in the 1950s, he occasionally used totalitarianism, it was mainly with regard to McCarthyism, in which respect it signified for him some evil beast lurking within us all, ready at all times to burst forth. Here, again, it was a convenient term for something he had always thought anyway, in this case the time-honored Calvinist belief that we are all inherently rotten. At the 1953 symposium, on which Pietz relies, Kennan had been asked to say something more specific about the subject, and thus shoved up against the wall, he conceded defeat by turning the term impressionistically into an image of something dreamlike, an exit symptomatic of his overall disinclination to pin down general abstractions and of his unease about the whole concept. He continued to use totalitarianism now and then as a designation for something almost indefinably evil, as an absolute negative. His overall view may otherwise be characterized as sporadic and contradictory. On the one hand he retained notions of instability and crusts over something volatile and hence brittle; on the other, he concluded that modern technology and the destruction of primary groups in society (everywhere) were important factors in the emergence of totalitarianism and that technological efficiency in fact rendered it largely impervious to resistance. Yet he had also expressed a belief earlier that totalitarianism was chiefly a problem pertaining to *development* and therefore historically of passing nature; and he was convinced that change would come in the Soviet Union as everywhere else, in which supposition he proved right. Noting towards the end of the 1950s a decline in "fanaticism," a greater openness, and impressive economic and technological gains, he began to think the nightmare was over. The Soviet Union appeared to be moving towards the "conservative-authoritarian" state he considered to have been "the norm" in the west during the Christian era, unlike totalitarianism a political form that was not "hideous in the sight of God." From then on the concept ceased to have anything but historical significance to him. In sum, Kennan thought variously and contradictorily but not particularly deeply about the concept of totalitarianism.

*

I have gone into detail to elucidate the historical superficiality of Pietz's argument. For his is a *historical* thesis. Historical epochs are distinguished and characterized. A continuity is detected between one period and another. Having found elements of orientalism, Pietz feels free to make generalizations about "cold war discourse." It is not small potatoes we are presented with: "How to save the myth of the West, with its essential ideological component of 'technology,' in the face of Nazi Germany? The theory of totalitarianism, with its adoption of accepted colonialist ideology, was the answer." A conspiracy perhaps? There are other examples of simplifications and errors: the reader would be well advised, for example, to ponder the validity of Pietz's views about the "end of ideology" thesis. However, the point is that, from a purely procedural viewpoint, one might have expected something rather more modest from the readings Pietz produces. His question is huge; his evidence is slim; his conclusion is huge. Yet the lit-crit industry is of course not known for its interest in historical research. Read a couple of texts, and pretty soon you can make totalizations about something or other.

All of which leads me to conclude on a note that goes beyond Pietz. The principle of creative misreading—"any interpretation, no matter how badly informed, is fine as long as it is interesting"—is perfectly sensible in the analysis of a novel or a film; it is wholly pernicious in the analysis of historical processes. The production of historical knowledge does not come about that way; nor can it, nor should it. Historical claims demand historical work. Otherwise, make other kinds of claims.

ROBERT SUTHERLAND

Eternity in Darkness at Noon *and the* Consolation of Philosophy

"Eternity" is not only the last word in the dying mind of Nicolas Salmanovitch Rubashov; it is the final word as well in the whole of Arthur Koestler's well-known novel devoted to Rubashov's character and fate. Such prominence suggests to a reader familiar with classical literature a reference to Boethius on eternity in the *Consolation of Philosophy*. Other parallels so strengthen the suggestion as to lead serious readers to trace the lines along which Koestler and Boethius develop their emphasis upon eternity. Among the most obvious of these parallels is that both are narratives in which unjust imprisonment is a central feature of the setting for each. Yet a surprise awaits those who expect the similarity in setting to result in a resemblance on eternity. Though the topic is important in both works, it is so in very different respects. The differences need marking in a broad, introductory way before turning to the specific terms in which they are developed.

For Boethius, the possession of eternity is paramount and on the scale of possession, God is far higher than man. Yet, according to Boethius, the human capacity to possess eternity is not only large but essential to happiness. By contrast, Rubashov is thoroughly immersed in time, in struggling for power, and in reducing all thought to historical terms. To possess eternity is beyond Rubashov's conception. About eternity, Rubashov's intellect is blank, even black. Only in his last moment of consciousness,

From *Classical and Modern Literature* 13, no. 1. (1992). © 1992 by CML, Inc.

described by the narrator, is eternity's power to lift Rubashov up affirmed just as mortality sucks him down.

The role of eternity in the life of Boethius becomes great while it remains minute for Rubashov. That it exists at all for either one is the point of departure for what follows. Before perceiving eternity, each undergoes a conversion in which a forgotten or lost identity is recollected. For Rubashov, the recovery is agonizing and uncertain. The difficulty of recovery is, in turn, related to how slightly Rubashov is connected to eternity. Yet to ignore the conversion and connection altogether has brought embarrassing results to at least one prominent and otherwise careful reader. In securing for others such a slender but important reference to eternity in *Darkness at Noon*, the conversion of Rubashov needs detailed treatment.

The context for Rubashov's conversion is the conclusion of a trial like the "show trials" in Moscow during the 1930s. Behind the trial is a revolutionary party very much like the Communist Party and a leader, called No. 1 in the novel, who is very much like Stalin. Rubashov appears in the novel as the last surviving member of the party's original central committtee. Much of the conflict in the novel turns on a revolution within the revolutionary party. On the one side is a new generation in the party, a brutal generation; Rubashov calls them "Neanderthalers" to emphasize their savagery. In the pursuit and exercise of power, this generation acknowledges no limits. On the other side is Rubashov's generation of intellectuals, who start out thinking in totalitarian terms but who remain civilized and cultured in their actions, even when they have the power to coerce. In the conflict, Rubashov is a transitional figure, formed in an earlier period but more adaptable to the brutal demands of a later one than many of his peers. He acts as though he has no conscience but, unlike the "Neanderthalers," he comes to hate himself for doing it.

The novel opens with the arrest of Rubashov, the shock and setting of his imprisonment, and his reconstruction of events leading up to the arrest. Three hearings provide titles for each third of the novel and the first third closes with an initial hearing that is conducted by Ivanov, a former friend and college classmate of Rubashov. Ivanov has gone even further than Rubashov in making compromises with the new generation of party leaders. They are in the process of consolidating power by a two-fold strategy. They execute summarily all those members of the older generation who have a perfect record of loyalty to the party and they conduct public trials of those whose record shows some deviation in loyalty. Ivanov closes the first hearing with instructions for Rubashov to confess his opposition to the party and prepare for a trial.

Ivanov's conduct of the second hearing, which dominates the middle of the novel, shows how clearly the new generation is a child of the old. The important details here will be considered later. The point is that Ivanov is not successful in getting a confession. He is executed immediately and the task of making Rubashov confess is given to Gletkin who brings to bear on Rubashov all the crude brutality of the new generation. The public trial based on Rubashov's confession is the third hearing and it concludes with Rubashov's execution. From the point of view of Gletkin, the time between the end of the trial and the execution is insignificant, but for Rubashov it forms the opportunity for conversion.

Rubashov's conversion comes in the novel's last ten pages and is presented in terms so brief and complex as to require not only extended explanation but a strong background in classical philosophy and especially Boethius' *Consolation of Philosophy*. Before turning to these sources and beginning an explanation, the text must be allowed to speak for itself.

> For forty years he had lived strictly in accordance with the vows of his order, the Party. He had held to the rules of logical calculation. He had burnt the remains of the old, illogical morality from his consciousness with the acid of reason. He had turned away from the temptations of the silent partner, and had fought against the "oceanic sense" with all his might.[1] So now it was over. He had nothing more to do with it [the Party or its proceedings]. He no longer had to howl with the wolves. He had paid, his account was settled. He was a man who had lost his shadow, released from every bond. He had followed every thought to its last conclusion and acted in accordance with it to the very end; the hours which remained to him belonged to that silent partner, whose realm started just where logical thought ended.[2]

Eternity's place in the conversion is indicated by the reference to "oceanic sense," which

> the mystics called "ecstasy" and saints "contemplation"; the greatest and soberest of modern psychologists had recognized this state as a fact and called it the "oceanic sense." And, indeed, one's personality dissolved as a grain of salt in the sea; but at the same time the infinite sea seemed to be contained in the grain of salt. (206–207)

The connection between such an oceanic feeling and Rubashov's experience with eternity is clear from the last moment of Rubashov's consciousness, as described by the narrator. The execution is accomplished by two bullets in the back of Rubashov's head, the second, a "smashing blow hit him on the ear. Then all became quiet. There was the sea again with its sounds. A wave slowly lifted him up. It came from afar and travelled sedately on, a shrug of eternity" (216). An "oceanic feeling" is thus the last one Rubashov experiences, a far travelling wave of "infinite sea" rolls on beneath him, lifting and transporting his soul.

A glance at the German edition reveals a bit more. The final phrase, "ein Achselzucken der Unendlichkeit,"[3] or "a shoulder-shrug of endlessness" is especially rich, pointing the reader in several directions at once. The most obvious one to a German reader is the association of *der Unendlichkeit* with Romanticism but readers with a background in classical literature, and especially in *De consolatione*, may well note the parallel to *interminabilis vitae* in the famous discussion of *aeternitas* offered by Boethius at 5.6.9–15. There Boethius directs both the living and the dying alike not only to "endless life" but to the whole, simultaneous, and absolute possession of it, "interminabilis vitae tota simul et perfecta possessio" (5.6.10–11). Such direction immediately raises questions, however, since the similarity of *der Unendlichkeit* and *interminablilis vitae* is compromised by the contrast between *ein Achselzucken* and *tota simul et perfecta possessio*. The prospect of possessing eternity thus fully, however distant it may be, looks very different from the "shoulder-shrug" which Rubashov experiences.

The difference may not, however, be as great as it first seems, especially given the contrast in contexts. Boethius refers to eternity at the end of his reunion with philosophy in the context of an inquiry concerning God's nature ("quis sit divinae substantiae status," 5.6.4) while Koestler's reference pertains to one who has recently been converted to thinking in terms of contemplative subjects. About eternity, the dying Rubashov is still very confused and deeply uncertain. For Rubashov, a "shoulder-shrug" is not only enough; it is, perhaps, as much of eternity as he can stand for the moment. Possession of it lies beyond his capacity to comprehend, much less experience.

Rubashov has no *Philosophia* to guide him on the long journey up the ascending path. The word "God" is out of place in the circles Rubashov has frequented and he dares not to say such a word as an affirmation. Rubashov has, instead of Lady Philosophy, only a "silent partner" whose existence Rubashov has often denied in conformity with Party-approved thinking. Rubashov thus resembles, not so much Boethius at the end of his journey where discussion of God and his nature makes sense, but Boethius as Lady

Philosophy first found him, a lost, deluded figure struggling against the best in his nature.

Darkness at Noon may be read, and will here be discussed, as a gloss on the first few books of the *Consolation of Philosophy*. The cement which binds these two works together is, put in the most general terms, an agreement on what ails the central figure in each and how a cure is accomplished for them. In similarly broad terms, many of the striking and fundamental differences between these two works are due to the gravity of Rubashov's illness and the very limited scope of his recovery before death overtakes him. He is a far, far sicker figure than Boethius, as will become clear by a comparison of their conditions.

Lady Philosophy makes the diagnosis of Boethius at 1.2.12. Boethius suffers from lethargy, not in its modern sense of lacking energy but in its root sense of forgetfulness. The Latin word *lethargus* transliterates λή θαργος, derived from λήθη. The disease is especially common among those who are being prosecuted for misdeeds they did not commit. Socrates was among the first to show the course of the disease. The *Apology* opens with Socrates' admission that the prosecution has been so persuasive in pressing the charges against him that "I myself actually almost forgot myself" (ἐγὼ δ' οὖν καὶ αὐτός ὑπ' αὐτῶν ὀλίγου ἐμαυτοῦ ἐπελαθόμην, 17A2–4). The remedy is, of course, a process of recollection, which Socrates seems to have prescribed and administered for himself as he reviewed the charges made against him and narrated the circumstances and conduct that had been misrepresented by his accusers (18D–28B). The *Apology* is thus a preface to the full doctrine of ἀνά μνησις or remembrance that later appears more fully at *Meno* 81-86 and *Phaedo* 72–76. There Plato presents the soul forgetting its eternity while suffering the harsh imprisonment of the body but then, as philosophy draws it nearer the truth, the soul recollects the knowledge of eternity.

Lady Philosophy extends Socrates' experience to the case of Boethius. She not only diagnoses the problem in terms of forgetfulness but actually specifies what Socrates and Boethius both forgot, "quid ipse sis, nosse desisti": you have forgotten what you yourself are (1.6.40). Furthermore, the climax of *De consolatione*, in book 3 where Boethius is reintroduced to eternity by Lady Philosophy, is marked by an ode to Socrates and his pupil, Plato. The ode begins with a reference to self-knowledge and ends by referring to recollection.

> Quisquis profunda mente vestigat verum
> Cupitque nullis ille deviis falli,
> In se revolvat intimi lucem visus
> ....

Quod si Platonis musa personat verum,
Quod quisque discit immemor recordatur.
(3.11.1–3, 15–16)

Compared to Boethius, much less Socrates, Rubashov's progress in recollecting eternity is painfully slow, thinly presented, and thus faintly realized. To understand why requires grasping the full wretchedness of Rubashov's condition. Boethius, even at his worst, seems almost aglow with health compared to Rubashov. The difference can clearly be seen by looking briefly at the lowest moments of each character. As the *Consolation of Philosophy* opens, Boethius is awake in his cell with pen in hand, reviewing the misfortune that has fallen upon him and framing the verses to express vividly his lament. Lady Philosophy appears above Boethius' head and he can see some of her features clearly, especially her outer garments, but her face and head are but dimly visible, partly because they rise to such heights that the clouds sometimes obscure them but mainly because the tears in Boethius' eyes prevent him from beholding what Lady Philosophy offers for him to see (1.1.44–45).

Rubashov is asleep in his prison cell, possessed by a nightmare of utter paralysis at the very moment in which his life may depend upon choice and action. The worst moment is yet to come, however, as the remembered reality of his arrest shatters the nightmare and the half-awake Rubashov is stranded between the nightmare of paralysis and the reality of imprisonment, unable to distinguish clearly one from the other, so profound is his disorientation (3–4). If the worst moment for Boethius derives from his impaired perception of philosophical truth, the parallel condition for Rubashov is far more debilitating. Boethius may have forgotten who he is and how closely he is linked to eternity, but Rubashov has no clear, enduring self left by which he can form the basis for distinguishing between reality and illusion. The only thing real to him for years has been what the revolutionary party dictates and an ambiguous impulse for physical survival which is tied to perpetuating the party. It is the only source of durability and direction Rubashov knows. Even worse, the party, as his guide, is dedicated to abolishing the self, all references to eternity or God, and any capacity to imagine what such references might mean.

In attacking the self, the party stalked its prey without guile or subtlety. Nothing less would satisfy it than a massive assault on common use of the first person singular. "I" was such a forbidden word that Rubashov referred to it as the "grammatical fiction" (121, 205). In the prison diary Rubashov kept, he noted how the party insisted that "Questions of personal pride; prejudices such as exist elsewhere against certain forms of self-abasement;

personal feelings of tiredness, disgust and shame–are to be cut off root and branch…" (137).

Rubashov's conversion from following the party comes as he, like Boethius, rediscovers or recollects who he is. The process begins with the entry of his "silent partner"; it is strongly advanced by the increasing importance of memory to Rubashov, and it culminates in Rubashov's acknowledgement of eternity and the "oceanic feeling" which he associates with it. An element of eternity emerges, however, even in the first moments at which Rubashov discovers "der stumme Partner" (*Sonnenfinsternis*, 99, 224), the "silent Partner" whose existence the party had denied by insisting that talking to one's self is but a vacant monologue.

> Rubashov had always believed that he knew himself rather well … he had no illusions about the phenomenon called the "first person singular,"…[But now] he made unexpected discoveries. He found out that those processes wrongly known as "monologues" are really dialogues of a special kind; dialogues in which one partner remains silent while the other, against all grammatical rules, addresses him as "I" instead of "you" … but the silent partner just remains silent, shuns observation and even refuses to be localized in time and space. (87-88)

The refusal to be localized in time and space is initially experienced by Rubashov in the form of memory. Yet what he remembers most seems, at first glance, unrelated to ἀνάμνησις in Plato and Boethius. Few, if any, of their philosophical commonplaces surface directly and explicitly in Rubashov's experience with memory. Much of it is devoted to recalling a sexual affair he had with a subordinate named Arlova (90–98, 119–120, 125–127, 205–206). She had loved him, had trusted him, and finally, when she was arrested and tried for opposing the party, she looked to him to lead her defense. He refused. He even disavowed her publicly, justifying the betrayal to himself by the logic of time and history. Such logic will be discussed below. What is relevant here is that the memory of Arlova eventually broke the logic of time and place and awakened in Rubashov a sense of personal responsibility and a strength of self that was sufficient to support Rubashov's conversion. Though Arlova bears little resemblance to Lady Philosophy, she is, given the circumstances, no less instrumental in breaking the chains upon Rubashov's mind and she deserves to be considered as Lady Philosophy's parallel in *Darkness at Noon*.

The chains are not easily broken, however, and the climax of Koestler's novel revolves around Rubashov's struggle with them. Even after recovering the memory of Arlova and discovering his "silent Partner," Rubashov easily slips back into his old way of thinking. "He was still fascinated by the problem as to whether to-day, after the experiences of the last few months and days, he would again send Arlova to her death. He did not know" (127).

Rubashov's uncertainty about such a "problem" is provoked and advanced by Ivanov, whose long interview with Rubashov marks the climax of the novel. The interview seems to end with the victory of Ivanov plus the moral and spiritual exhaustion of Rubashov but it is followed by the execution of Ivanov and the severe restriction in the novel of all that he represents. Extended analysis is required to explain how the anomaly relates to Rubashov's conversion and the limits of space here permit little more than a sketch of the relationship between Rubashov and Ivanov, especially its background and significance for the struggle within Rubashov.

Koestler provides Rubashov and Ivanov with a common background and an apparently common fate. They are both revolutionary "theorists" in the age before revolution becomes an excuse for tyranny and theory is still associated rather with decisions about policy than with compulsion and coercion. The new age of absolute and arbitrary rule by No. 1 in the party is represented in the novel by Gletkin, a tireless, almost mindless extension of the party *apparat*. Rubashov and Ivanov seem equally at odds with the "crudity" of No. 1 and his slavish instrument, Gletkin, who supervises the brutal elimination of all who might compete with No. 1 for power.

The point of most extreme contention between Rubashov and Ivanov emerges near the end of their interview, when Ivanov observes:

"There are only two conceptions of human ethics, and they are at opposite poles. One of them is Christian and humane, declares the individual to be sacrosanct, and asserts that the rules of arithmetic are not to be applied to human units. The other starts from the basic principle that a collective aim justifies all means, and not only allows, but demands, that the individual should in every way be subordinated and sacrificed to the community—which may dispose of it as an experimentation rabbit or a sacrificial lamb." (128)

Rubashov objects:

"To me it sometimes seems as though the experimenters had torn the skin off the victim and left it standing with bared tissues, muscles and nerves...."

"Well, and what of it?" said Ivanov happily. "Don't you find it wonderful? Has anything more wonderful ever happened in history? We are tearing the old skin off mankind and giving it a new one. That is not an occupation for people with weak nerves; but there was once a time when it filled you with enthusiasm. What has so changed you that you are now as pernickety as an old maid?"   (130)

Koestler's German provides "zu einer wehleidigen alten Jungfer geworden bist" for the last line and *wehleidigen* is perhaps inadequately rendered by a word so archaic as "pernickety" is today (144). A more literal translation would offer: "you have become a whining old maid." Rubashov considers briefly a reply which invokes memory, especially the memory of friendships he has betrayed and the people who are executed or tormented because of his failure to help them. Arlova is the most promient and extended example but numerous others leap to his mind as well and each is a prospective source of regret, shame and woe to him. The more Rubashov rejects Ivanov and all he stands for the more conspicuous becomes his tendency to whine.

Rejection of Ivanov was a struggle for Rubashov and Ivanov knew it well. Ivanov even draws from Christian imagery to mock Rubashov's difficulty:

"*Apage Satanas*!" repeated Ivanov and poured himself out another glass [of brandy]. "In old days, temptation was of carnal nature. Now it takes the form of pure reason. The values change. I would like to write a Passion play in which God and the Devil dispute for the soul of Saint Rubashov."   (121)

The "reasoning" of the Devil echoes in Rubashov's mind throughout his interview with Ivanov. The following is but one of many examples, though an especially significant one because it returns attention to unexplained terms in the first quotation to appear here from *Darkness at Noon*.

When a year ago he had sent Arlova to her death, he had not had enough imagination to picture the details of an execution. Would he now behave differently merely because he now knew some of its aspects? Either it was right—or it was wrong to sacrifice Richard, Arlova, and Little Loewy. But what had … [their suffering and death] to do with the objective rightness or wrongness of the measure itself?"   (125–126)

When at novel's end Rubashov's conversion is as complete as his life will permit, he looks back upon his past to observe that he has lived as the Party demands, he has "held to the rules of logical calculation. He ha[s] burnt the remains of the old, illogical morality from his consciousness with the acid of reason" (209). The "rules ... of calculation" to which Rubashov refers here determine the "objective rightness or wrongness" of any means, including executions, and the rules are derived from what Rubashov calls "das Gesetz des historischen Kredits" (90), "the law of historical credit" (79).

"He who is in the wrong must pay; he who is in the right will be absolved ... [such] was our law" (79). And it was a law full of surprises for many, including Rubashov. Before turning to specifics, the importance for Koestler's novel of time and history needs to be emphasized.

From the opening admonition to study history, which Rubashov gives to a young policeman who arrests him (8), to the end of Gletkin's interrogation, when Rubashov is promised that he will be vindicated according to "history's textbook" (194), the weight of time contributes much to securing both the plot for the novel as well as the line of development along which the major characters move. Certainly in Rubashov's character, only the struggle within and the theme of conversion take precedence to time and history in explaining the experiences associated with him. Furthermore, confusion about why Rubashov "gives in" to Gletkin and the party can be partially dispelled or avoided by preliminary attention to the importance of time and history.

Above all, the reference to eternity at the end of the novel remains largely inexplicable so long as Rubashov's references to time and history are discounted or neglected. While time and history remain a central issue for Rubashov, eternity, and all that it represents, lies beyond his grasp, but once "his account was settled" (205), then he gains release from the law of historical credit and turns to meet the lifting wave of eternity.

The plot of *Darkness at Noon* is explained in terms of time and history by the first extract provided by the novel from Rubashov's diary. Before turning to it, some introduction to the diary is needed. Material for the diary comes from Ivanov, who supports it as the best method to accomplish the crushing of Rubashov's resistance to the party. According to Ivanov, keeping a diary serves to advance Rubashov's thinking in ways which affirm the power of the party and thus the diary is an easy substitute for harsher methods, like torture and interrogation. As Ivanov observes to Gletkin, "When Rubashov capitulates ... it won't be out of cowardice, but by logic. It is no use trying the hard method with him" (82). Rubashov's diary thus becomes a surrogate for Ivanov long after the mind of the man, and even the man himself, has been eliminated. The resemblance, especially in historical and temporal terms, is clear from the following lines of the diary:

We have learnt history more thoroughly than the others. We differ from all others in our logical consistency. We know that virtue does not matter to history, and that crimes remain unpunished; but that every error had its consequences and venges itself unto the seventh generation. Therefore we concentrated all our efforts on preventing error and destroying the very seeds of it. Never in history has so much power over the future of humanity been concentrated in so few hands as in our case. Each wrong idea we follow is a crime committed against future generations. Therefore we have to punish wrong ideas as others punish crimes: with death.... We lived under the compulsion of working things out to their final conclusions. Our minds were so tensely charged that the slightest collision caused a mortal short-circuit. Thus we were fated to mutual destruction.

I was one of those. I have thought and acted as I had to; I destroyed people whom I was fond of, and gave power to others I did not like. History put me where I stood; I have exhausted the credit which she accorded me; If I was right I have nothing to repent of; if wrong, I will pay.   (80)

Darkness at Noon develops along lines which demonstrate the accuracy of Rubashov's observations about what time will bring, though in more subtle ways than are indicated above. As time tells, both the party and those who resist it are right at some periods and wrong at others, each alternating with the other the privileges of vengeance. At the end of Rubashov's interrogation, Gletkin confirms the point for the new age of the party. He admits to Rubashov that future ages will reverse the condemnation of Rubashov. Rubashov will be vindicated while Gletkin and his associates will implicitly be vilified, "And then you, and some of your friends of the older generation, will be given the sympathy and pity which are denied to you to-day" (194). Such an admission by Gletkin serves to fulfill the observation which Rubashov makes in his diary—"Thus we were fated to mutual destruction" (80). As one age gives way to another, each side takes its turn at being the victor and the vanquished in the temporal cycles of mutual destruction.

Rubashov's tentative affirmation of eternity enables him to begin breaking out of time's destructive cycle and his conversion in this respect parallels the development of Boethius as Lady Philosophy leads him along at the end of book one and throughout books two and three. The variability of *fortuna* is *Philosophia*'s lesson here. The rich and the poor, the powerful and the weak, the glorious and the obscure are all subject to the reverses of time. The people most in need of consolation are not those who happen now to be poor, weak, and obscure, for they are the least subject to the blindness which pretense brings. Delusion clings fiercely to the strong, rich, and glorious, however, as they project today's triumph into the prospect of a dominance everlasting. To avoid nasty surprises, the temporal goods of life are best regarded as on loan to us, subject to recall at a moment's notice. *Philosophia's* opening appeal to Boethius in book two concludes with her own version of the law of historical credit.

> Si ventis vela committeres, non quo voluntas peteret sed quo flatus impellerent, promoveres; si arvis semina crederes, feraces inter se annos sterilesque pensares. Fortunae te regendum dedisti; dominae moribus oportet obtemperes. Tu vero voluentis rotae impetum retinere conaris? At, omnium mortalium stolidissime, si manere incipit, fors esse desistit.   (2.1.55–62)

In stressing the parallel here between the *Consolation of Philosophy* and *Darkness at Noon*, caution is required to grasp the limits of Rubashov's progress in these terms. The calm of a soul quite free of the world's many distractions remains beyond Rubashov. The most that can safely be said of him is that he turns his back on the clang and clamor of contending sides as they cancel each other out across the ages of vengeance and recrimination.

Furthermore, Rubashov's aversion is by no means a source of enlightenment for him. Immediately before feeling the impact of the executioner's first bullet, Rubashov contrasts his condition to that of Moses.

> Moses had not been allowed to enter the land of promise either. But he had been allowed to see it, from the top of the mountain, spread at his feet. Thus, it was easy to die, with the visible certainity of one's goal before one's eyes. He, Nicolas Salmanovitch Rubashov, had not been taken to the top of a mountain; and wherever his eye looked, he saw nothing but desert and the darkness of night. (215)

But with the second bullet, the desert and darkness yield to a wave which, slowly coming from afar, lifted Rubashov up, a shrug of eternity's shoulder.

So small is the opening which Koestler allows to eternity here that even the most careful and serious reader may miss it altogether. Efforts to read *Darkness at Noon* in its historical and political context complicate even further any effort to understand the importance of Koestler's reference to eternity. Consider, for example, George Orwell's reading of the novel.

Few writers active in the early 1940s were better qualified to relate the novel to the events that surrounded it, especially the rise of totalitarianism and the threat it posed to nations affirming the rule of law and the protection of individuals from mistreatment by the state. From the mid-1930s on, Orwell was a first-hand observer of the kind of mentality and practices described in Koestler's novel. Furthermore, Orwell clearly demonstrated a desire to give credit to Koestler when he deserved it. Thus, Orwell observed that *Darkness at Noon* "reaches the stature of tragedy."[4] The choices Rubashov confronted were fully developed on what Orwell called an "aesthetic level" well above the "polemical tract" so characteristic of most efforts by novelists to address the issues raised by Communism and Fascism.

Yet, such an able, appreciative, and well-informed reader comes up empty-handed in an attempt to read the novel in a way that explains its end. According to Orwell, the main issue is not Rubashov's conversion or his struggle for an identity that transcends politics and finds an opening to eternity. Instead, "the whole book centres round one question: Why did Rubashov confess?"[5] Orwell asserts that three explanations are possible for all those who confessed in "show trials" like the one Koestler represented in the novel. The accused confessed because of (1) guilt, (2) torture and blackmail, or (3) "despair, mental bankruptcy and the habit of loyalty to the Party."[6]

Orwell insists that utter despair prevails in Rubashov's soul.

> Rubashov ultimately confesses because he cannot find it in his mind any reason for not doing so. Justice and objective truth have long since ceased to have any meaning for him. For decades he has been simply the creature of the Party, and what the Party now demands is that he shall confess to non-existent crimes…. What is there, what code, what loyalty, what notion of good and evil, for the sake of which he can defy the Party and endure further torment? He is not only alone, he is also hollow.[7]

Having thus misread the novel, Orwell goes beyond it to attribute to Koestler himself views which are an extension of Rubashov's character. According to Orwell, Koestler's disillusionment with the Russian Revolution and its consequences had resulted in a pessimism so deep that he abandoned all hope for major political change and thus all effort to organize and effect it. All that remains, as Orwell says of Koestler's position, is "to keep out of politics, make a sort of oasis within which you and your friends can remain sane, and hope that somehow things will be better in a hundred years."[8]

Closer attention to the end of Koester's novel against the background of Boethius' *Consolation of Philosophy* may have saved Orwell from such an obvious misreading of the novel and misrepresentation of the author. To Orwell's credit, however, he quickly corrected the mistake in an essay published a year after the erroneous account described above.[9] Koestler made the correction easier by his writings on the importance of a contemplative approach to politics. Put briefly and generally, Koestler claims that the crisis posed by Communism and Fascism is a spiritual crisis which results from the decades of approaching politics in reductionistic terms that stresses little more than biological or socio-economic utility. To avoid such crises in the future, and perhaps the destructive consequences associated with them, our contact with eternity must be recognized and enlarged. Only from the perspective of eternity do the limits of political power become clear to the point that the ambition for it can be checked and contained. "Neither the saint nor the revolutionary can save us; only the sythesis of the two."[10]

In the very different context of classical philosophy as represented in the Platonic dialogues, Koester's novel can be considered as an imaginative postscript to the story of Callicles or Thrasymachus. Each in a different way has embraced power as the love of his life, fully expecting that his devotion to it will insure that power will always be his. Each says with the pride of those who prevail for a day that might makes right forever (*Republic* 339A; *Gorgias* 484A). Plato does not permit us to see Callicles and Thrasymachus when the sun has set on their day in the precincts of power. We may well envision them as tyrants who have been betrayed and overwhelmed by those whose hunger for power is even greater than their own. Had we been allowed to see Callicles or Thrasymachus so abused and crushed, they may well have resembled Rubashov as he attempts to recollect an identity based on something beneath, or even better, beyond the perpetual confusion and contention ever associated with struggles for power. If their recollection reaches the point of a conversion and, like Rubashov, they find and opening to eternity, then they may well say of their past that they were "omnium mortalium stolidissim[i]," "the most foolish of all mortals" (*De consolatione* 2.1.61).

NOTES

1. Arthur Koestler, *Darkness at Noon*, trans. Daphne Hardy (New York: Bantam, 1966), 209. Hardy's translation is the original edition, which appeared in 1941, and all quotations are taken from it, except where otherwise indicated in direct and specific terms. The reader thus has some assurance that the argument is not dependent upon equivocal or self-serving translations which an author with a point to prove may unwittingly provide.

2. Ibid., 205.

3. *Sonnenfinsternis* (Stuttgart: Karl M. Fraas, 1948), 216. The German edition, not published until 1946, some five years after the English translation appeared, offers the following as the final sentence: *Sie kam von ferne und reiste gemächlich weiter, ein Achselzucken*

der Unendlichkeit (235). Charles Connell saved me from at least one error in working with the German edition; John Gruber-Miller helped me to avoid several others in representing Boethius' text.

4. *The Collected Essays, Journalism and Letters of George Orwell*, ed. Sonia Orwell & Ian Angus (New York: HarBrace, 1968), 3: 238.

5. Ibid.

6. Ibid., 3: 239.

7. Ibid.

8. Ibid., 3: 244.

9. Ibid., 4: 17–19.

10. Arthur Koestler, *The Yogi and the Commissar and Other Essays* (New York: Macmillan, 1945), 247.

DAVID CESARANI

War, 1938–42

The years 1938 to 1942 were among the most creative and chaotic of Koestler's life. He wrote and published his first two novels, *The Gladiators* (1939) and his masterpiece *Darkness at Noon* (1940). He also produced a brilliant analysis of the fall of France in 1940, interwoven with the story of his personal experiences and escape from Nazi-dominated Europe. This book, *Scum of the Earth* (1941), had the added distinction of being the first that he wrote entirely in English. It marked yet another language shift, with all the profound effects on mental processes involved in translation from one language, political culture and artistic heritage to another. Throughout these writings he was trying to figure out where he belonged.

In April 1938, somewhat later than he made out in his memoirs, he finally left the Communist Party. Despite all that he had witnessed in Russia in 1932–3, and had subsequently learned about the country, he retained a deep loyalty to the Soviet Union, its people, their heroic efforts to modernise a relatively backward empire and the particular idea of revolution which animated this gigantic enterprise. His last illusions were destroyed by the Nazi–Soviet Pact in August 1939. From that point onwards he was doubly, or trebly, an exile: uprooted from the country of his birth and spurned by those he had adopted, he had broken with the Party, an international haven, and was now deserted by Russia. Where was his home?

From *Arthur Koestler: The Homeless Mind*. © 1998 by David Cesarani.

This question was more than theoretical. When war broke out in September 1939 the French turned on foreigners in their midst. Koestler was interned twice. On the first occasion he was freed thanks to a strenuous campaign by friends and allies. The second time he took his fate in his own hands and escaped, living on the run from the French authorities and the invading Germans. He sought anonymity in the French Foreign Legion, eventually escaped to North Africa and from there made his way via Portugal to England. However, he was not given official permission to enter the country and arrived illegally, as a result of which he spent a further stretch in prison. Once he was released, by dint of another campaign, he enrolled in the Pioneer Corps of the British Army. Even though he was now in uniform and subject to military discipline, Koestler continued to write and also engaged in political crusades. Jewish preoccupations were to the fore. Despite being an alien he campaigned for the rescue of refugees from German-occupied Europe in 1941–2 and monitored the Nazi persecution of the Jews.

Jewish themes repeatedly emerge in his writing from this period. Spartacus, the hero of *The Gladiators*, receives inspiration from a prophetic Jew. *Scum of the Earth* is punctuated with references to the role of anti-Semitism in the demoralisation of France and full of observations on the singular plight of Jewish fugitives such as himself. The central figure in *Darkness at Noon*, Nikolai Salmanovitch Rubashov, *is* a Jew. But it was as an ex-Communist, someone who had freed himself from the simultaneously reassuring and perilous embrace of the Party at the expense of becoming an alien or outsider in every sense, that Koestler at last achieved real fame and permanent security as a writer.

I

After his Middle Eastern adventure and rediscovery of Zionism, Koestler returned to France for a few weeks. In January 1938 he travelled to England for a lecture tour to promote *Spanish Testament*. The book had become a popular success and an effective propaganda tool, as Münzenberg had hoped. According to the biographer of Victor Gollancz, founder of the Left Book Club (LBC), 'Of the books on the Civil War published by the LBC, the most influential was Arthur Koestler's *Spanish Testament*, which came out in December 1937 and was followed up in January by the author's speaking tour to groups. Koestler's experiences as a prisoner of Franco expecting imminent execution gave his book and his talks an immediacy that added feverishness to the LBCs support for the Popular Front forces.'[1]

By now Koestler knew he was not a Communist, but had not summoned the courage to break openly with the Party. He realised it would mean adding homelessness to exile and obloquy to self-pity. The lecture tour offered a device to break the impasse, a gentle way of provoking his expulsion. At almost every one of the dozens of Left Book Club meetings which he addressed a member of the audience asked for his thoughts about the treatment of POUM—the Trotskyist-dominated militia force that had had been broken up by the Republican authorities at the behest of the Communists in 1937. Koestler answered that members of POUM might have been misguided in certain ways, but they were sincere anti-Fascists. This contradicted the Party line which denounced POUM as renegades who showed an independence of thinking alien to Communist practice. However, the English Communists merely expressed their disapproval by silence or argued with him politely and reasonably. The Party seemed willing to ignore his *faux pas* for the time being: England was a side-show. Nevertheless, Koestler felt relieved that he had recorded his dissent from the Party line. The Left Book Club was only a dress rehearsal for what he knew he had to do in the real political and ideological cockpit: the *émigré* German community of Paris.[2]

Events hastened his next move. In March 1938 the trial of Bukharin and other old Bolsheviks began in Moscow. Then Eva Weissberg arrived from the USSR bearing the incredible story of her own arrest, interrogation and imprisonment. Two years earlier she had been the object of fantastic accusations of sabotage and anti-Soviet espionage. She was arrested and held for eighteen months until representations by the Austrian consul secured her release. Even though Alex had separated from her in 1934 and knew that the penalty for supporting his ex-wife was almost inevitably to suffer the same fate, he had worked tirelessly to free her. Eva was eventually expelled from the USSR in September 1937; true to form, Alex Weissberg was arrested in March 1937 and was still in prison. Fired up by this further evidence of Communist perfidy, Koestler prepared for a talk on Spain to the Association of German Writers in Exile in April 1938.[3]

As a celebrity he attracted a large audience, mainly composed of German Communist refugees. Beforehand, the organisers asked him to stick to Party orthodoxy in his comments on Spain, but he refused. At the end of his talk he drew three provocative conclusions: that no individual or party was infallible; that it was wrong to persecute allies who took a different route to the same goal; and that Thomas Mann was correct when he declared: 'In the long run, a harmful truth is better than a useful lie.' His listeners understood exactly what he meant and immediately the meeting broke up he was cold-shouldered. To the Party he had instantly become a non-person; and just as quickly he was engulfed by loneliness. 'It was not a physical loneliness, for after the break with the Party I found more friends than I have had before. But individual friendships could never replace the knowledge that one belonged to an international brotherhood embracing the whole globe; nor the warming, reassuring feeling of a collective solidarity which gave to that huge, amorphous mass the coherence and intimacy of a small family.'[4]

Despite this the Party did not expel him, probably because it did not want a public breach with a famous survivor of Franco's jails. So in a mood of 'bridge burning' euphoria on 22 April 1938 he wrote a letter of resignation to the 'Writers Caucus' of the German Communist Party. The letter, which has only recently come to light in the former KGB 'Special Archive', is remarkably ambivalent. In it he promises not to join any oppositional group and pledges his loyalty to the Soviet Union which he regards 'as a decisively positive factor in the political balance of our time'. He begs his former comrades to regard him still as 'an ally'. Finally, he pleads for his breach to be kept secret to avoid embarrassing those who helped him in 1937 under he impression that he was not a Communist.[5]

It was followed by a much longer letter, sent a week later, explaining his motives. Koestler denounced the 'moral degeneration of the Party, which began long before 1933'. The Moscow Trials and the events in Spain forced Party members either to believe the unbelievable or abase their intellects. The 'Trotskyite–Nazi conspiracy … is gradually beginning to occupy for us the role *The Protocols of the Elders of Zion* occupies in the minds of the Nazis'. But the problem went deeper. The movement lacked a revolutionary ethics: Communists denounced bourgeois morality and utilitarianism, but had no adequate substitute. The only guide to practical action was that the end justified the means. Marxist theory had 'ossified' too. There 'is not a hint of an explanation in our theory for the laws that impel the masses' to act against their own 'objective class interests'. Koestler ended by reaffirming his loyalty to the USSR, but asserted that this could be combined with free inquiry and debate. 'I feel I am being suffocated by you, and I have the elementary need to breathe, to think, to write freely again, to dare to speak my mind.'[6] His profession of fealty to a country which he had seen at its worst is not the only odd facet of his 'breach' with Communism. Koestler broke with the Party at a rather late stage, long after his mentor Münzenberg, and remained on good terms with the 'apparat' for some time after that.

In *The God That Failed* Koestler asserted that Münzenberg 'broke with the Comintern in 1938, six months after myself'. Actually, Münzenberg had effectively broken with Moscow a year *earlier*. From January 1937 he deflected calls that he present himself in Moscow, at first pleading ill-health, then simply rejecting them. At a German Popular Front conference in Paris in April 1937 he condemned the mistakes the Party had made in the early

1930s, taking a barely veiled swipe at Stalin. Moscow then sent an emissary of the KPD to sequester the funds of the 'Münzenberg Trust', but Münzenberg refused to co-operate. In the summer he held talks with exiled liberal politicians and bourgeois figures such as the writer Leo Schwarzchild, the ex-Ullstein editor Georg Bernhard and the novelist Heinrich Mann about creating a new party. This would subsequently take shape as the Deutsche Freiheits Partei. In September 1937 his book *Propaganda als Waffe* appeared. It was a searing attack on the lies used by totalitarian regimes and could as easily be read as a critique of the techniques used by the Soviets or the Nazis. Sure enough, it was attacked in the exile German Communist press in November 1937. There are conflicting versions of precisely when Münzenberg was expelled from the German Communist Party, but it is most likely that the decision was taken in March 1938 although it was not published until May.[7]

Whichever date is selected as the moment that Münzenberg cut his ties with the Comintern, it is certain that by the time Koestler returned to Paris in September 1937 Münzenberg had lost his power base. Koestler recalls that 'Otto greeted me at the Gare du Nord, most incongruously and touchingly equipped with a huge bouquet of roses. We must have looked like a couple of gangsters out of an American film carrying a wreath at a funeral.' In effect, they were and it was Willi's funeral. Despite the fact that Katz was now acting as Münzenberg's undertaker, Koestler remained on good terms with him and continued to live in his old appartment on 10 rue Dombasle (where Walter Benjamin was a neighbour and fellow Saturday-night poker-player).[8]

Koestler's inexactitude regarding the timing of Münzenberg's departure from the Party signifies the intense difficulty he had in making his own break. The blurring of dates suggests that in retrospect he wished he had left earlier, pre-empting his mentor rather than trailing in his wake. What lies beyond doubt, however, is that during the first half of 1938 he was sawing through the ideological and emotional shackles that bound him to Communism. Perhaps the most important tool at his disposal was the novel about Spartacus, *The Gladiators*.

Thanks to the success of *Spanish Testament* he had negotiated a contract with Jonathan Cape to publish the novel in English. The advance of £125 enabled him to concentrate on the writing, even though he had to set aside some of the money to pay for the translation. It was an important turning point in his career for he was now able to think of himself primarily as a writer and 'writing as a purpose in itself. The book provided the material means for his emancipation from writing as propaganda and the intellectual leverage he needed to free himself from the ideological compulsion.[9]

In *The Gladiators* Koestler makes the late Roman Republic resemble modern Europe. Its economic system is a parody of late capitalism, prone to all the same crises. A revolutionary situation develops when Spartacus, the leader of a group of runaway gladiators, forges an army out of rebellious slaves and discontented elements. A member of the Essenes, a Jewish sect, outlines to Spartacus a vision of society based on primitive Communism and he sets out to create the perfect society. Unfortunately, he falls victim to the 'law of detours'. As explained by the Essene, 'the worst curse of all is that he [man] must tread the evil road for the sake of the good and the right, that he must make detours and walk crookedly so that he may reach the straight goal.'

Using Spartacus, Koestler obliquely examined the dilemmas of the Bolsheviks in the years after 1917. Spartacus demands complete obedience from those who will follow him to the Utopian, egalitarian 'Sun City' he proposes to establish. But Spartacus is forced to make a series of compromises to preserve his Utopian community and is driven to ever more brutal measures to ensure internal discipline. The hoped-for rising of all the slaves of Rome, a metaphor for the world revolution, does not occur and Sun City, which is modelled on the kibbutz, remains isolated. In the end he wearies of leadership: he berates the masses for their lack of revolutionary discipline but refuses to bully them any longer. The rebel horde is defeated by the Romans whose commander, Crassus, tells Spartacus, 'you should have invented a new religion'. Spartacus dies in battle; his followers are crucified.[10]

The Gladiators is full of vividly drawn action and rich with characters. For a first novel it is an astonishing accomplishment. Admittedly it is replete with anachronisms, such as Roman houses equipped with 'fire escapes', even though Koestler laboured over the period detail. But none of this matters by comparison with the narrative drive and intense rumination on the dilemma of means and ends. The novel reflected a deep shift in Koestler's political thinking. In it he suggested that a revolution can only succeed if its leaders are ruthless and indoctrinate people with a new set of beliefs. Any humanity or toleration of dissent is fatal. Spartacus fails because he still has old-fashioned scruples and applies repression inconsistently, continuing to value human life over the cause he champions. This is a chilling message which can be read in two ways, according to the reader's taste. In essence, however, it is a pessimistic, un-Marxist novel. Unlike his contemporaries, Ignazio Silone and André Malraux, socialist writers who had also been through a long involvement with the Communist Party, he saw little hope for spontaneous revolution amongst the people, and equally little hope that uncorruptable leaders would offer them decent direction.

During 1938 Koestler had contemporaneous experience of revolutionary ruthlessness at work. In the spring, having received Eva Weissberg's news about her husband, he mounted a campaign to help save Alex. He persuaded Frédéric Joliot-Curie and Jean Perrin, Nobel Prize winning physicists, to intercede with Stalin on Weissberg's behalf. He also saw Martin Ruhemann, an English-born scientist who had known Weissberg during a spell in Kharkov. Ruhemann refused to help because he was sure that Weissberg must have been a saboteur if that was what the charges said. Koestler was disgusted by this response: it was another demonstration of the Party's corrupting effect.[11]

The Gladiators was finished in July 1938. Over the summer, Koestler spent some time at Sanary-sur-Mer, a small resort on the French Mediterranean coast between Marseilles and Toulon, where the exiled German-Jewish writer Lion Feuchtwänger had lived since 1933. Feuchtwänger's home had become the meeting place for a circle of writers who were Communists or fellow travellers. Even though Koestler laboured under the stigma of a renegade, he was still welcome there. Alfred Kantorowicz remembers him visiting along with Heinrich Mann, Arnold Zweig, Ernst Toller, Ellen Wilkinson, the Labour MP, and Robert Neumann. He was frequently engaged in passionate argument with the other guests. Ludwig Marcuse recalled that Koestler would come to the house and make 'wild speeches' on the veranda in the presence of Kantorowicz and other stars of the Party.[12]

As soon as *The Gladiators* was completed he started work on the novel that was to emerge as *Darkness at Noon*. It began life entitled 'Watchman, What of the Night', later slightly improved as 'The Vicious Circle'. According to the publication proposal submitted to Jonathan Cape: 'the first volume of a trilogy on modern Russia, [it] opens with the arrest of the former People's Commissar, Rubashov on the charge of plotting against the state.' Koestler recorded that originally it was supposed to deal with some prisoners in a totalitarian country, under sentence of death, who re-evaluate their lives and realise that they are guilty of sacrificing men for an abstract ideal of mankind.[13] If it was serendipitous that the title and precise content changed, it was nothing short of miraculous that the novel was ever finished and published. It was written in spite of the usual distractions that afflicted Koestler and some that were unprecedented. Its composition, which was stretched over nearly two years, was haunted by the events of the time, such as the Nazi–Soviet Pact, another spell of imprisonment and Koestler's beleaguered, pessimistic mood.

Manès Sperber has given an affecting portrait of Koestler in the last year before the war. 'Koestler and I were going on 32 and both of us were homeless in more than one sense and extremely sensitive, yet hardened to blows and deprivations, the dangerous allure of success and the inspirations of loneliness.' Although they disagreed on matters of taste and lifestyle, they concurred on the 'essential' things. 'Our friendship was like that of rock-climbers who are exposed to the same enticements and dangers and expect no less from each other than they do from themselves.' Both found comfort in their Jewish heritage. 'No matter how depressing the events of the day might be, the Jewish wit and gallows humour that each new day provoked determined the tone in which each of us expressed his fears and hopes. In fact, we felt more bitterness than is required to hate one's own life and all one's contemporaries, and yet we had a lot of fun when we were together and could often be heard laughing heartily.'[14]

In October 1938 Sperber and Koestler were drawn into Willi Münzenberg's last great publishing venture: a weekly anti-Fascist paper based on the principles of the Popular Front. Münzenberg acquired financial backing from the French Socialists and rented an apartment to serve as an editorial office. He recruited Koestler to act as co-editor and Ludwig Marcuse, the novelist, to edit a cultural section. Sperber became a consultant editor. In the early autumn Münzenberg's diminished circle of friends and supporters met regularly to hammer out a programme for the paper, christened hopefully *Die Zukunft* (The Future). The first issue appeared on 12 October 1938.[15]

Koestler writes rather dismissively that *Die Zukunft* was 'stillborn' and soon went stale. In fact, it continued until the fall of France in May 1940 and performed a multitude of important functions. It was a rallying point for disillusioned Communists and anti-Fascists of all hues. The paper was loosely tied to the Deutsche Freiheits Partei and together they represented one of the first attempts to create a progressive, anti-Stalinist and anti-Fascist politics for Europe.[16] Typically, Koestler worked on it for only about three months, leaving before the end of 1938. He later said that he had been attracted to the project mainly because he wanted to fill the void left by his split from the Party, and he certainly seemed ill at ease, displeasingly glum one moment and engagingly euphoric the next. Marcuse remembered him as 'a melancholic who had enormous potential when he wanted to succeed'.[17] According to Sperber, Koestler resigned because the success of *Spanish Testament* 'made him decide to pursue a literary career and write only occasional articles and reports'. He wanted to concentrate 'on a novel that was intended to reveal the criminal and political background of the Moscow Trials'. Koestler was resentful that because of the paper he could write only at night.[18]

It was probably also through Münzenberg that around this time he met

Paul Willert, the only son of Sir Arthur Willert, a former correspondent for *The Times* who moved into diplomacy via the News Department of the Foreign Office in 1920, remaining in the foreign service until 1935. Like his father, Paul Willert had been to Eton and Balliol where he became 'extremely left-wing'. He visited Berlin in the 1930s, encountering Willi Münzenberg and Otto Katz. From 1937 to 1939 he worked for Oxford University Press in Europe and America. Thanks to his eminent father and his Communist associations Willert was well placed to help left-wing German exiles. During 1938–9 he attended lunches which Münzenberg organised to cultivate important contacts. Willert was useful: he knew people at the British embassy in Paris and had access to journalists and politicians in Britain, including Harold Nicolson, MP. In a few months' time he would play a critical role in Koestler's life.[19]

In April 1939 there came another, familiar interruption to Koestler's writing. Jonathan Cape had accepted his proposal for the novel, but the advance ran out and he was forced to break off while he and Sperber worked together on a third sex book for the Aldors. For two months they and another exile, Fritz Kuenkel, concocted *L'Encyclopédie de la famille*, a vast tome exceeding 800 pages attributed to Drs A. Willy, A. Costler, R. Fisher and others. The revised English version was entitled *The Practice of Sex*. Like its predecessors, the book did very well and was translated into several languages. The first French edition was published in 1939 and was reprinted three times by February 1940, selling over 12,500 copies.[20] Like the other sex books with which Koestler was involved, it has been unjustly neglected.

The Practice of Sex began boldly by claiming that there was a crisis in erotic and family life due to 'systematic suppression by silence of the sexual instinct'. The book was dedicated to alleviating these woes by placing sex, love and the family in a correct scientific and historical perspective. The influence of its neo-Freudian, ex-Marxist (and mainly Jewish) authors was unmistakable, but they cleverly managed to blend earnest social psychology with soft pornography. A survey of sexual mores amongst 'primitive and other races' with the aim of establishing the 'natural forms' of sexual activity and human relations also allowed for much titillating detail. In order to supply the knowledge necessary for the achievement of a 'full sex life' the authors provided graphic chapters on women's anatomy and sexual development as well as po-faced studies of marriage in England, America and the USSR. By its mid-point the book became increasingly repetitive and ill-organised, although there was interesting and sensitive material on why marriages fail.[21]

Koestlerian preoccupations were evident throughout. The description of sexuality in France strikingly resembles the brothel passages in Koestler's autobiographical works of the 1950s. A section on 'Heredity and Eugenics' discussed Darwinian and Mendelian theories of evolution in terms and a style which recur in Koestler's later scientific writing. There is also an interesting Jewish thread running through it. In a section devoted to the erotic life of 'other races' there are comments on Jews and Judaism that prefigure much of Koestler's later writing on the subject and suggest not only that he authored these passages, but that certain attitudes were formed long before they are usually attributed to him. A closing chapter on 'Mixed Marriages' condemns Nazi racism and attacks the stigma attached to Jewishness.[22]

Sperber was grateful for the work on *L'Encyclopédie de la famille* since he, too, was desperately hard up and it was not uncongenial employment. He and Koestler were now inseparable and were often to be seen in the cafés of the Left Bank where the *émigrés* assembled, the one short, hair thinning and full of animated gestures, the other lanky, with a thick oily crop and nervy movements. They also met weekly with the great 1920s German writer Alfred Döblin, now an exile too. With him they thrashed out questions concerning Communism and the Jewish Question. Years later Koestler recalled: 'As I regarded Döblin as one of the most original and independent minds of the Left, I proposed that we should start a sort of seminar or *Arbeitsgemeinschaft* to clarify our outlook. I think the three of us met three or four times, but the project petered out as so many others among émigrés.' Unlike Koestler, in his memoirs Sperber added that Döblin was, like them, a Jew and that anti-Semitism was one of the topics which interested him. At their informal 'seminar' they spent a great deal of time discussing the Jewish Question and Döblin's plan for a 'new Jewish movement'.[23]

Sperber did not get on well with all Koestler's friends. In the summer of 1939 Németh and his girlfriend turned up in Paris. By now Koestler was as close to Sperber as he had been to Németh in the old days. They discussed all their ideas and collaborated on money-making literary projects. But Sperber could not stand the sloppy, shabby and importunate Németh, whom he regarded as a lazy parasite. This was a recipe for constant friction until Koestler left Paris for the South of France in July 1939, accompanied by his new girlfriend, Daphne Hardy.[24]

Hardy was born in England in 1917, and grew up in Switzerland and Holland where her father worked at the Court of International Justice. Educated at the German Realgymnasium in the Hague and a French convent school, she was fluent in French and German. She studied sculpture at the Royal Academy School of Art and in 1938 won a scholarship to go to Paris. Friends in London gave her an introduction to Koestler and they quickly became attached to one another. She moved into his flat on 10 rue

Dombasle, although in his accounts of the period Koestler pretended that she had her own place in the same building. He held out great hopes for this relationship. Hardy was not conventionally pretty but she had a lithe figure and sparkling eyes. She was intelligent company and a gifted artist. Although prone to insecurity, which meant that she was easily dominated, and occasional bouts of self-pity, most of the time she had a cheery disposition. It seemed as if he had at last found Helena.[25]

II

During August 1939 Koestler and Hardy rented a ramshackle villa near the village of Roquebilliere in the Alpes Maritimes. It was an idyllic location but the climate and the international situation grew oppressive. French troops were being called up and were massing close to the Italian border. When Koestler learned of the Russo-German pact on 22 August 1939 he realised that war was inevitable. The pact fatally undermined the faith in Russia that had nourished him for nearly a decade, and to which he clung even after his break with the Communist Party. He also knew that it doomed Europe to an apocalyptic conflict, which would settle his fate one way or the other. He was to be plunged into a war against Fascism, but for a cause that was hazy and hardly inspiring.[26]

To Koestler's irritation Hardy found events less of a distraction and set off for Switzerland to visit an art exhibition in Geneva. Koestler fretted in her absence, but made some progress with the novel. The passages in which Rubashov meditates on the betrayal of foreign comrades in order to defend the 'bastion' of communism, actually the national interest of the USSR, are imprinted with his reaction to the Russo-German pact. By the time Hardy returned the international crisis dictated that they make for Paris as quickly as possible. From there, Koestler intended to proceed to London and enlist in the British army. On 29 August they left the villa. Three days later, in Le Lavandu, they heard that Germany had invaded Poland. The homeward journey continued at a snail's pace. Their battered old car couldn't go very fast without overheating, while the roads were clogged with military traffic and panic-stricken city dwellers who anticipated imminent bombing raids.[27]

The constant delays had a fortuitous result. Almost overnight the mood in France had darkened. Fifth Column hysteria was intensified by the Russo-German pact, which added the Left to the forces of the Right as a possible source of subversion: the press spewed out anti-foreigner sentiment directed against the left-wing exiles. Anti-Fascist foreigners like Koestler were instantly suspect. Police raided his Paris apartment building on 2 September in search of 'aliens' and alleged subversives, but in his absence had to settle for carting off a sickly German-Jewish refugee doctor who occupied the neighbouring flat.[28]

Once back in Paris, Koestler presented himself at the local police station, relying on the fact that Hungary was a neutral country to protect him from detention. He was twice waved away and returned to his flat relieved, if rather puzzled. His encounter with the British consular authorities was less pleasing. A passport officer told him that his visa for entry to the UK had been cancelled, along with all other visas, on 4 September. Koestler insisted that he wanted to return in order to join the British army, but to no effect. He was instructed to apply for a new visa, which might take several weeks to come through. He briefly considered joining the French army, but he was not inclined to risk his life for a country that was locking up refugees and foreign anti-Fascists. Unwilling to sit passively, he asked a well-connected and friendly lawyer to enquire of the police and judicial authorities why he was a suspect. The lawyer told him that a rightwing clique in the government was hunting down political opponents and simultaneously appeasing Spain by arresting anti-Fascists who had supported the Republicans. He advised Koestler to get to Britain as quickly as possible. The chances of this were slight. The British authorities were dragging their feet over the entry visa and the French would not let him leave the country.[29]

For a month Koestler waited for the inexorable return of the police, a packed bag ready for his departure. They finally appeared on 2 October when he was having his morning bath. Once the first shock had subsided Hardy set about organising provisions for Koestler's involuntary journey. She waved forlornly from the entrance to the building as he was led off to the police station. He was held there for several hours among a congerie of other 'suspects' before they were taken to the Salle Lepine, a lecture hall. The detainees spent three boring days in the hall and two uncomfortable nights in the building's coal cellar. Each day batches of prisoners were removed by the police. Finally the last contingent, including Koestler, was taken to a more permanent detention centre in the converted Roland Garros tennis stadium, near Auteuil. The conditions there were much worse, but the internees stayed long enough to improvise facilities and to develop some kind of collective spirit.[30]

Within a few days he was among a group of 500 men, including Gustav Regler and Hans Schultz, Münzenberg's former secretary, who were loaded on to a train heading south-west towards Le Vernet, an internment camp in the department of Ariège, near the Spanish border. Le Vernet had been established to hold Spanish Republicans who had fled into France when the Civil War ended: it had an odious reputation. Regler described the camp as 'a collection of ramshackle huts at the foot of the Pyrenees, without beds, without light, and without heating'. It was 'an eerie cemetery. The huts stood like great coffins on the plains.' When they arrived, the detainees 'lay on planks and were forgotten'. Koestler complained that facilities in the camp were so primitive that the inmates were reduced to living like Stone Age men.[31]

Having also recently left the Communist Party, Regler was bitter about being arrested along with dozens of genuine CP members, including the entire Central Committee of the exiled German Communist Party. But Regler had been a political commissar in Spain during the Civil War and his natural leadership qualities soon asserted themselves. He was elected spokesman for the 150 men in his block, which numbered many veterans of the International Brigade. Despite even his best efforts morale soon began to break down. These German exiles wanted to make war on Fascism, even if it meant fighting their countrymen. They felt useless and vulnerable held behind wire, hundreds of miles from the front line. 'There was constant repudiation and fighting among friends. Feelings were relieved by sheer baseness; it was a dysentery of the soul.' Regler dreaded the moment when he had to douse the lights in the hut, plunging the men into darkness and introspection. 'We sought to understand our time. No kind of evaluation could have withstood our grief at our imprisonment. For a time, everything seemed to us mere senseless chaos.'[32]

Koestler, who was in another hut (Quartier C, Barrack 24), was particularly demoralised. 'Internment in a concentration camp during a war is not in itself a pleasant experience. In my case it came too soon after imprisonment in a civil war.' Within a short time he had a physical and mental collapse. According to Regler, Koestler 'lived withdrawn in his own hut'.[33]

In *Scum of the Earth*, written in England in 1941, Koestler describes the routine that was soon established in the camp. The internees had to perform manual labour, mainly road building and construction. They were forced to stand for hours while roll calls were taken at the start and conclusion of every day. As the weather deteriorated both the work and the parades became almost unbearable. The camp administration was 'run with that mixture of ignominy, corruption and *laissez-faire* so typical of the French administration'. French officers and guards relied on a system of trustees and elected block leaders. Few were as upright as Regler, who constantly fought for better conditions for the men in his barrack. Instead, Koestler had to deal with a string of petty, venal tyrants. To his acute eye it was a mark of how far civilisation had fallen that veterans of Franco's prisons or Nazi camps reacted with equanimity to these conditions.[34]

The Communists were, inevitably, the best organised and most disciplined group. Non-and ex-Communists also tried to organise, but with less success. Koestler, Regler and Leo Valiani, an Italian anti-Fascist, made an early attempt to resist the camp authorities and instil backbone into the non-aligned detainees. When it was announced that the men would have their hair shaven Regler drafted a petition of protest, while Koestler and Valiani drummed up support in the various huts. The petition was rejected by the camp commandant. This was not the end of the business. According to Regler, 'We had been herded like sheep to the shearing, and I remember that the humiliating nature of the proceedings was relieved only by the fact that Arthur Koestler, who was otherwise very reserved and furious about his arrest, had snatched the scissors from the barber before it was his turn, and in wild delight had cut great handfuls of hair from his splendid crop. "I've been wanting to do it ever since I was a child!" he cried, and then went quietly back to his place.'[35]

As soon as Koestler was sent to Le Vernet, Hardy made efforts to obtain his release but organisation was not her forté and she 'hadn't a clue how to set about this sort of thing.' In desperation she turned to Dorothea Koestler who loyally contributed her redoubtable skills and experience. The extent of their campaign is shown by the many letters and papers, which were confiscated by the French police in 1940 and ended up in the KGB's 'Special Archive'. On 10 October Hardy wrote to Jonathan Cape alerting Koestler's English publishers to his detention and begging for their help. She also enlisted the aid of the Duchess of Atholl who had written the introduction for the Left Book Club edition of Spanish Testament. Atholl, in turn wrote to Georges Mandel, a prominent radical politician, and a Jew, who became Minister of the Interior in 1940, assuring him that Koestler was anti-Nazi.[36]

In a demonstration of the affection he retained in the hearts of ex-girlfriends and ex-wives, Dorothea wrote to Anthony Eden and Sir Robert Vansittart, reminding them of the crucial part they had played in freeing Koestler from a Fascist jail in 1937. Her letters, however, were less than honest about Koestler's situation. She told Eden that the French must have misinterpreted the reasons for his incarceration in Spain and taken him to be a pro-Communist. She insisted that he had only had 'nominal relations with German Communist circles, which were finally and completely terminated over two years ago'. Dorothea warned that Koestler was ill and unlikely to survive a winter in a concentration camp, and implored Eden to intervene with the Hungarian embassy, which could establish that Koestler was a neutral. The use of English in these letters was superior to Dorothea's normal command of the language, which suggests that they were drafted by Daphne Hardy. It was an intimate collaboration.[37]

Hardy mobilised Koestler's colleagues and friends. Edgar Mowrer, the journalist, cabled Harold Nicolson urging him to act and telling him that Koestler had 'abjured Communist doctrine last year', a somewhat different line from that being spun to Eden. André Malraux offered the Ministère des affaires étrangères a personal guarantee on behalf of Koestler if he was freed, and completed one of the forms which were being used in the applications on behalf of hundreds of other internees. He also gave Hardy essential financial support. Jean Paulhan, editor of the prestigious *Nouvelle Revue française*, signalled his willingness to assist. At her request, Frédéric Joliot-Curie signed a letter calling for Koestler's release. Hardy also wrote to Ferenc Aldor demanding that he send the final payment for the work on *L'Encyclopédie de la famille* to Koestler in Le Vernet so that he could use it to buy extra food and cigarettes. Meanwhile, in London, Rupert Hart-Davis at Cape was rallying PEN via Cecil Day Lewis and trying to get the *News Chronicle* interested in Koestler's arrest. David Scott, the paper's Paris correspondent, repeatedly questioned officials as to the reasons for Koestler's arrest.[38]

Paul Willert enlisted his parents on behalf of both Koestler and Regler, whom he also knew. Hardy combined forces with the wives of the Communists Gerhardt Eisler and Gustav Regler, and with Paul Willert, to procure food to be sent to the camp. Subsequently the internees were delighted to receive a goose accompanied by tins of dripping. Regler and Koestler shared their portion with their immediate circle, but Regler noted sardonically that Eisler, a KPD Central Committee member, hoarded his and ate alone.[39]

At the turn of the year winter closed in and conditions in Le Vernet worsened. Illness, suicide and madness claimed more prisoners each week. Because it was too cold to sit in the latrines, the men became constipated. Koestler's health and spirit weakened. For two weeks he was assigned to the latrine squad, unpleasant and heavy work pushing a trolley carrying barrels of waste to a nearby river. Only the intense comradeship of the camp maintained his resistance, an experience memorialised and celebrated in *Scum of the Earth*.[40]

The campaign to free Koestler finally bore fruit. The most influential helper was probably André Le Troquer, a Socialist deputy and lawyer who acted for the former Popular Front Prime Minister Léon Blum. At Hardy's behest Le Troquer made an intervention with the Ministère des affaires étrangères. The ministry responded with alacrity, although initially in non-committal fashion.[41] Few other internees could command such illustrious support and the weight of pressure on the authorities finally had effect. On 17 January 1940, with almost no advance notice, Koestler was discharged from Le Vernet.

III

A day later he was back in Paris where he celebrated by going on a 'drunken binge' and sleeping for twenty-four hours. But his position remained precarious. Officially he was under a deportation order, which could not be carried out due to wartime conditions. The Interior Ministry would only permit a short respite to the enforcement of the order, so each time the period of remission neared its end Koestler had to re-enter the bureaucratic maze to seek another extension or face detention. His indeterminate status confounded his attempts to volunteer for the French army or to serve as an ambulance driver for the Red Cross. Another request for a visa to travel to Britain and join the British army was refused.[42]

His anxiety was heightened when his flat was raided by the police on 12 March 1940. The officers made a terrible mess but he and Hardy could only watch as many of his papers and manuscripts were taken away. All attempts to find out why he was being harassed were rebuffed; any explanation was left to his ample imagination and persecutory fantasies. One evening he met Malraux who was about to depart for the front, announcing his readiness to die with the proletariat. There is a strong hint that Koestler envied him and felt his own macho self-image, a foible he shared with Malraux, was impugned by enforced passivity.[43] Despite everything Koestler kept working on *Darkness at Noon*. The first draft was wrtten in German, so Hardy translated it into English at a desk at one end of the flat with Koestler working over her initial translation, sitting on the bed or pacing around. It was finally sent off to his French publisher on 1 May 1940, an ironic date for what was destined to become one of the most significant literary attacks on Communism and the Soviet Union. Hardy retained one copy of the manuscript for the publication of the English edition. A fortnight later German armoured divisions broke through the French lines in the Ardennes and crossed the Meuse at Sedan.[44]

France was gripped by a Fifth Column mania: wave after wave of arrests decimated the immigrant and refugee communities. Those who had fled the Nazis were subjected to a double torture: apprehensive of detention by the French authorities and terrified of what would be in store for them if the Allies failed to stem the German advance. Koestler was in a frenzy. He discussed suicide methods with German *émigrés* and secured a supply of cyanide. Sperber recalled: 'At one of our last meetings Koestler gave me a white pill, to be used if a quick death was the only way out.' Even in the midst of this crisis Koestler did not forget his comrades still in the internment camps. He urged the PEN organisation in Paris to engineer the release of foreign anti-Nazi writers held in Le Vernet and elsewhere before the Germans reached them.[45]

The long-predicted police visit occurred on the morning of 22 May 1940, soon after German tanks had reached the French coast. Koestler was escorted to a converted sports stadium in a southern district of Paris and placed among dozens of 'enemy aliens', all in fact refugees who were as afraid of the Germans as were the French. He took with him a suitcase containing food, drink and the suicide pills. While he waited in the stadium he consumed a bottle of brandy and by the time he was called for interrogation he was drunk. Heedless of the consequences, he lied prodigally, asserting that he was a foreign journalist who had been mistakenly arrested. The interrogating officer was so impressed by his Hungarian passport, his press card and other papers that he didn't bother to check the facts with the policemen who had carried out the arrest. Koestler carried the bluff still further and insisted that he had to attend a vital press conference at the Ministry of Information that afternoon. The officer decided a mistake had been made and promised to look into it; meanwhile, Koestler was free to go.

For the moment he was in the clear, but he knew it would not be long before the authorities noted his absence. He went to the apartment of the writer and publisher Adrienne Monnier, where he was hidden for a night, before being passed on to another safe house, the French PEN Club, run by Henri Membre. While he was concealed Monnier went to Henry Hoppenot, a sympathetic official in the Foreign Ministry, and obtained a travel permit that would enable Koestler to leave Paris for Limoges. After a week in hiding, Koestler and Hardy (who had been staying with Andor Németh) made their escape.[46]

They arrived in Limoges on 3 June 1940 and stopped there for two weeks, watching France collapse before their eyes and taking stock of their predicament. All Koestler's endeavours to reach Great Britain had been rebuffed; he lacked the necessary papers to enter the United States. The international refugee organisations and PEN might eventually get him a passage out of France, but how long could he hang on if the Germans occupied the whole country? Even if the German advance was halted Koestler was still a fugitive in the eyes of the French police. He had to change his identity, get new papers and 'go underground'. The easiest way to do this was by joining the Foreign Legion. On 16 June 1940 Koestler went to the Limoges recruiting office and enlisted in the Légion étrangère as one Albert Dubert, a Swiss taxi-driver, claiming that he had lost his identity card. After a few cursory questions and a medical check he was given the papers necessary to establish his new identity. Despite orders to proceed to the Legion's depot at Angers, which was under German control, he and Hardy went south, intent only on staying ahead of the invaders.[47]

The saga of the following months was recorded by Koestler in cramped writing on the pages of a tiny diary. This later furnished the material for the final third of *Scum of the Earth*, but the printed version differs in several respects from the original notes. The order of events is rearranged to give them more dramatic colour. Characters are elaborated upon and several passages of an intimate nature are not reproduced. In particular, a number of encounters with women and some rather negative thoughts about Daphne Hardy are omitted. Otherwise, the powerful observations which made *Scum of the Earth* such a success when it appeared in 1941 were transcribed from the notes he had made at the time.[48]

On 17 June 1940, the day that Marshal Pétain formed a new government and ordered the French army to lay down its arms, Koestler and Hardy headed south. Such was the disruption of rail and road traffic that they got no further than the edge of Limoges. When night fell they took refuge in a wayside restaurant and slept on the tables. The following day they took a bus to Périgueux. On arrival, Koestler went to the Busseaux Barracks and presented himself as Légionnaire Dubert. While Hardy found a room with a local family, Koestler had his first taste of life in the military. It was initially an easy regimen. He spent the mornings hanging around the barracks or on labour duties and met with Hardy in the afternoons and evenings. Soldiers regularly disappeared in anticipation of demobilisation, but Koestler stayed on, hoping to be assigned to a depot in another town and given the necessary travel documents. On 21 June they learned that Périgueux would fall within the German Zone of Occupation. Koestler skipped over the barracks wall and joined Hardy. By a combination of lifts, lorry rides and buses, slipping through police and army roadblocks on the way, they reached Bordeaux two days later.[49]

Bordeaux, seat of the evacuated French government, was a scene of demoralisation and chaos. The British consul had departed and the last ships had left the port. From the quayside they rushed to the United States consulate, where they recognised Edgar Mowrer, the American journalist. He had a car and offered them a lift to Bayonne-Biarritz, where it might still be possible to get a boat to safety. Koestler and Hardy argued for several hours whether they should leave together or split up. He insisted that she leave him since his papers were useless. Hardy obstinately refused to abandon him, driving him to heights of frustration and provoking 'a sort of nervous breakdown'. Finally, they resolved to stick together and in the evening kept the rendezvous with Mowrer. All went well until they reached Biarritz and drove into a military check-point. Mowrer and Hardy passed inspection, but Koestler was hauled out of the car, questioned and told he would be held pending investigation. Hardy capitulated to circumstances and the car continued to Bayonne and, with luck, a ship home. Koestler was taken to the local jail, where he spent the night in the company of an inebriated French airforce officer who had gone absent without leave.

In the morning Koestler was escorted by a policeman to the military barracks at Bayonne, only to be dumped amid more chaos. Thousands of uniformed men, many of them foreign volunteers, clamoured at the docks for a place on non-existent boats. Alone and in despair, Koestler left the port area and drifted through the town. He thought of committing a petty crime that would get him locked up for a few months out of sight of the Germans and knocked on the door of a lawyer's house to ask his advice on the matter. The kindly lawyer gave him some wine and warned him that he was more likely to be shot for looting. That night he returned to the barracks exhausted, his feet throbbing with pain from his new army boots. At some point between 21 and 25 June, he records making a suicide attempt by taking the potassium cyanide which he had been given in Paris. It was 'no good' and he vomited it up. It was his third failed suicide bid.

To adapt Oscar Wilde, to fail to kill oneself once is misfortune, to fail to do so three times is suspicious. At this very time many other exiles and *émigrés* managed it with distressing efficiency. The fact that all the while Koestler kept a diary recording what he saw and experienced must suggest that he had an eye to writing it up one day and casts doubt on the seriousness of his intentions. His suicidal endeavours may have been more like gestures of despair, calculated to jolt him out of his despondency, for which purpose failure had to be built into the attempt.

On 25 June the radio broadcast the terms of the armistice. Bordeaux, Biarritz and Bayonne were all to fall within the German occupied zone. At 3 p.m. the men in the barracks were assembled and told they were being transferred to the unoccupied area. Koestler was attached to an *ad hoc* unit which marched out of Bayonne about three hours later. The Germans arrived soon afterwards. On the first leg of the march the '22ième Compagnie de Passage' covered a mere eight kilometres, but at least they were out of harm's way. They marched for several days, lugging a miscellany of personal belongings and military equipment. Each morning there were fewer men in the company and fewer pieces of martial hardware. Koestler's feet were now in bad shape and he sought relief whenever the column passed a pharmacy. Fortuitously, he met a sympathetic old couple who gave him a lift in their car as far as St Palais, a village adjacent to the demarcation line.

Koestler didn't wait to reach safety with his unit. He hobbled across the boundary between the occupied zone and the 'Free Zone', spending the night by himself in open fields. The next morning he set off eastwards, at first painfully on foot and, later, by lorry, in search of the others. For days he hitch-hiked through the foothills of the Pyrenees looking for his company, staying overnight at camps for soldiers separated from their commands. On 29 June he reached Audage. His feet were in such an appalling state that he found an infirmary where they could be treated. Somewhat restored, he bought toiletries, including a comb and toothbrush, and cleaned himself up. Since he was no longer capable of walking more than a few yards he took a bus to the next depot. On 1 July 1940, after more fruitless searching, he opted to stay at Susmiou, a picturesque hamlet near Navarreux, where about 120 assorted soldiers were billeted in farm buildings. This was to be his home for the next eight weeks.

He spent the first night in a barn with a representative collection of disgruntled soldiery. Over successive days he shuffled around the countryside in a pair of slippers lent him by a young Breton. In Castelnau he tracked down his unit and reacquainted himself with a priest he had met in Bayonne and marched beside on the first leg of the evacuation. On 4 July he limped to Navarreux and had his feet treated in the local hospital. Then he purchased a pair of espadrilles and whiled away some time in a café in the company of a young girl. A routine established itself: mornings were passed reading, sun-bathing and speculating whether Hardy had reached Britain. He listened to the radio, read what papers he could get his hands on and talked to the soldiers, soaking up their views on the war, politics and life in general. On several evenings he met German and Jewish refugees, including internees who had been released from the notorious internment camp at nearby Gurs. Their situation was even more desperate and the encounters, particularly with the women, were heart-breaking.

On Bastille Day, 14 July, he learned that Carl Einstein, a fellow writer, nephew of Albert Einstein and a veteran of the Spanish Civil War whom Koestler had met in Paris in 1939, had committed suicide. This was the pattern for a string of despairing *émigrés* and refugees, although only the most famous casualties would be reported at the time. Koestler's diary reveals that he too regularly descended into a suicidal melancholy. He was grateful for his conversations with the priest, which stirred his intellect and revived his combative spirit. But most of the time he was depressed and lonely. Self-recrimination, enforced idleness and a poor diet took its toll. He visited the infirmary again, but this time for mental as well as physical relief. When the priest got his demobilisation orders he handed Koestler the key to a hut in Castelnau which a local farmer permitted him to use for reading and writing. Koestler went there regularly, but spent most his time in the hut regretting Hardy's absence and falling into erotic reveries. His mood was not improved by the daily flood of fatuous decrees from the Vichy regime, the guileless propaganda in the press and on the radio, or the news that Vladimir Jabotinsky had died in New York. It seemed to Koestler as if he had been totally abandoned.

Orders for the demobilisation of alien volunteers arrived at Susmiou on 10 August 1940. Koestler was eventually directed to the Foreign Legion depot at Marseilles, which had always been his goal. After four days of travel, and with a huge sense of relief he reached the port. For the first time in five months he had a hot shower. He attended to his health and bought a pair of comfortable shoes. He was also able to buy newspapers and catch up with events, albeit filtered through the slanted Vichy French press. One of his first acts was to fire off cables to find out if Hardy was safe. It was not until 1 September 1940 that he received a message from her announcing that she had reached England some time ago.

While in Marseilles, Koestler bumped into a number of prominent German émigrés. They all carried stories of suicides and deaths among the refugee community. Sperber, who had reached Marseilles after serving in the French army, described the city in the summer of 1940 as 'a tragic drama that was staged like a vaudeville show'. On every corner refugees ran into acquaintances who were in a similarly parlous state. 'A completely unexpected encounter was with Arthur Koestler, and for an instant this was shattering as well as surprising. He was wearing the same Legionnaire's uniform that I had finally taken off the day before.' Koestler told Sperber that he had a scheme to get to Africa; it was 'very daring but prudent'. The quayside at Marseilles was the scene of innumerable poignant farewells. 'When we embraced at parting, I felt inexplicably sorry for him, and he probably feared the worst for me.' Kantorowicz also spotted Koestler, but characteristically thought it 'was not advisable to speak to him'.[50]

Amid the turmoil Koestler's life resumed a semblance of conviviality: he began to have 'a lovely time'. During the day he was given nothing more to do than stand guard outside the depot or, because he was posing as a Swiss who therefore spoke German, run errands to the Germans now supervising the operations of the port. In the evenings he mixed with the large community of refugees, émigrés and relief workers from neutral countries who were based in Marseilles. He had an affair with a woman called Jacqueline. One evening he sat with Walter Benjamin in a bistro overlooking the Old Harbour. Benjamin told him of his plans to reach Spain by crossing the mountains. In case of failure, he had procured a supply of morphine or 'sedatives'. Since he had more than he needed he offered half to Koestler who gratefully accepted. Having been turned back at the border, Benjamin took his own life a few weeks later.[51]

Like all the refugees, Koestler's main concern was to get out of France as quickly as possible. He visited the American consulate and contacted various international refugee organisations. After a week of frustration he ran across a large group of escaped British prisoners of war who were interned at Fort St Jean. Since the American consulate proved 'hopeless', he joined their elicit escape scheme concocted with covert assistance from Varian Fry, an

American who represented the New York-based Emergency Rescue Committee. Fry had previously worked as an editor in New York, but was recruited by the committee, which sent aid to refugee writers, artists and intellectuals. After he arrived in Marseilles in mid-August he also arranged the departure of prominent refugees. He listed Koestler and 'his wife' as one of his 'clients', although there are no details to indicate what this involved. However, Fry admitted later that he did co-operate with the British embassy in Lisbon to facilitate the escape of the British soldiers.[52]

Koestler obtained his discharge papers from the French military authorities at the end of August. On 3 September he and a party of fugitive British servicemen led by Lieutenants John Ray, John Hopkins and Ian McCallum, and Staff Sergeant Richard Newman, embarked on a ship bound for Oran. The voyage lasted four days. As they passed the coast of Spain, Koestler entertained the others with stories of his Spanish Civil War adventures.[53] On 6 September the party disembarked at Oran and proceeded to Morocco. Although there were difficulties at the frontier they were allowed to transfer to a military train and arrived in Casablanca on 7 September.

Koestler went immediately to the American consulate which was handling British interests. From there he was referred to E. E. Bullen, the local representative of Shell du Maroc, a subsidiary of the Anglo-Dutch oil corporation. Bullen was actually a British diplomat on a covert mission. Formerly the British resident in Lisbon, he had been sent to Casablanca to organise an escape route for British servicemen who managed to reach North Africa. Once in Casablanca, he made contact with Baron Rüdiger von Etzdorf, an anti-Nazi German who was working for British intelligence and smuggling escaped POWs out of France. Bullen met Koestler in a café and set up a rendezvous with Etzdorf, whose cover-name was Ellerman. Bullen also arranged accommodation in a cheap pension for Koestler and the British servicemen, while 'Ellerman' worked out an escape plan to get them away from Vichy-controlled Morocco to more neutral territory.[54]

Two days later Koestler received a British Emergency Identity Certificate and within a week a visa. However, the next stage of his odyssey was via the covert route set up by British military intelligence.[55] At five in the morning on 14 September he clambered aboard the El Mar Azul, a small 'ignoble' boat, chartered by 'Ellerman' to carry over fifty escaped British troops to Lisbon. It was a long and unpleasant passage, and Koestler was seasick for much of the time. They finally reached Lisbon on 17 September.[56] When at last he was permitted to land he made straight for the Bar Anglais to celebrate. He was in a neutral country and relatively safe from German hands for the first time in four months. He could get English newspapers and send telegrams to London. Thanks to Macmillan, his publishers in the United States, he could take money from his accumulated royalties and was not even short of cash.

IV

Koestler's sojourn in Lisbon lasted for seven weeks. Despite all his efforts the British authorities seemed unwilling to let him re-enter the country, even to join the army. He found his enforced stay frustrating, but Lisbon was not without compensations. It was a comfortable exile, with plenty of bars, restaurants and hotels. The city was filled with refugees among whom he encountered Babette Gross, Münzenberg's wife and assistant. They met regularly to exchange stories about Berlin and Paris, Willit, his now scattered circle and the catastrophe that had overtaken their cause. On the occasion of their first meeting they talked until four in the morning. However, Koestler would not learn that Münzenberg was in fact dead, probably murdered by Stalin's agents, until he reached England weeks later.[57]

A typical day began with a visit to the British passport office or the military attaché. On some mornings he would be occupied sending telegrams to London or New York. These activities were followed by lunch, alone or in company. In the afternoons he read, slept or went for walks. Evenings were filled by seeing friends, going to the cinema or amorous adventures. Koestler spent a lot of time with Ellen Hill, a married American woman who was on her way to the United States. By mid-October their relationship had become stormy and his diary reported 'scenes'.[58] At the end of September Koestler heard of Walter Benjamin's suicide at Port Bou on the French–Spanish border. His death was an uncomfortable reminder that Fascist Portugal was no safe haven. In *The Invisible Writing* he claims that this information so depressed him that he attempted suicide yet again, but failed because of a 'weak stomach' that caused him to vomit up the poison. There is no mention of this in his diary, although there are indications that he redoubled his efforts to get to Britain. He saw 'Ellerman' a number of times and learned from him that the Home Office in London was obstructing his departure.[59]

He fired off telegrams to the *News Chronicle* and Hardy, and wrote to Macmillan in New York. Vernon Bartlett, MP, the foreign editor of the *News Chronicle*, urged Koestler to get in touch with David Scott, their local man, who would do what he could on the spot. In the meantime Bartlett took up Koestler's case in London. Walter Lucas, *The Times* correspondent in Lisbon, was also enlisted in his capacity as a member of the Unitarian service committee, one of a network devoted to assisting refugees.[60]

Notwithstanding Bartlett's efforts, the *News Chronicle* could neither secure Koestler a visa to enter Britain nor discover why he was being refused one. The paper passed his case on to Julian Layton, who was well known at the Home Office as an intermediary for Jewish refugees and exiles. Koestler meanwhile was frantic: the situation was 'hellish'. He felt a 'sudden craving for life in the USA—the first time—and betrayal of Daphne'. He was becoming increasingly resentful of Hardy, whose cables reached him only intermittently. By comparison with Dorothea Koestler she seemed to have let him down. This was rather unfair since Britain was experiencing major disruption due to the Blitz and Hardy was not always in London, near to post offices. But as days passed with no reply from her, Koestler became tetchy. At one point he wrote of their relationship in his diary '*la fin approche*'. He confided, 'Almost wish Daphne were dead—to be able to die in piece [*sic*], undisturbed.'[61]

With the help of Harry Donaldson, the American consul in Lisbon, he contacted the Exiled Writers Committee in New York (a subsidiary body of the League of American Writers) and asked them to sponsor his entry into the United States. Towards the end of October he learned that the Committee of Publishers had advanced $200 to purchase him a passage from Lisbon to New York and the Exiled Writers Committee had submitted affidavits on his behalf to the President's Advisory Committee on Refugees. The way to America was all but clear.[62]

By the end of October 1940 Koestler could no longer contain his impatience. Rejecting the option of going to neutral America in favour of joining the British army, he planned to leave Portugal illegally and throw himself on the mercy of the British authorities. At least then he would be in a position to make his case directly. He prepared for his illicit departure by writing to the British passport control officer in Lisbon with a summary of his case to ensure that, once he was discovered in Britain, he could show he had never intended to slip into the country and remain there illegally.[63] He also warned the British consul general in Lisbon, Sir Henry King, leaving no doubt about his motives. He explained that all efforts to obtain an entry visa, including appeals by the *News Chronicle* and his friend Harold Nicolson, had failed. He attributed this to 'either a libellous denunciation or some inevitable mistake'. He was therefore taking the desperate step 'to have myself arrested on British soil in order to have some means of defending and rehabilitating myself'. Since he was a well-known anti-Fascist, who had twice been arrested for his beliefs, it was unsafe to remain any longer in Portugal. While he was happy to die for an ideal, he said, he refused to perish because of red tape.[64]

In fact, Sir Henry was privy to Koestler's flight from Portugal and the letter was part of an elaborate charade. Koestler arrived at Bristol airport on board a BOAC plane on 6 November 1940. He had with him one small suitcase containing personal effects and about $60 in cash. On disembarking, he reported to the immigration officials and was duly detained. He was taken under escort to London the next day. (In a typically good-humoured and generous gesture, on his release from internment six weeks later he sent the Bristol police two shillings for cigarettes and thanked them for making the journey to London so pleasant.) After two nights in Cannon Row police station and a rather ludicrous interrogation by a hooded German ex-refugee, he was transferred to Pentonville Prison. It was his third period of confinement, without trial or fixed duration, in four years.[65]

Of course, this time the circumstances were hugely improved. On learning of his arrival influential friends, including Vernon Bartlett, Harold Nicolson, Harold Laski and Lady Atholl, wrote to the Home Office with assurances that Koestler was a trusted anti-Fascist who only wanted to volunteer for the British army. In view of his paranoia about the reasons for his exclusion from Britain, the most intriguing intercession came from inside Military Intelligence (Research), possibly from the rising Labour Party politician and future cabinet minister Richard Crossman. It was suggested in a letter that Koestler could offer valuable information on French trades union officials and left-wingers now working with the Vichy regime. The German Department of MI(R), run by the *Guardian*'s former Berlin correspondent F. A. Voigt, 'feel that they may also be able to make use of him'. The letter-writer was under the illusion, unless he was lying, that Koestler had never been more than 'in close touch with' the Communist Party: 'I doubt if he was ever a member.' He stated that, 'I am not prepared to say that he is 100% all right, but I cannot imagine that it would be possible for him to do any harm whatsoever and he might well be quite useful to us, but also to the Ministry of Information and other propaganda organisations.'[66]

The letters of intercession paid off. Koestler was released on 13 December 1940 and issued with alien's papers. In gratitude for the exertions on his behalf he had Cape send copies of *Darkness at Noon*, which had just come out, to Laski, Lady Atholl, Bartlett, Sir Peter Chalmers-Mitchell and Henry Wickham Steed, an ex-editor of *The Times* who had taken an interest in Koestler some time earlier. Laski modestly replied, 'You do not need to thank me. I am only ashamed that the trouble should have to happen to one who has done so much for democracy.'[67]

V

While he was in Pentonville *Darkness at Noon* appeared and was instantly well received. Praise for the novel flowed in from all quarters. Wickham Steed thought it was 'not far from being a masterpiece. It is the most devastating exposure of Stalinism that I have read.' John Strachey, the Left Book Club selector, remarked wickedly that it contained the best defence of Stalinism he had come across. Kingsley Martin, editor of the *New Statesman*, was no less impressed and asked Koestler to write for him.[68]

Darkness at Noon is one of those books that has ceased to be a work of literature and has instead become a monument. Read purely as a novel it is dark, static and obsessive It takes an effort to recapture the *frisson* it caused in readers when it was published, especially among the Communists and ex-Communists to whom it was addressed and for whom the issues it raised were more important than the artistry with which they were presented.

Much has been written about the novel. It has been seen as a historic milestone in the journey from the Pink Decade of the 1930s to the Cold War and a key text in the intellectual counter-attack against Communism. It has been read on a philosophical level as a debate about the 'dilemma of means and ends', the potentially destructive effect of universal Utopian ideologies that sweep aside the suffering of individuals for a greater good and a powerful assault on determinism, notably the crude Marxist theory of history. Finally, it has been taken as an historical curio, a reflection on the Moscow Trials of the 1930s.[69]

The most important fact about the novel is the one that is least remarked upon in critical studies: the central character, Nicolas Salmanovich Rubashov, is a Jew. In *The Invisible Writing* Koestler comments somewhat improbably and in a suspiciously offhand way: 'Incidentally, the second name, Salmanovich (Solomonson) made my hero a Jew, but neither did I notice this, nor has any reader ever pointed it out to me.' This is implausible for a number of reasons. It may be that Koestler really 'forgot' that Salman Rubashov (later Shazar) was the name of an editor of the Hebrew socialist daily *Davar* with which he had been familiar in Palestine in the 1920s. But could he have forgotten that of the three models for the character, Bukharin, Radek and Trotsky, two were Jewish?[70]

Finally, there is a great deal of Koestler in Rubashov: the novel is a fictionalised reworking of *Dialogue with Death*. Scenes in the cell and the prison are taken from Koestler's experiences in Seville. The references could not be stronger: in Seville he was in Cells 40 and 41: Rubashov is in Cell 404. Rubashov, like Koestler, is a deracinated Jew who has given up the messianism natural to Judaism, or any religious system of thought, only to find it in a materialist political philosophy.

Several critics writing on *Darkness at Noon* and Koestler's other novels have noted their Christian symbolism, but Rubashov's most explicit religious references are to Jewish tradition.[71] At the end he wonders about the fate of the revolution: 'What happened to these masses, to this people? For forty years it had been driven through the desert, with threats and promises, with imaginary terrors and imaginary rewards. But where was the Promised Land?' Just before his execution he compares himself with Moses, who 'had not been allowed to enter the land of promise either'.[72] At one level *Darkness at Noon* is a perceptive examination of the attraction which Marxism exerted on many Jews between the 1880s and 1940s. While the novel and the lure of Marxism cannot be reduced to ethnicity, it would be perverse to ignore the specific identity of both the chief character and the author, who together constitute a case study in the phenomenal and ultimately tragic relationship between the Jews and Communism.[73]

Although the book deals with Koestler's general problem with Communism, its trigger was the series of Moscow Trials of 1936–8. He wanted to explain why hardened old Bolsheviks like Bukharin confessed in captivity to crimes they could not possibly have committed, and repeated these falsehoods during the show trials, incriminating themselves and others in what appeared to be a wholly craven fashion. Manès Sperber, one of the first to read the finished manuscript, recalled, 'For years Arthur and I had been discussing the question that concerned and even obsessed us: why did the defendants in the Moscow trials … confess to imaginary crimes instead of turning the tables on their accusers in these public trials and sharply attacking them, and thus Stalin as well?'[74]

Koestler deduced that the logic of their own political philosophy, with which he believed he was familiar, compelled the old Bolsheviks to act thus as a 'last service' to the revolution.[75] Sperber concurred at the time, but was doubtful that it would be possible to convey this to ordinary readers. 'During the many months in which Koestler was working on his book we had carried on many discussions about his plan, in particular the difficulty of convincingly presenting this absurdity even to those who were trying to shield themselves from the truth. And now the finished manuscript was lying before me one afternoon. I immediately began to read it and I did not put it down until I had read the last page. It was almost dawn.' Sperber was convinced that Koestler had succeeded in penetrating the mystery and presenting it in such a way that neutral readers would be convinced of the 'confession theory'.[76]

Unfortunately, the most authoritative account of the trials refutes this interpretation. Stephen Cohen, Bukharin's acclaimed biographer, comments: 'Owing to Koestler's powerful art, this image of Bukharin—Rubashov as repentant Bolshevik and morally bankrupt intellectual prevailed for two generations. In fact, however, as some understood at the time and as others came to see, Bukharin did not really confess to the criminal charges at all.' In the courtroom he actually turned around the charges against him. Bukharin mocked his own confession, but pleaded guilty to the accusation that he had opposed Stalin—which was precisely the message he wanted to leave behind him.[77]

Darkness at Noon is more Koestler's confession than Bukharin's. It is his attempt to understand how he had been suborned by the logic of the revolution and how he had betrayed men for the sake of mankind: most obviously 'Nadeshda' in Baku, but also all those who had been lured into Communism by his propaganda. The novel's wide and enduring resonance is partly due to the mistaken identity of the protagonist (as Bukharin, rather than Koestler) and the belief that it could explain the show trials. Its initial powerful appeal, rooted in a specific period, was to tens of thousands of ex-Communists who wanted their disillusion explained and their transgression forgiven. Koestler offers such a powerful case for the revolution that no ex-Communist could feel ashamed of his or her youthful idealism. Yet he also exposes the amorality of the Communist Party and the Soviet Union, thus justifying and pardoning those who turned their back on them. Anti-Communists, of course, absorbed only the latter and revelled in the compelling refutation of revolutionary doctrine.

Darkness at Noon tells the story of Rubashov, an old revolutionary and veteran of Fascist jails who is arrested for treason on the orders of the authoritarian figure who controls the Party and the state. While he knows he is innocent of the charges against him, he cannot quell the suspicion that: 'The Party can never be mistaken ... The Party is the embodiment of the revolutionary idea in history ... History knows her way. She makes no mistakes.' Yet, he reflects in prison, the more the Party tried to build the Utopia which reason and the logic of history dictated was possible and necessary, the more repression was needed. Loyal Party members became schooled in deception and murder.[78]

In his 'diary', one of Koestler's favourite literary devices, Rubashov explores the 'dilemma of means and ends'. He once believed that revolutionary ethics had replaced bourgeois liberal notions of 'fair play' and that a useful lie might serve mankind better than the truth; but his faith was shaken. Doubt was connected with the discovery of the self: the 'I' which was rendered a 'grammatical fiction' in materialist theory. He began to reflect critically on the betrayals he had committed for the sake of the cause. At that time 'he had not enough imagination to picture the details of an execution'. Now that he could connect himself, the 'I', with the suffering of others, his deeds appalled him.[79]

His first interrogator, Ivanov, another old revolutionary, tells him that revolutionaries cannot afford the bourgeois luxury of sentiment and pity. 'Most great revolutionaries fell before this temptation, from Spartacus to Danton and Dostoyevsky ... The principle that the end justifies the means is and remains the only rule of political ethics.' However, alone in his cell Rubashov concludes that history is not a science, that human beings are not predictable. If the future cannot be predetermined it is wrong to justify terror because it is in accord with the 'laws of history'. Gletkin, a younger and rougher interrogator, nevertheless traps Rubashov by getting him to interpret his thoughts and actions according to the revolutionary ethics to which he was once bound and which he still cannot deny. Condemned by his own words he agrees to sign a confession and is even convinced to incriminate the 'opposition' as the 'last service the Party will ask of you'.[80]

In his cell awaiting death Rubashov experiences the 'oceanic feeling', the sense of himself as a human being, a part of humanity and perhaps something larger. It seemed to him that 'for forty years he had been running amuck—the running amuck of pure reason'. What could supplant revolutionary logic? Rubashov/Koestler speculates that it might be like a new religion or movement that would combine 'economic fatality *and* the "oceanic sense"', in which 'only purity of means can justify the ends'. It would forge individuals into a new collectivity that would 'develop a consciousness and an individuality of its own, with an "oceanic feeling" increased a millionfold, in unlimited yet self-contained space'. Moments later, Rubashov is executed.[81]

Darkness at Noon is a *tour de force*. Once Koestler began it, the novel virtually wrote itself. It spoke with searing passion to cohorts of Communists and ex-Communists in the 1940s and 1950s, but since Communism collapsed so precipitately, and left so little behind except ruins and the memory of pain, it is hard to recall the hold that the ideology exerted over millions of people, the shock when its dark underside was exposed and the liberating results of Koestler's book. Forty years later Michael Foot recalled its effect on him in words that may stand for a whole generation: 'Who will ever forget the first moment he read *Darkness at Noon*? For socialists especially, the experience was indelible. I can recall reading it right through one night, horror-struck, over-powered, enthralled. If this was the true revelation of what had happened at the great Stalin show trials, and it was hard to see how a single theoretical dent could be made in it, a terrifying shaft of darkness was cast over the future no less than the past.'[82]

The novel was regarded as a potent anti-Communist weapon from the 1940s to the 1970s when, alongside Orwell's *Animal Farm* and *1984*, it was a set text in schools in the USA and Britain. It was hated and feared by the

Communist Party which did its utmost to refute the text and discredit the author, something in which Koestler gloried. Like the greatest political novels it rapidly passed from literature into the realm of concrete action. It became a weapon in the arsenal of the Cold War and now stands as a monument to that conflict.

VI

On the strength of *Darkness at Noon* Koestler approached Victor Gollancz with a proposal for a personal account of the fall of France and his escape to England. It was immediately accepted for the Left Book Club and Koestler obtained an agreement from Gollancz for the book to be published simultaneously by Jonathan Cape. He began work on it as soon as he left prison.[83]

On his release, he moved in with Daphne Hardy at 26a Bute Street, South Kensington. She had visited Koestler in prison, but it was such a painful experience for both of them that he asked her not to return. For many weeks each had thought the other dead; to meet divided from one another by wire and glass added insult to injury. Although they subsequently lived together for several months, their relationship never recovered from the traumas in France and the months of separation. As soon as Koestler moved to Bute Street they started quarrelling. The virtues which had once attracted him to her now became vices. Her carefree, Bohemian and slightly irresponsible ways and lack of concern for domestic niceties, which were fine in Paris and the South of France, became irksome to him in their cramped London quarters. Koestler criticised her for alleged 'vices of laziness, schlampig-ness [slovenliness], casualness etc'. Hardy, who was trying to combine sculpting with a full-time job at the Ministry of Information, naturally resented this. She would sink into rancorous moods before exploding with rage. The separation enjoined by Koestler's military service dealt a further blow to their tottering relationship.[84]

True to his word, Koestler presented himself to the Alien Recruitment Office on the Euston Road soon after his departure from Pentonville and volunteered for service in the British army.[85] At the time, the army did not have the equipment for battalions of foreign-born volunteers who were of low priority and he was told to return in two months' time. This enabled him to work on *Scum of the Earth*, banging away on a rented typewriter and living off the five pounds a week advance from Cape. It was intended to last for twelve weeks and Koestler needed all that time. But in mid-February the army decided it needed him. Jonathan Cape appealed to the recruiting office to defer Koestler's call-up for another two weeks. This was accomplished without demur. Koestler was astonished at the casual handling of the matter, but grateful for the extra time since the writing did not come easily.[86]

It was the first book he had written from scratch in English and it was composed during the worst of the Blitz. It also had to be vetted. When each instalment was completed he sent it to Jonathan Cape who, in turn, sent a copy to Harold Nicolson at the Ministry of Information to make sure that it contained nothing that would aid or comfort the enemy. Nicolson found it 'admirable stuff'. Like *Darkness at Noon* it benefited from Daphne Hardy's attention to grammar and vocabulary. Indeed, without her ministrations it is hard to see how it could have been such a *succès d'estime*.[87]

By the end of February he had a typescript of 250 pages and was ready to begin polishing it. He sent Nicolson the final draft on 1 April, just a fortnight before he was due for call-up. Nicolson disagreed with Koestler's pessimism about France and gently requested the deletion of a passage illustrating the depth of French hostility to Britain. With that minor change the book was cleared. Gollancz was pleased with the finished product and made it a Left Book Club choice to coincide with the publication by Cape on 30 May. Paul Willert was deputised to correct the proofs of *Scum of the Earth* if Koestler was prevented from doing so by his army service.[88]

Scum of the Earth blends reportage and autobiography. It covers the period from the Nazi-Soviet Pact to Koestler's internment in 1939, his arrest and detention in Le Vernet, the fall of France, his wanderings around southern France and escape. Koestler brilliantly dissects the mood of the French public and the sources of their demoralisation, including the pervasive xenophobia and anti-Semitism. He excoriates the theory and tactics of the Communist Party, accusing it of being out of touch with real people, such as the soldiers he marched alongside in the catastrophic days of May–June 1940. 'In three weeks here I have learned more about mass psychology than in seven years of Communist busybodiness. Good God! In what an imaginary world we have lived. Have to start quite afresh—all of us.'[89] The portrayal of Le Vernet includes a devastating insight into the plight of International Brigaders: 'Ten years of constant defeat had reduced them to what they were; and their fate merely exemplified what had happened to all of us, the European Left. They had done nothing but put into practice what we had preached and believed; that had been admired and worshipped, and thrown on the rubbish heap like a sackful of rotten potatoes, to putrefy.'[90]

Scum of the Earth is remarkable, bursting conventional genres, rich in analysis and prediction. It perfects the unique style of combined reportage, diary and political commentary that Koestler had tried out in *Spanish Testament*. If *Darkness at Noon* signalled his arrival as a novelist of the first rank, *Scum of the Earth* confirms his place among the greatest journalists of the century.

Ever economical with his literary products, and keen for their potential to be maximised while he was a name, Koestler also proposed to Gollancz to publish the second half of *Spanish Testament* as a separate book. If the LBC didn't want to do it he asked Gollancz to release it to Penguin. With Gollancz's permission Penguin accepted the proposal at the start of April, although various delays and Koestler's service in the Pioneer Corps prevented *Dialogue with Death* from appearing until February 1942.[91]

Meanwhile, *Darkness at Noon* was taking America by storm. During February Koestler had pressed Cape rather irritably to speed up the book's publication by Macmillan in the USA in order to capitalise upon its *succès d'estime* in Britain. At the end of March he was delighted to learn that it had been selected as a Book of the Month Club choice, guaranteeing a large sale and healthy royalties.[92] Such success lifted Koestler far above the other exiles and refugees in London, although they continued to play a major part in his life. He received many letters from less well-off Continentals imploring him for assistance, which he dutifully passed on to his political and literary contacts.[93]

In January 1941 the publisher Freddie Warburg had suggested that Koestler contribute a study of the Gestapo to the 'Searchlight' series which George Orwell and Tosco Fyvel, the Jewish writer and journalist, were co-editing. Koestler met Fyvel and lunched with Orwell in mid-February, but counter-suggested a book on the way ordinary people in Europe viewed their countries. Orwell approved the project and a contract was issued, but Koestler's service in the Pioneer Corps made it impossible to complete.[94] On 15 April 1941, at No. 8 Recruiting Office, Euston Road, Arthur Koestler took the oath as a member of His Majesty's armed forces. Three days later he jokingly wrote to Tosco Fyvel: 'Now at last I can relax, mainly by peeling for Victory.' But military life was not going to be a lark. The eleven months he was to spend in the army turned into an agony of frustration that culminated in another nervous collapse.[95]

VII

Koestler's first posting was to No. 3 Training Centre, Pioneer Corps, Ilfracombe in Devon. Barely a month passed before he was moaning bitterly to Hardy, 'I am working now eight hours a day in the bloody open air and it is really no fun.' Inoculations made him feel ill and he had no chance to recover. 'We are living in a terrible rush and strain, heavy work from 6 a.m. to 5 p.m. and afterwards still drill; I have not left the camp since I arrived and barely manage to find the time to read a newspaper; and at night there is firewatching.' He proposed to endure it for another two weeks and, if there was no improvement, try to find a way out.[96]

In May he joined 251 Company, Pioneer Corps, at Shirehampton near Bristol. The hard manual labour combined with news of the German invasion of Russia was debilitating. He wrote to Willert: 'Since it began I live in a sort of daze, and there is nobody with whom I could discuss it and try to get some order into my thoughts.' He had not totally surrendered his idealistic aspirations for the revolution. 'Whether the Soviets are victorious or defeated, Stalin and his bureaucracy will disappear. The great question is, what will come after? In the first case—perhaps the rebirth of all our hopes and not only hope but fulfilment. In the second case some sort of Asiatic Soviet Republic will probably survive east of the Urals...' John Strachey, who heard from Gollancz that Koestler was unhappy in the Pioneer Corps, was just as desperate to discuss the new world situation, although in his view the change was '*potentially* for the better'. By mid-August it was hard to be optimistic. Each day Koestler read about familiar Soviet cities falling to the Germans, often in the wake of devastating battles.[97]

Strachey had been greatly affected by *Darkness at Noon*. According to his biographer, Hugh Thomas, the novel and the Communist Party's anti-war line before June 1941, 'completed Strachey's political re-education'. He was now an RAF adjutant with 87 Fighter Squadron, stationed near Bath, and one of those whom Koestler went to for company while he was posted to the West Country. Strachey recalled the impression which Koestler made during a visit to his RAF base: 'There entered the rumpled, battle-dressed figure of Private Koestler of the Pioneer Corps, surely one of the oddest men ever to dig a British latrine.'[98] In fact, Koestler and the other men in 251 Pioneer Company had been excavating pools in which oil would be poured ready for burning to divert German bombers attacking Bristol. Many years later, in a lecture to the British Academy, he recalled that the men were so eager to help the war effort that they asked for the tea-break to be abolished, to the consternation of the British NCOs and officers.[99]

During the summer Koestler started lecturing for the Army Educational Corps. He gave talks on 'Vichy France', 'The history of the Fifth Column' and 'The war on the Eastern Front' to British troops in the neighbourhood of his new posting, Oakley Farm Camp near Cheltenham, Gloucestershire. The lectures were tiring, but his encounters with British servicemen were instructive. He found the troops 'shockingly ignorant of real Nazism'. He told Willert that 'I find again and again by this contact with British soldiers how totally ignorant they are about mass-feeling. If we survive this war we all should sit down modestly on our arses for 2 or 3 years and shut up and learn the ABC of what human thinking, feeling, the laws which govern their actions and inactions are really like. We have all lived more or less in a phantom world.'[100]

Koestler's commanding officer adapted uneasily to running a company filled with European coffee-house types. He refused to allow Koestler to lecture without specific permission and reserved the right not to give it. Nor was he prepared to relax the usual camp regimen in his favour. This meant that he put in several hours of fatigues in the morning and was often exhausted when the time came to give the talks. Koestler could not simply apply for a transfer to the Education Corps since it did not accept aliens.[101]

He began to pull strings to get out of the Pioneer Corps. When *Scum of the Earth* was reviewed in *Horizon* by Major Bonamy Dobrée, a pre-war academic employed in the Ministry of Information (MOI), he wrote to him explaining his difficulties and asking if Dobrée would write to his CO in support of his work for the Education Corps. He confessed: 'I'm rather at the end of my tether.' Towards the end of October he reported to Guy Chapman, husband of the writer Margaret Storm Jameson, who was also attached to the MOI, that after five months' lecturing he had been sent back to digging. It seemed impossible to get official sanction for his lecturing work except on an *ad hoc* basis.[102]

Was Koestler really so badly treated in the Pioneer Corps? True, it would have been better for all concerned if he had never been stuck there, but once in he was permitted a great deal of latitude. During his eleven months in the army he was granted at least two substantial leave periods, not to mention weekend passes which enabled him to stop over in London or stay with friends in their country houses. While he was based at Cheltenham he had 'no lack of social life', seeing Strachey, Michael Sadleir and Cecil Day Lewis, who lived in the Cotswolds. He was first granted a five-day leave in early September to enable him to speak at a PEN congress in London. It took a bit of lobbying on his behalf by Storm Jameson and Guy Chapman, but in the end the army recognised the importance of his participation. The furlough allowed him time to dine with Stephen Spender, Fyvel and Robert Neumann, the *émigré* German novelist.[103]

Koestler quickly became a member of several overlapping social, literary and political groups. Through Gollancz and the LBC he had met Strachey and Laski. Through Warburg he met Fyvel and Orwell. He met Cyril Connolly, the editor of the new and hugely influential literary magazine *Horizon*, soon after the publication of *Scum of the Earth*. They quickly became friends. Koestler was invited to contribute to *Horizon* and introduced to Connolly's circle. Even while Koestler was in the Pioneer Corps, Connolly arranged a party for him at which he met the journalist and newspaper proprietor David Astor, the poets Stephen Spender and Louis MacNeice, the writer Philip Toynbee and other *Horizon* contributors. In 1974 Koestler remembered that the '*Horizon* crowd was a very cosy one'. He told Iain Hamilton that 'I couldn't say I was an insider in the clique. I was, of course, a strange bird on the periphery but I felt at home.' He was always grateful to Connolly because he 'took me under his wing'.[104]

Via Laski and Strachey he met the Labour politicians who founded *Tribune*: George Russell Strauss, Michael Foot and Nye Bevan. Foot took him on to write a column for the *Evening Standard*, which led him into contact with Frank Owen and eventually with Lord Beaverbrook himself. He met Lord Victor Rothschild via John Strachey and in due course Koestler became close to Victor's sister, Miriam. She added a second branch of the Rothschild dynasty to his collection of acquaintances by introducing him to Guy de Rothschild, her cousin. Guy's wife Alix was from an old Hungarian Jewish family, which aided the bonding process. This connection would later lead him back into Zionist politics. Paul Willert introduced Koestler to Freddie Ayer, with whom he had been at Eton and Oxford. Ayer had 'read and admired' *Scum of the Earth* and *Darkness at Noon*, although he soon found Koestler's pronouncements on philosophy rather irritating.[105]

Most of those who met Koestler at this time recall a tremendously vital, attractive and even glamorous figure who breathed commitment. Their first encounter was imprinted in Astor's memory: Koestler was 'dressed in a battle dress with his hair cut short, sort of army length, in a collection of writers in the home of Cyril Connolly ... and here was this figure, standing out in contrast to all the others who had not got their hair cut short and were not in uniform'.[106]

Yet Koestler grew restless with the constraints imposed on him by the army. He complained about 'mental deformation by cockeyed values'. He now felt guilty reading philosophy in the morning, but at ease sweeping corridors. His exasperation increased when he damaged his hand in an accident during a work detail on 20 September. Nursing his injury back at camp his thoughts yet again turned to suicide. 'Why not?' he asked his diary–notebook. There is no explicit reply, only the suggestive comment: 'Like a postman killed before able to deliver the contents of his bag.' Koestler, as usual, toyed with suicide, but was held back by a supervening consciousness of his mission and his own importance.[107]

Separation from Hardy created more discomfort. While he was stationed near Ilfracombe, she arranged to stay in Totnes and tried to find lodgings for him nearby. Since it was difficult for an unmarried couple to take a room in a boarding house these fleeting rendezvous, so hard to organise for both of them, were especially frustrating. When Koestler was posted to Shirehampton Hardy was transferred to Buckinghamshire. He encouraged her to get a job with the BBC in London, but she was eventually posted to Oxford. Visits to her were awkward because she lived in a house dominated by a fearsome landlady. An attempt to make room for Koestler to stay over during a leave weekend in early June only provoked a row.[108]

Hardy was angry that Koestler wrote to her infrequently, but her irritation turned to guilt when she learned how badly he was faring. She gallantly promised that next time she had leave she would travel from Oxford to wherever he was stationed. They managed to see each other in London in June, August and November 1941, but Koestler was in town more often than that. Hardy felt she was becoming an incidental part of his very busy London schedules. After one blazing argument he wrote to Cyril Connolly, 'I am sorry Daphne got hysterics in the taxi when I saw you last time, it was not serious, only a legitimate protest against my alcoholic talkativeness.'[109]

Hardy's sense of injustice and the quarrels were not simply hysterics. He owed the title of *Darkness at Noon* and much of its literary success to her. She was still collaborating with him on his writing and at least one dispute flared up because, as he later explained, 'I made her work too hard on polishing an essay I had written'. Hardy read, commented upon and improved his English, making sure it was elegant as well as intelligible. However, while Koestler mentioned this assistance to friends such as Paul Willert, apart from her translation of *Darkness at Noon* she never received public credit. It was little consolation that he referred to her sometimes as 'my fiancée' or 'my wife': he took her for granted and that rankled.[110]

Despite the inconveniences of army life Koestler remained astonishingly productive and assiduous at 'networking'. At the beginning of May he sent off *Dialogue with Death* with corrections and production notes. During stop-overs in London in the summer he saw Crossman and Neumann, and spent a weekend with Gollancz at his country home in Brimpton. The PEN congress in London on 11 September provided the opportunity to see Jonathan Cape, Storm Jameson, Tosco Fyvel, Cyril Connolly and E. M. Forster, with whom he was soon on friendly terms.[111] In October Koestler also started broadcasting for the BBC Home Service. His first radio performance was in a scripted discussion, but a few weeks later he was invited to write and present his own material. He was soon being granted special leaves to broadcast. His scripts, such as 'Europe in Revolt', transmitted on the Home Service in mid-1942, usually dealt with events on the Continent. His guttural accent, as well as his background, gave these broadcasts an authenticity and authority much sought after by the BBC.[112]

Due to the bombing of their printer, Cape were not able to meet the deadline for publication of *Scum of the Earth* in May 1941, so the Left Book

Club edition appeared first and with rather less of a fanfare than Gollancz had hoped. The Cape edition arrived in September and was an immediate hit.[113] It further heightened Koestler's celebrity status. George Russell Strauss, the left-wing millionaire and Labour MP, invited him to stay at his London house when he was next in town and asked him to contribute to the first weekly issue of *Tribune*. Laski, who was sent a complimentary copy of the book, which he dubbed a 'historic document', invited Koestler to dinner. Koestler was diligent about turning such contacts to good use and soon asked Laski to write references on Hardy's behalf when she applied for a job at the LSE.[114]

The book turned Koestler into a hero figure for all the *émigrés*, exiles and refugees who had experienced flight and internment either on the Continent or in Britain. From September 1941 onwards, letters flooded in from members of the Pioneer Corps, erstwhile comrades and even family members who had lost track of him. On Christmas Eve, Koestler heard from Leo Valiani, Mario in *Scum of the Earth*. Writing under the name Leo Weiczen, he told Koestler that he had reached French Morocco and thence travelled to Mexico. He asked Koestler to help him join the British army and also requested money so that he could continue writing a book on Croce. Typically, Koestler did his utmost to help.[115]

Koestler's Pioneer Corps blues were temporarily lifted by a week's leave in London between 30 October and 6 November, into which he fitted a prodigious number of social engagements and meetings. He stayed at the house in Drayton Gardens, off the Fulham Road, which Cyril Connolly rented from Celia and Mamaine Paget. Peter Quennell, the writer, lived on the top storey. Koestler found the place in rather a mess when he arrived and 'made some order' before launching into twenty telephone calls before dinner. The next morning was also heavily devoted to the phone. He dined with Stephen Spender and the Connollys and then went to a party attended by Count Károlyi, the ex-Hungarian premier, David Astor, Arthur Calder-Marshall, a writer now at the MOI, Quennell, the poet Louis MacNeice and the painter Augustus John. Over the next days he saw Orwell, Neumann and Fyvel, and had meetings at Cape. Another day he dined with the co-editors of *Tribune*, George Russell Strauss and Aneurin Bevan, who he thought was 'a nice boy but a tipler [*sic*]'. In the course of the week Koestler lunched or dined at the Reform Club, the Travellers, the Dorchester and David Astor's home.[116]

Pleasure was not the only reason for this exhausting schedule. He wrote in his diary on his return that he was 'back from eventful leave, crusaide [*sic*] for Virgin Island settlement'. Koestler had developed a scheme for extricating some of the 80–100,000 internees and stateless aliens in

France, of whom 45,000 were in internment camps. Most of these were Jews and the remainder left-wing exiles or former members of the International Brigades, all of whom were in peril. Many had already been sent to Germany, committed suicide to avoid repatriation or been transferred to labour camps in French North Africa. Yet rescue from Vichy France was still possible. His plan was for the United States to offer to intern the aliens on territory under its control, possibly the Virgin Islands, for the duration of the war.[117]

With this in mind he contacted Eleanor Rathbone, who had been stirred to action about Le Vernet after she read *Scum of the Earth*, Harold Laski, David Astor, Sir Edward Hulton, proprietor of *Picture Post*, and the secretaries of the main refugee organisations in London. During his stay in town he saw Rathbone, Lady Asquith, Lady Cripps and Astor several times. The most important meetings were with G. Kuhlman, the Deputy High Commissioner for Refugees, and John Winant, the United States ambassador. The critical objective was to persuade the Americans to take up the plan. To publicise it Astor asked Koestler to write an 800-word article for the *Observer* on the position of political refugees in Vichy France. Koestler also drew up a lengthy memorandum detailing the scale of the refugee problem there, the threat the refugees faced and the possible solution. Astor subsequently presented the memo to Winant, who seemed amenable. Afterwards Koestler, Astor and Rathbone had a 'victory tea' to celebrate.[118]

Koestler was buoyed up by the meetings, but he was driven frantic by the restrictions he faced once back in camp. He told Astor that 'I feel cut off and buried alive while burning to carry on with this thing. Last thing I heard was that the Nazis are sending German Jews to camps in Poland which are even more horrible than the French camps.' The celebrations were anyway premature. Winant passed the matter on to an embassy official, Lewis Einstein, who displayed little interest or energy. Then the entry of the United States into the war altered everything. Rathbone told Koestler on 12 December that the scheme's chances of success were ruined. Soon afterwards Koestler's health broke down.[119]

His collapse can be attributed to the failure of the refugee scheme coming on top of the cumulative frustration of army life. In order to get some privacy for his writing he had taken up residence in a room that served as the 'Company's library-plus-sports-stores-room, surrounded by boxing gloves, cricket-bats, old volumes of *Punch* and a Jewish holy shrine containing two Thora-rols [sic] wrapped in gold and velvet'. These rather unusual quarters were far from ideal. During November relations with his superiors deteriorated. The quartermaster confined him to barracks for two weeks over a petty incident involving the distribution of tickets for a dance.

This meant that he would miss a PEN conference in London. The CO's decision was only reversed after PEN officials intervened with the War Office. It was little wonder that he willingly signed the *Horizon* manifesto 'Why Not War Writers', which Connolly had concocted in an attempt to persuade the government to support writers, as well as artists, and to help aliens like Koestler get out of stupid Pioneer Corps jobs.[120]

During November he had discussed an idea for a propaganda film with Arthur Calder-Marshall, who was at the MOI film unit, and pleaded with him to ask the War Office Public Relations Office to secure him leave so that he could work on it. Even better, he suggested that Calder-Marshall arrange for his transfer. Koestler concluded his letter tersely 'this is an SOS'. He managed to write an outline—despite the fatigues, digging and lecturing—which was sufficiently promising for Calder-Marshall to offer him ten pounds for a rough treatment. Calder-Marshall also tried to help Koestler get some time off so that he could do research in libraries and write in peace, but the next thing he knew was that Koestler was in hospital.[121]

It is not clear exactly what happened. He told Michael Károlyi that he had suffered 'a nervous breakdown'. In a letter to Neumann he said: 'I was brought in with rather melodramatic nervous collapse ... I feel pretty rotten.' He informed Sir Herbert Read that 'I have been in hospital after a nervous breakdown—the first I have ever had. It must have been accumulating for years.' The medical notes for his discharge from Mill Hill Emergency Hospital specify a carefully controlled diet of milk, rusks, eggs, cream, olive oil and orange juice. The drugs prescribed are sodium citrate, atrophine mixture and magnesium trisilicate. Rather hopefully he was advised not to smoke.[122] The treatment suggests that Koestler had a stomach complaint, possibly ulcers, brought on by tension.

Messages of sympathy poured in to the emergency hospital in Cheltenham to which he was first sent. Hardy was terribly worried about him, but could not visit at once. By letter she advised him to adopt her philosophy and 'be passive', though she knew he wouldn't agree. George Russell Strauss sent best wishes from himself and Nye Bevan, and told Koestler not to worry about an overdue article for *Tribune*. Astor expressed his concern and Calder-Marshall sent a box of chocolates. Kingsley Martin wrote soothingly, 'Don't forget that you have masses of friends in this country and that we treasure you as one of the people we are most proud to know and whose books we believe will last.'[123] More practically, Calder-Marshall made a final push on Koestler's behalf. He discussed his case with Sir Arthur Willert, Paul Willert's father, who was head of the MOI Office for Southern Region. He also asked Louis MacNeice to put Koestler's name forward for the BBC European Service. One promising avenue seemed to be getting Koestler work on propaganda films so Basil Wright, at the MOI Film Unit, put in a request for his release.[124]

On Christmas Eve 1941 Koestler was transferred to Mill Hill Emergency Hospital for convalescence. Things were looking up. Connolly had called him the day before to say that the War Office had agreed to second Koestler for propaganda work: only a technical blunder had delayed his discharge. But Koestler was in no rush. He told Hardy that the hospital was 'so efficiently run you would think it is in a different country'. He was well fed and cared for; several of the doctors had read his books and fussed over their famous patient. He rose at 7 a.m., bathed, breakfasted, then did light gym for an hour. He had a siesta after lunch and was allowed to work in a room put aside specially for his use. In the evenings he attended lectures on such useful subjects as car engines and electronics. It was, in short, 'a near miracle—an eldorado-island in the midst of general army-muddle'.[125]

At the end of December Koestler went for an interview at the MOI where Calder-Marshall and Richard Crossman were pressing for his immediate release from the Pioneers. He was discharged from medical supervision in early February and took up temporary residence at 102a Drayton Gardens, Chelsea. On 10 March 1942 he was formally discharged from the British army for 'ceasing to fulfil army physical requirements'. His discharge notice recorded that Private Koestler had been 'A good soldier during his period of service'.[126]

NOTES

1. Ruth Dudley Edwards, *Victor Gollancz: A Biography* (London, 1987), pp.269–70.

2. IW, pp.382–4. Albrecht Betz, 'La Problematique du renégat: Münzenberg, Sperber et Koestler à la fin des années trente', in *Willi Münzenberg. 1889–1940: Un Homme Contre*, Colloque International, Organisé par Bibliothèque Méjunes, L'Institut de L'Image (Marseilles, 1993), pp.135–43.

3. IW, pp.385–7; Weissberg, *Conspiracy of Silence*, pp.x–xi; Alfred Kantorowicz, *Exil in Frankreich* (Bremen, 1971), pp.17, 167.

4. IW, pp.386–9.

5. See Michael Scammell, 'Arthur Koestler Resigns', *New Republic*, 4 May 1998, pp.27–33. Scammell made the find and the translation is his.

6. Ibid. IW, pp.388–90.

7. TGF, pp.71–3; Gross, *Willi Münzenberg*, pp.299–309, 311–13; Harald Wessel, *Münzenbergs Ende* (Berlin, 1991), pp.136–42, 143–50; R. N. Carew Hunt, 'Willi Münzenberg', in David Footman (ed.), *International Communism*, St Antony's Papers, No. 9 (London, 1960), pp.72–87.

8. IW, pp.365, 386, 406.

9. IW, p.393. Münzenberg contracted to publish the German version, but the printing was overtaken by the war.

10. TG, pp.156, 169, 333–53.

11. IW, p.411. Weissberg, *Conspiracy of Silence*, pp.71–2.

12. Kantorowicz, *Deutsche Tagebuch*, Vol.1, pp.59, 340; Ludwig Marcuse, *Mein Zwangzigstes Jahrhundert* (Munich, 1960), p.244.

13. IW, p.393. See also publication proposal, probably for Jonathan Cape, MS2308/2.

14. Sperber, *Until My Eyes*, p.134.

15. Ibid., p.138.

16. Gross, *Willi Münzenberg*, pp.323–4, 325–8; Wessel, *Münzenbergs Ende*, pp.200–17.

17. Marcuse, *Mein Zwanzigstes Jahrhundert*, p.234.

18. IW, pp.406–8; Sperber, *Until My Eyes*, p.138.

19. Interview with Paul Willert, 28 August 1994. See also Stephen Koch, *Double Lives: Stalin, Willi Münzenberg and the Seduction of the Intellectuals* (London, 1995), pp.82, 93, 308–9; Sam Tanenhaus, *Whittaker Chambers: A Biography* (New York, 1997), pp.134–5, 137, 147–8, 149.

20. IW, pp.214, 222, 401; Sperber, *Until My Eyes*, p.134.

21. Drs A. Willy, A. Costler, R. Fisher and others, *The Practice of Sex* (London, 1940), Introduction and pp.48–9, 111–12.

22. Ibid., pp.86–91, 103–7, 438, 451–4.

23. Koestler to Heinz Grueber, 29 November 1971, MS2387/2; Sperber, *Until My Eyes*, pp.151–2.

24. IW, p.413.

25. SOS, p.24; *Scum of the Earth* [STE], p.58. Interview with Daphne (Hardy) Henrion, 8 June 1998.

26. STE, pp.1, 6–10, 16–18.

27. Ibid., pp.20–1, 24–32.

28. Ibid., pp.32–3.

29. Ibid., pp.35–40.

30. The following account of Koestler's internment is based on STE, unless otherwise indicated.

31. STE, pp.97; Regler, *Owl of Minerva*, pp.333–4, 352–3.

32. Regler, *Owl of Minerva*, pp.336–7.

33. STE, pp.105–6; IW, p.416; Regler, *Owl of Minerva*, p.350.

34. STE, pp.107, 111–19.

35. Ibid., pp.99–102; Regler, *Owl of Minerva*, p.350.

36. Interview with Daphne (Hardy) Henrion, 8 June 1998. Daphne to Cape, 10 October 1939; Daphne to Atholl, 14 October 1939; Atholl to Daphne, 21 October 1939 and 5 January 1940, CCHDC, 619/1/3.

37. Dorothea Koestler to Eden, 31 October 1939; Dorothea Koestler to Vansittart, 1 November 1939, CCHDC, 619/1/3.

38. STE, pp.141–5; IW, p.142; Mowrer cable to Nicolson, nd, probably November 1939; Malraux guarantee, 27 November 1939; Paulhan to Daphne, 12 December 1939; Rupert Hart-Davis to Daphne, 10, 22, 23, 25 November 1939, CCHDC, 619/1/3. Curtis Cate, *André Malraux: A Biography* (London, 1995), p.274.

39. Interview with Paul Willert, 28 August 1994. Regler also benefited from the intercession of the French politician Georges Mandel, Ernest Hemingway, whom he had known well in Spain, Eleanor Roosevelt and Martha Gelhorn. Regler, *Owl of Minerva*, pp.340, 349, 352–3.

40. STE, pp.146–8. Regler, *Owl of Minerva*, pp.342–3.

41. Le Troquer to Daphne, 28 November 1939 and Ministère des affaires étrangères to Le Troquer, 30 November 1939, CCHDC, 619/1/3.

42. STE, pp.158–62; Cate, *André Malraux*, p.274.

43. STE, pp.162–7, 172.

44. Ibid., p.167. Daphne Hardy gave the novel its famous English title when she was

handling it for Cape and Koestler was *incommunicado* in France. Interview with Daphne (Hardy) Henrion, 8 June 1998.

45. STE, pp.171–4; Sperber, *Until My Eyes*, p.161.

46. Koestler to Gisele Freund, 5 October 1955, MS2380/3; STE, pp.175–9 and preface to Danube Edition (London, 1968), pp.8–9; IW, p.420.

47. STE, pp.179–88. A few of the papers of 'Private Albert Dubert' survive in MS2308/2. His demobilisation documents record 16 June 1940 as his date of enlistment in Limoges.

48. See diary 1939–40, MS2304. The following narrative is based on the memoir of the fall of France in *Scum of the Earth* and the unpublished version of the diary. Where the text of the diary coincides more or less with the version published in *Scum of the Earth* the page references to the published version are given. Koestler wrote a third version for a *Daily Telegraph* magazine article, 17 August 1973, reprinted as 'A Sentimental Pilgrimage', in *Kaleidoscope* (London, 1981), pp.285–305. Several details differ in this narrative. Daphne disappears from it completely.

49. For the following paragraphs see diary and STE, pp.193–261.

50. Sperber, *Until My Eyes*, p.183; Kantorowicz, *Exil in Frankreich*, p.187.

51. STE, p.278; IW, pp.420–1; 'A Sentimental Pilgrimage', p.303; Martin Domke to Koestler, 12 October 1941, MS2371/2. For minor inconsistencies in the two accounts of this meeting, see Ingrid and Konrad Scheurmann (eds), *For Walter Benjamin*, trans. Timothy Nevill (Bonn, 1993), pp.275–6.

52. Varian Fry, *Surrender on Demand* (New York, 1945), pp.76–9, 105–13. Koestler's name and that of his wife appear on a list of 'clients' prepared by Fry around 1941; information from Dr Elizabeth Berman, Guest Curator, 'Assignment: Rescue' exhibition at United States Holocaust Memorial Museum June 1994–January 1995. In 1967, Koestler was considered for writing a preface to a book celebrating Fry's wartime work, Document 10, Varian Fry Papers, ed. Karen J. Greenberg, *Archives of the Holocaust*, Vol.5, *Columbia University Library* (New York, 1990), p.129.

53. Richard Newman to Daphne Hardy, 9 December 1940, MS2371/1, reference to Lt Hopkins, 8 September 1940 and for the voyage, see 3–6 September 1940, diary 1939–40, MS2304. Koestler to Miss Fitzgerald, 26 June 1942, MS2372/1, refers to a Jack Pollock. Ian McCallum to Koestler, 29 October 1946, MS2374/4.

54. E. E. Bullen to Koestler, 12 September 1978; Koestler to Bullen, 30 September 1978, MS2391/2. According to Norman Bentwich, Etzdorf deserted from the German army in 1938 or 1939 and was interned in France when war broke out. Norman Bentwich, *I Understand the Risks* (London, 1950), p.102. Interview with Anita von Etzdorf, 1 June 1998.

55. Proposed Sending of British ex-soldiers to Martinique from Casablanca, 12 October 1940, FO371/24303, PRO. Communications between the acting consul in Casablanca listed Koestler among sixteen British personnel. Strangely, the FO correspondence places them in Casablanca in October 1940, a month *after* Koestler's diary. Koestler was described as a 'naturalized British subject' with Palestinian nationality dating back to March 1928.

56. Preface to the Danube Edition, STE (London, 1968), p.11; unpublished memoir by Rudiger von Etzdorf, courtesy of Anita von Etzdorf.

57. See diary 1939–40, MS2304; IW, p.407; Wessel, *Münzenbergs Ende*.

58. Ellen Hill to Koestler, 31 August 1941, MS2371/1. See also Ellen Hill to Daphne Hardy, 27 February 1941, MS2371/1.

59. IW, p.421; Koestler to D. R. Darling, 8 September 1973, MS2388/3.

60. *News Chronicle* to Koestler, 2 October 1940, MS2308/2; 15 October 1940, diary 1939–40, MS2304.

61. *News Chronicle* to Koestler, 21 October and 1 November 1940; Kesler to Koestler, 22 October 1940, MS2308/2; 22 and 29 October 1940, diary 1939–40, MS2304; Daphne to Koestler, 6, 24 and 31 October 1940, MS2308/2 and undated telegram from Daphne to Koestler, MS2301/3.

62. Leonard Mins to Koestler, 28 October 1940. Early in December 1940 the Committee recommended that Koestler's visa application receive 'expeditious consideration'. Harry Donaldson to Koestler, 13 December 1940, MS2414/1.

63. Koestler to British Passport Control Officer, Lisbon, 21 September 1940, MS2414/1. The dating is probably an error.

64. Koestler to Sir Henry King, November 1940, MS2414/1. See also Sir Henry King to Koestler, 11 March 1953 and Koestler to King, 24 March and 8 April 1953, MS2332/5.

65. IW, pp.421–2. Koestler to Aliens Department, Home Office, 29 December 1940, MS2372/1. He claimed that the governor of Pentonville said that his belongings had been sent to MI5: Koestler to Aliens Department, Special Branch, 29 December 1940, MS2372/1; Koestler to Bristol Police, 23 December 1940, MS2372/1. Koestler insisted it was a KLM plane, but other documents refer to a BOAC airliner.

66. See letter, author unknown, to Under Secretary of State, Home Office, 3 December 1940, MS2308/2. Letter to Major Sinclair, 9 December 1940, MS2308/2. According to Tom Bower, Koestler did do work briefly for MI5; see Tom Bower, *The Perfect English Spy: Sir Dick White and the Secret War 1935–50* (London, 1995), pp.46–7.

67. Laski to Koestler, 21 December 1940, MS2371/1.

68. Wickham Steed to Koestler, 25 December 1940 and Strachey to Koestler, 23 January 1941, MS2371/1; Koestler to Kingsley Martin, 2 April 1941, MS2414/1.

69. For a useful guide to the various critical studies, see Frank Day, *Arthur Koestler: A Guide to Research* (New York, 1987).

70. IW, p.394. Schneour Zalman Rubashov (1889–1974), who became Salman Shazar in Israel, was born in White Russia and emigrated to Palestine in 1924. He was a leading figure in the Palestinian labour movement and an editor of *Davar*, its main daily paper, until he became its chief editor from 1944 to 1949. He was Minister of Education in two Labour cabinets and twice served as President of Israel from 1963 to 1973.

71. Pearson, *Arthur Koestler*, pp.56, 66–7.

72. *Darkness at Noon* [DAN], pp.210–11.

73. See Jonathan Frankel, *Prophecy and Politics: Socialism, Nationalism and the Russian Jews 1862–1917* (Cambridge, 1981); Robert Wistrich, *Revolutionary Jews from Marx to Trotsky* and *Socialism and the Jews* (Oxford, 1982); Gitelman, *A Century of Ambivalence*; W. D. Rubinstein, *The Left, the Right and the Jews* (London, 1982).

74. Sperber, *Until My Eyes*, pp.157–9.

75. IW, pp.394–401.

76. Sperber, *Until My Eyes*, p.158. Sperber, unlike Koestler, goes on to acknowledge that they had been wrong about the 'confession theory'.

77. Stephen F. Cohen, *Bukharin and the Bolshevik Revolution: A Political Biography, 1888–1938* (New York, 1975), pp.372–80.

78. DAN, pp.18, 40, 65.

79. Ibid., pp.81–4, 90.

80. Ibid., pp.124–8, 186–90.

81. Ibid., pp.206–7.

82. Michael Foot, *Loyalists and Loners* (London, 1986), p.217.

83. Koestler to Gollancz, 23 December 1940; Gollancz to Koestler, 26 December 1940, MS2371/1; Koestler to Gollancz, 7 January 1941, MS2372/1.

84. Iain Hamilton interview with Arthur Koestler, 5 March 1974, p.10, MS2436/5; SOS, p.25; Daphne to Koestler, 31 May 1941, MS2301/3.

85. Documents pertaining to Koestler's alien status and application to join the British army are in MS2308/2. On 22 December 1940 the foreign editor of the *News Chronicle* wrote to the officer in charge of the No. 3 Recruiting Centre for Aliens confirming that Koestler had acted as a reporter for the paper and reiterating his anti-Fascist credentials, MS2414/1. Although, even now, Koestler hedged his bets. Early in December 1940 the Exiled Writers Committee in New York had recommended that Koestler's visa application receive 'expeditious consideration'. On 4 January 1941 he wrote to them to explain that since he had reached Britain he had no *immediate* need of the fare money or entry visa to the USA. 'I have no desire to leave this country as long as I am allowed to be at liberty and to do my share. But I am a Hungarian subject and Hungary, as part of the Axis, might reenter [*sic*] the war at any moment. This might mean internment again... So it would be a great reassurance if I could know that the way to the USA was open to me, should such an emergency arise': Koestler to Miss Sherman, secretary, Exiled Writers Committee, 4 January 1941, MS2414/1.

86. Lilian Herbert (of Cape) to Koestler, 31 January 1941 and Jonathan Cape to Koestler, 14 February 1941, MS2342/3; Army Recruitment Office to Cape, 12 February 1941, MS2371/1; Iain Hamilton interview with Arthur Koestler, 5 March 1974, p.10, MS2436/3.

87. Nicolson to Koestler, 27 January 1941, MS2371/1; see also 'A Sentimental Pilgrimage' in *Kaleidoscope*, p.300; interview with Miriam Rothschild, 4 April 1998.

88. Koestler to Jonathan Cape, 19 and 26 February 1941, MS2372/1; Gollancz to Koestler, 7 March 1941, MS2371/1; Koestler to Gollancz, 28 March 1941; Koestler to Nicolson, 1 April 1941, MS2372/1; Nicolson to Koestler, 7 April 1941; Gollancz to Koestler, 2 April 1941; Gollancz to Koestler, 5 May 1941, MS2371/1.

89. STE, pp.16–17, 42–50, 244–5.

90. STE, pp.66–7, 78–83, 89–91, 119–22.

91. Koestler to Gollancz, 26 February and 2 April 1941, MS2372/1; Trevor/Phyllis Blewitt to Koestler, 29 March 1941, 6 May 1941, 28 May 1941, 31 July 1941, MS2371/1.

92. Koestler to Jonathan Cape, 26 February 1941; Koestler to Gollancz, 28 March 1941, MS2371/1.

93. Haffner to Koestler, 3 March 1941; Neumann to Koestler, 19 March 1941, MS2371/1; Koestler to Laski, 12 February 1941, MS2372/1; 8–9 March 1941, diary 1941, MS2304.

94. Warburg to Koestler, 7 and 20 January 1941, MS2371/1; 4, 5 and 17 February 1941, MS2371/1; Fyvel to Koestler, 13 and 27 February 1941, MS2371/1; Koestler to Fyvel, 15 February and 18 April 1941, MS2372/1; 11 February 1941, diary 1941, MS2304.

95. Attestation and enlistment forms, 15 April 1941, MS2308/2; Koestler to Fyvel, 18 April 1941, MS2372/1.

96. Koestler to Daphne, 10 May 1941, MS2301/3; Daphne to Koestler, 21 April 1941, MS2301/3.

97. Koestler to Willert, 1 July 1941, MS2372/1; Strachey to Koestler, 11 July 1941, MS2371/1; Koestler to Neumann, 13 August 1941, MS2372/1.

98. Hugh Thomas, *John Strachey* (London, 1973), pp.209–10; John Strachey, *The Strangled Cry* (London, 1962), pp.11–12.

99. 'The Lion and the Ostrich', Lecture to the British Academy 'Thank-Offering to Britain Fund', 27 June 1973, reprinted in *Kaleidoscope*, pp.275–7.

100. Koestler to Sheila, 26 August 1941; Koestler to Willert, 4 September 1941, MS2372/1.

101. Koestler to Willert, 4 September 1941, MS2372/1; Capt. S. B. Denison, Education Corps to Koestler, 6 November 1941, MS2371/2.

102. Koestler to Dobrée, 30 September 1941, MS2414/1; Koestler to Chapman, 28 October 1941, MS2372/1; diary-notebook [DN], 28 October 1941, MS2305.

103. Jameson to Koestler, 18 and 26 August 1941, MS2371/1; Jameson to Koestler, 15 September 1941, MS2372/1; see diary 1941, MS2304; Iain Hamilton interview with Arthur Koestler, 5 March 1974, pp.14, 19, MS2436/5.

104. Iain Hamilton interview, pp.19–20.

105. Ibid., pp.18–24; Strachey to Koestler, 1 April 1942, MS2371/3; Koestler to Strachey, 9 April 1942, MS2372/1; Rothschild to Koestler 19 April and 27 April 1942; Koestler to Rothschild, 28 April 1942, MS2372/1; DN, 8 April 1942, MS2305; 30 June and 30 July 1942, diary 1942, MS2304; Foot, *Loyalists and Loners*, pp.215–20; Guy de Rothschild, *The Whims of Fortune* (London, 1985) p.137; A. J. Ayer, *Part of My Life* (London, 1977), pp.244–5. Interview with Miriam Rothschild, 4 April 1998.

106. Interview with David Astor, 8 June 1995.

107. Report on injury, 20 September 1941, Oakley Camp Farm, MS2307/1; DN, 29 September 1941, 29 September 1941 to 22 May 1943, MS2305; DN, 8, 17, 19 October 1941, MS2305.

108. Daphne to Koestler, 21 April, 6 May 1941; Koestler to Daphne, 10 May 1941; Daphne to Koestler, 28 May, 4 June 1941, MS2301/3.

109. Daphne to Koestler, 8, 10, 27 June 1941, MS2372/1; Koestler to Willert, 4 September and to Connolly, 19 September 1941, MS2372/1.

110. Koestler to Willert, 2 October and to Helen Lidiski, 17 October 1941, MS2372/1; Strauss to Koestler, 8 October 1941, MS2371/2.

111. Diary, 10 August 1941, MS2304; Koestler to Gollancz, 2 and 4 August 1941; Koestler to Neumann, 13 August 1941; Koestler to Cape, 4 September 1941, MS2372/1; diary, 11 and 13 September 1941, MS2304; Connolly to Koestler, 16 September 1941, MS2371/2; Koestler to Forster, 26 September, 1 and 17 October 1941, MS2372/1; diary, 2/3 November 1941, MS2304.

112. Christopher Salmon, BBC, to Koestler, 16 October and 19 November 1941, MS2372/1; Trevor Blewitt, BBC, to Koestler, 13 January 1942, MS2371/3. For 'Europe in Revolt', see MS2363/2. Iain Hamilton interview with Arthur Koestler, 5 March 1974, p.14, MS2436/5.

113. Koestler to Trevor/Phyllis Blewitt, 2 May 1941; Koestler to Cape, 3 May and 30 July 1941, MS2372/1; Gollancz to Cape, 5 May and 11 June 1941, MS2371/1. For praise of the book, see Storm Jameson to Koestler, 8 July 1941, MS2371/1. Robert Hewison, *Under Siege. Literary Life in London 1939–45* (London, 1988), pp.42–4.

114. Strauss to Koestler, 8 October 1941, MS2373/2; Strauss to Koestler, 16 December 1941, MS2371/2; Strauss to Koestler, 20 January and 18 May 1942, MS2371/3; Laski to Koestler, 22 September and 1 October 1941, MS2371/2; Koestler to Laski, 28 September 1941, MS2372/1.

115. See MS2371/2. Weiczen to Koestler, 24 December 1941, MS2371/2.

116. DN, 7 November 1941, MS2305. Michael Sheldon, *Friends of Promise: Cyril Connolly and the World of Horizon* (London, 1990), p.71.

117. 'Scheme for the rescue of Alien Refugees in Unoccupied France and French North Africa' encl. with Koestler to Paul Strage, Secretary of the Friend's Service Council, nd, probably September 1941, MS2413/2. See also Eleanor Rathbone to Koestler, 28 September 1941 and 14 October 1941, MS2371/2.

118. Koestler to Laski, 28 September 1941, MS2372/1; Astor to Koestler, 1 October 1941, MS2413/2; Edith Pye, International Committee for War Refugees in Great Britain, to Koestler, 20 October 1941, MS2371/2; Koestler to Rathbone, 9 November 1941; Koestler to Astor, 9 November 1941, MS2413/2; DN, 7 November 1941, MS2305.

119. Koestler to Astor, 23 November 1941, MS2372/1; Einstein to Koestler, 28 November 1941, suggesting a meeting between them; Astor to Koestler, 25 November 1941; Rathbone to Koestler, 12 December 1941; Rathbone to Koestler, 18 December 1941, MS2371/2; Koestler to Rathbone, 7 January 1942, MS2372/1;

Rathbone to Koestler, 24 January 1942, MS2371/3; interview with David Astor, 8 June 1995.

120. Koestler to CO, 24 and 25 November 1941; Koestler to Connolly, 26 November 1941; Koestler to Calder-Marshall, 26 November 1941, MS2372/1. Sheldon, *Friends of Promise*, pp.83–4.

121. Calder-Marshall to Koestler, 7, 22, 28 November and 1 December 1941, MS2371/2; Koestler to Calder-Marshall, 26 November 1941 and to George Campbell, MOI Films Div., 26 November 1941, MS2372/1.

122. Koestler to Károlyi, Koestler to Neumann, 6 December; Koestler to Sir Herbert Read, 23 December; Koestler to Carus Wilson, 25 December 1941, MS2372/1; Daphne to Koestler, 4 and 20 December 1941, MS2301/3; Notes for discharge, MS2307/1.

123. Kingsley Martin to Koestler, 2 December 1941, Arthur Calder-Marshall to Koestler, 5 December 1941; Astor to Koestler, 10 December 1941; Strauss to Koestler, 23 December 1941, MS2371/2.

124. Calder-Marshall to Koestler, 5, 12 and 18 December 1941; Paul Willert to Koestler, 16 December 1941, MS2371/2.

125. Koestler to Daphne, 27 December 1941, MS2301/3.

126. Calder-Marshall to Koestler, 29 December 1941, MS2371/2; Crossman to Koestler, 1 January 1942; Calder-Marshall to Koestler, 6 January 1942, MS2371/3; Koestler to Phyllis Bottome, 13 February 1942, MS2372/1; Army Discharge Notice, to March 1942, MS2308/2.

MARTINE POULAIN

A Cold War Best-Seller: The Reaction to Arthur Koestler's Darkness at Noon in France from 1945 to 1950

Arthur Koestler's *Darkness at Noon* served as the pioneer publication denouncing Stalinist strategies. First released in 1940 in London, Jewish publishers reissued subsequent French editions of *Darkness at Noon* in the mid-1940s amidst a climate of Communism, facing major obstacles that included a paper shortage. The Communists regarded paper as a rare commodity in war-torn Europe, and it would not easily be turned over to anti-Communist movements. Publicly heralded in France, *Darkness at Noon* survived Cold War Communist censorship and underground book sales. While French Communist party members abhorred Koestler's message and his successful publications, Western critics and democratic-minded European readers clung to the revolutionary statements envisioned in the book. This essay describes the difficulties, from lack of funds to political warnings, the author and publishers experienced when attempting to release the work. It also follows the various reactions to *Darkness at Noon*, both exceedingly positive and sharply negative.

From *Libraries & Culture* 36, no. 1 (Winter 2001). © 2001 by the University of Texas Press.

Jonathan Cape published *Darkness at Noon* in London in 1940. Arthur Koestler, the author, was a Hungarian Jew who had lived in Berlin and Paris and had belonged to the German Communist party, been a reporter for an English newspaper during the Spanish Civil War, been imprisoned in Málaga and released through the intervention of his newspaper, and chose to recount the Moscow trials of 1938 in a work of fiction. Arthur Koestler's novel, the first important book denouncing the Stalinist reign of terror, had worldwide success and prompted unusually far-reaching discussions. These debates became particularly virulent, and more so in France than elsewhere.

Publication of the English Edition

In *Hieroglyphs*, Arthur Koestler related the genesis of the idea and the writing style of *Darkness at Noon*.[1] The novel, written in German and translated into English by his companion of that time, Daphne Hardy, was begun during the summer of 1936 and completed in April 1939. The first edition was published in 1940 in London, where Koestler was a refugee.

In France, Pierre and Robert Calmann-Levy, descendants of an important dynasty of publishers of Jewish origin, only published the book after the war, in December 1945.[2] The Nazis had closed down the publishing house during the war, a measure consistent with their policy of keeping French publishing Aryan.

Robert Calmann-Levy got in touch with Allen Lane, the publisher of the pocket edition during the war, perhaps in 1943 or 1944. The French edition, entitled *Le Zéro et l'infini*, was an immediate success. In this essay, I hope to analyze the tormented triumph of the book. The reading of Koestler's novel was greatly affected by the international political context of the moment, when the Cold War commenced in 1947. French national politics were directly influenced by its presence in terms that became increasingly conflictual, even to the point that discussions turned into harmful denunciations.

Let me remind my foreign colleagues that the French Communist party (FCP) had an important following at the end of the war. It was part of the government in 1947, and until 1956 it represented more than a fourth of the electorate. The deterioration of relations among political currents that had been allied during the Resistance was aggravated in 1947. This uncompromising political context in France had a direct impact on the reception of Koestler's novel.

The French Edition

The Calmann-Levy archives include a wealth of documents concerning the French editions of Arthur Koestler's work, but they do not solve all the mysteries. The French translation, under the direction of Penguin Books, was late in coming.[3] Throughout 1945, Robert Calmann-Levy, who had acquired the rights to another of Koestler's books (*Arrival and Departure*, or *Croisade sans croix*), planning to publish it after *Darkness at Noon*, worried and complained that he had not received the long-awaited translation. His major problem, apart from the delay in receiving the translation, was the paucity of available paper. In France, where the war had just ended, the paper supply was strictly controlled,[4] and there was very little of it. At last, on 28 December 1945, Arthur Koestler received a telegram from Robert Calmann-Levy announcing the publication of his book in an edition of 20,000 copies, according to Koestler's wishes. From the moment of publication, the editor intuited the success that the book was to have.

It is interesting to observe the precision and the regularity (about a letter a week) of Robert Calmann-Levy's correspondence with Koestler, keeping him informed of his book's success. Throughout 1946 and 1947, Robert Calmann-Levy sent Arthur Koestler an abundance of clippings discussing the book, gave him details about sales, and informed him of further editions, which often delayed the publication of other books by Koestler because paper was so scarce. Arthur Koestler faithfully answered all these communications on his blue paper. An initial good feeling developed into a real friendship between the two men.

The publisher prepared a new edition of 10,000 copies in February 1946.[5] It was immediately sold out. On 28 March he let Koestler know that a third edition of 20,000 copies is planned.[6] That edition turned out to be 44,000 copies—immediately out of print.[7] On 3 May 1946 Robert Calmann-Levy told Arthur Koestler that a fourth edition of 20,000 copies is planned (30,000 will actually be printed), while 15,000 copies of *Arrival and Departure* have already been reserved by bookstores.[8] On 11 July 1946 Calmann-Levy wrote Koestler that 115,000 copies of *Darkness at Noon* had been sold, and a fifth edition of 20,000 copies was under way.[9] Seventy thousand copies were immediately reserved by bookstores in Paris and throughout France. Robert Calmann-Levy undertook an edition of 100,000 copies early in 1947. More than 300,000 copies of *Darkness at Noon* were sold in France between 1945 and 1948.[10]

Public Acclaim

Clearly, there was an impassioned public acclaim for *Darkness at Noon*. The press did not lag behind this general acclamation. From the time of its publication and throughout the entire year, numerous reviews were dedicated to the book.

Le Figaro published an article full of praise for the book on 9 February

1946, appreciating that it had "violently stirred public awareness" and that "hallucinating scenes leave the reader with vivid impressions." The author of the review, who briefly recounted the accusations of the Moscow trials and evoked "the rise of the Stalinist dictatorship," which is the context of the book, emphasized that Arthur Koestler's novel is a perfect illustration of "the conflict between revolutionary action and moral ideas."[11]

In *La Minerve* of 22 February 1946, Yves Gandon praised the novel as well. In his summary of Koestler's theme ("is the individual only a pawn on a chess board, or has he an independent existence?"), he considered that the novel illustrates the conflict between "two moralities which cause dissension in the world," one Christian and humane, the other materialist with its point of departure being that "the end justifies the means." Observing that Arthur Koestler was able to write as analyst as well as novelist, the critic judged *Darkness at Noon* to be "without question, a work of exceptional merit."

There are endless examples of critical acclaim for Koestler's book, praising his qualities as an analyst and a writer. All accounts of the work assess it as a lucid exemplification of the tendencies of the Communist regime in the U.S.S.R. (the term *totalitarian* is often used) as well as an examination of the effects of power on human psychology. The book was to play an important part in the reflections of many liberal Democrats and to inspire certain evaluations of the Soviet regime. This was the case with Raymond Aron, for example, when he published *Le Grand Schisme* in 1948.[12]

Communist Hostility: A Growing Campaign of Denunciation

The Communists' attitude toward *Darkness at Noon* can only be understood in the context of the Cold War, which exacerbated their outlook and their behavior. Hardly favorable, and that is a euphemism, toward a book that denounces the Stalinist trials or an author who is an ex-Communist, during the early months of 1946 the Communists maintained a contentious posture while they established a strategy of suspicion.[13]

In *Action* of 5 April 1946 Claude Roy dissipated illusions and instilled doubts.[14] Is Roubachof's indecision not that of "a counterfeit man, completely cut off from the universe and other men?" "In this book written in 1939 and published in 1940, it could be said that there is no national-socialist menace, no *Wehrmacht*, that Munich had never been, that Mussolini was never born, that Hitler is inconceivable, that Soviet Russia reigns without peril, alone in the world, its existence concerning only itself."

If all the ingredients of the future campaign of denunciation are there, they are present in a euphemistic form. Arthur Koestler's theses are discussed, not denounced. The tone will become harsher, since Communist strategy will change in the autumn of 1947. A new strategy dictated by

Moscow replaced that of the sacred union adopted during the Resistance and then at the Liberation: confrontation was the new tactic. The FCP's attitude had already evolved since it left the government in May 1947. During a meeting of nine European Communist parties in the autumn of 1947, Andre Jdanov presented this new direction and introduced the creation of the Kominform. The French and Italian Communist parties were roundly reproached for their attitudes of collaboration with their governments. The enemy was designated: American imperialism. This radicalism had immediate effects on the attitudes of the FCP concerning cultural and intellectual matters: *Les Letters Françaises* was taken in hand, all "class enemies" were denounced, and so on. Arthur Koestler, like Victor Kravchenko, whose French translation of *I Chose Freedom* appeared in the fall of 1947, took on symbolic values.[15] They both became active renegades who falsified the image of the Soviet Union and of Communism as it was evolving. They had to be denounced.

Censorship and Censure

The Communist press alternately applied silence (boycotting the book, no longer discussing it), censorship, and invective. According to several Koestler specialists, the Communist party went to see Robert Calmann-Levy to ask him to renounce further editions of the novel.[16] Koestler echoed this pressure in his autobiographical essays: "The communists tried to intimidate the publishers of the book. When they did not succeed, they bought up entire stocks of it in bookstores in the suburbs and throughout the country, and destroyed them. As a result, the book was sold on the black market, for four or five times its real price, between editions."[17] He queried his publisher in a letter of 8 June 1946 and was reassured that there had been no pressure put upon him.[18] Did Calmann-Levy try to dissimulate the intensity of pressure and censure under which he had to work? No further archival information is available to help us clarify that question today.

The Communists found the success of Koestler's book intolerable and, even more so, the discussion of the Soviet regime that it incited. In 1947 Roger Garaudy, member of the party's National Committee, published a pamphlet entitled *Literature for Gravediggers* in which he harshly denounced *petit-bourgeois* writers one by one: Jean-Paul Sartre, François Mauriac, André Malraux, and Arthur Koestler.[19] The FCP clarified its doctrine during the late 1940s before engaging in "the battle of the book" during the fifties.[20] Laurent Casanova, member of the National Committee, presented this doctrine in June 1947: "There is a reactionary art just as there are reactionary politics.... There is an avant-garde art just as there are avant-garde politics."[21] What should be encouraged are "the exalting virtues of an optimistic literature," based upon the values of the masses: "using the people's life experiences as a point of departure, a certain number of moral values belonging to our time and our nation may be defined.... As long as there is action among the masses, the essential cultural values may really be found in the struggles of the masses." Intellectuals and artists should serve those values, and their enemies are denounced:

> Mr. Koestler and Mr. Dos Passos formulate their ideological arguments in a foreign country, and many defeatists in countries weakened by the war draw strength from those arguments, which find resounding echoes in France. American films bearing a foreign ideology invade our cinemas, American books inundate our bookstore shelves, foreign film companies and publishing houses, through economic and cultural exchanges, even settle in France, contributing to the degradation of our own national character.

This thesis, presented as a defense of a popular, anti-imperialist tenet, displays an overt nationalism that merits further discussion.

In 1950 Jean Kanapa published an even more virulent attack in the form of a pamphlet entitled. *The Traitor and the Proletariat, or Koestler and Company, Ltd.*, dedicated to *Darkness at Noon*.[22] Kanapa condemned the support and solidarity that consistently helped Koestler in his role as head of an organized campaign. The disparagement not only targeted *Darkness at Noon* but Arthur Koestler himself: "Koestler's activity, beginning with the *Testament of Spain*, is entirely devoted to a literary justification of the unjustifiable: first, desertion and then, still worse, treason."[23] His heroes are merely "traitors to their people, to the revolution, turncoats among the proletariat." Arthur Koestler represents nothing more than the derisive efforts of a bourgeoisie literature "to disclaim an already existing socialism, the workers' movement, the enormity of its aims, the courage of its militants, the nobility of its leaders."[24]

Neither Darkness nor Noon: *Esprit, Les Temps Modernes*

Faithful to what was to become its tradition, *Esprit* sought a "middle way." Martin Brionne dedicated an article to Koestler's book in May 1946 with a significant title: "Neither Darkness nor Noon."[25] Reproaching the conspiracy of silence as well as the imprecations of the Communist press, Martin Brionne did not really confront Koestler's book; he digressed endlessly in his arguments and did not conclude anything. Considering that Koestler's novel posed the question of modern Machiavellianism (does the end justify the means?), Brionne proposed a parallel between the early stages of Communism and early Christianity. Shouldn't Communism, as a young religion, be pardoned for its errors?[26]

A year later, *Esprit* discussed the book once again, this time in an article by Bertrand d'Astorg.[27] Admitting the book's success, he criticized the Communist party's diatribes against it but at the same time indicated his reservations.[28] Even the American ambassador in Moscow understood that the Russians were waging a battle against a fifth column, d'Astorg argued.

Doesn't every revolution pass through phases when one must consider that the end justifies the means? Spelling out the real reasons for his reticence, his need to believe in a brighter future, Bertrand d'Astorg pointed out, "For if the U.S.S.R. is not the country of socialism—even a faltering, marred socialism—where can the socialist look for it: in the United States, because there is an antitrust law there dating from 1904?"[29] He concluded his article with an appeal to a new European intelligentsia, a third force, ready to reconstruct a church, be it without God or clergy, a third force from which Koestler would be excluded because of his skepticism toward the European Left.

We know that Arthur Koestler's relations with Jean-Paul Sartre, who founded *Les Temps Modernes* in 1945 in collaboration with Raymond Aron, Maurice Merleau-Ponty, Simone de Beauvoir, Jean Paulhan, and others, were stormy.[30] When Koestler returned to Paris in 1946, he met with Sartre and his group. In February 1949 their relationship was severed on the grounds of political incompatibility. But between 1949 and 1950, *Les Temps Modernes*, Sartre, and Beauvoir were not yet fellow travelers of the FCP, as they became in 1952. Even though it was impossible for them to condemn the Communist regime, they did publish critical articles in their magazine.[31] Between October 1946 and January 1947, Maurice Merleau-Ponty published three articles in *Les Temps Modernes* directly inspired by his reading of Koestler's works, *Darkness at Noon* and *The Yogi and the Commissar*. These articles form the core of his book, *Humanism and Terror*, which was published by Gallimard in 1947.[32] As Claude Lefort recalled in the preface to a later edition of the book, "The planning of *Humanism and Terror* took shape when Merleau-Ponty was reading Arthur Koestler's *Darkness at Noon*."

Far more ample than his earlier analytical works, this book by Maurice Merleau-Ponty was several hundred pages long and quite close in spirit to the assessments in *Esprit*. After 1950, when he radically refused Stalinism, he left *Les Temps Modernes*.[33] Within the limited framework of this essay, it is impossible for me to give a detailed account of Merleau-Ponty's position. As Claude Lefort so rightly emphasized, throughout his book Merleau-Ponty and his double are present, confronting each other and disagreeing without ever seeing each other. Maurice Merleau-Ponty summed up his incapacity to take a firm stand, considering himself to be "in an inextricable situation": "One cannot be an anti-Communist and one and not be a Communist." He constantly weighed the blemishes of capitalism against the abuses of Communism.[34] Declaring himself a Marxist, Merleau-Ponty reproached Koestler for not being the least bit of an historian, for being pre-Marxist.[35] The accused in the Moscow trials may therefore be subjectively innocent and objectively guilty. The Yogis are not at grips with the Commissars; the same man is perhaps now Yogi, now Commissar, according to the point of view he adopts toward a given historical act.[36]

Maurice Merleau-Ponty, haunted by the fear of a third world war, which he deemed imminent, was equally put off by the inadequacies of both liberal and Communist worldviews (one must "remind the Marxists of their humanist inspiration" and "remind democracies of their fundamental hypocrisy"). However, in expressing an argument that will be used for a long time thereafter, he considered that "any criticism of Communism ... really aims at the very existence of the U.S.S.R. and must be considered as an act of war," a war that must be avoided at all cost.[37]

Conclusion

The study of reactions to Arthur Koestler's novel sheds a good deal of light on postwar and Cold War French society. Hundreds of thousands of readers evidently tried to formulate an opinion with the help of a book. Can that not be considered an outstanding example of the role of reading as a public exercise in reasoning? Readers' horizons and expectations influence their way of reading. One can estimate that there were three types of readers: those who modified their worldview and acquired a fuller understanding of the Communist system through reading Koestler's book; those, on the contrary, who reinforced their own outlook, either because they shared Koestler's views and found grounds to confirm their points of view in the book or because they disagreed entirely with Koestler's opinions and considered that the book shamelessly presented events in a distorted, invented, or falsified manner (such was the reaction of the Communists);[38] and those who might include readers such as Merleau-Ponty or d'Astorg, whom the book would leave at an intermediary stage–their previous points of view were neither confirmed nor weakened. Successive reading will lead the reader to an eventual modification of his or her world outlook.

This incident shows how deeply France was divided between two radically opposed currents of influence. The intelligentsia was most often sympathetic toward the pro-Communists. Today, such a lack of awareness of Soviet totalitarianism seems not only incomprehensible but also reprehensible. However, it is also useful to understand what led to this blindness. There is no doubt that the nearness to the war explains the gratitude felt toward the Soviet Union. But the reluctance to acknowledge the Stalinist oppression for what it was must have to do with a rapport with oneself and with the world, as Claude Lafort remarks so rightly in his preface. The mourning for a lost ideology, mourning for a lost belief in a better world was—at the end of the war—the most terrible bereavement in history; for many people, it was intolerable. It was the need to believe that constituted the group of readers who were willingly impervious to some of their reading.

NOTES

1. All references to Arthur Koestler's various autobiographical writings are taken from the remarkable edition of his collected *Oeuvres autobiographiques*, re-edited by Phil Casoar in the Robert Laffont edition (Coll. Bouquins, 1994). In his preface, Phil Casoar evokes the facts we are concerned with within this text.

2. For the history of the Calmann-Levy editions, see Jean-Yves Mollier, *Michel et Calmann-Levy ou la naissance de l'édition moderne: 1836–1891* (Paris: Calmann-Levy, 1984).

3. The agreement between Penguin and Calmann-Levy that relegated Calmann-Levy to the role of a subcontractor with Penguin for the French rights was an example of the singular conditions in publishing after the war. This situation soon became unacceptable for Robert Calmann-Levy, who corresponded with Allen Lane about procuring full rights as French publisher of *Le Zéro*. Arthur Koestler seconded him in this effort. A good sport, Allen Lane quickly agreed to withdraw and allow Calmann-Levy and Koestler to establish a direct contract, which was signed in 1946.

4. *Action*, founded in September 1944, was increasingly directed by the FCP: "*Action* was a refuge for the intellectual Communists in discord with Jdanovism. But it was a short-lived refuge and, through an elaborate process that escaped its participants, it became a strictly Communist publication." Jeanine Verdes-Leroux, *Au service du parti. Le Parti communiste, les intellectuels et la culture, 1944–1956 et 1956–1958* (Paris: Fayard-Minuit, 1983, 1987).

5. Letter to Arthur Koestler, 18 February 1946: "You will see from the enclosed clippings that almost all the critics have been immensely enthusiastic!" Letter of 27 February 1946: "Only a thousand copies left of first edition of *Zero*. Second edition at twenty thousand in course of print. Congratulations." Letter of 14 March 1946: "Almost 10,000 copies of the new editions, which should be out within the week, is already reserved." Calmann-Levy Archives.

6. "I'm doing my utmost to find the paper for a third edition of 20,000 copies." Letter from R. Calmann-Levy to A. Koestler, 28 March 1946, Calmann-Levy Archives.

7. "The new edition, of which 30,000 copies are already ordered, will be on sale within ten days." Letter from R. Calmann-Levy to A. Koestler, 25 April 1946, Calmann-Levy Archives.

8. Letter of 3 May 1946, Calmann-Levy Archives.

9. "We are thinking of a fifth edition of 22,000 copies, but if we manage to get hold of more paper, we'll print more." Letter of 11 July 1946, Calmann-Levy Archives.

10. After this success, Calmann-Levy became A. Koestler's official French publisher, while prior to this, Koestler had accepted the proposals of various publishing houses.

Charlot had published *Le Yogi et le commissaire* in 1945. In its articles, the press often associates the two books, very much related in content but different in form (one a novel, the other an essay). In 1946 Charlot published *La Lie de la terre*, an autobiographical book recounting Koestler's war years and particularly his internment in the Vernet prison camp. Before the war, Albin Michel had published *Un Testament espagnol* in Denise Van Moppes's French translation.

11. "Le Zéro et l'infini," signed Les Alguazils (*sic*), *Le Figaro*, 9 February 1946.

12. Gallimard, 1948. Raymond Aron is also responsible for another collection (*Liberté de l'esprit*), with the collaboration of Manes Sperber. Both men are Arthur Koestler's friends. Koestler, in his letters, often suggests that his editor consult them for their advice on matters concerning the publication of his work.

13. In January 1946, *Les Lettres Françaises* published an article on *Le Zéro* with a tone that astonishes R. Calmann-Levy, who writes to Koestler: "Enclosed you will find three reviews of *Le Zéro*: a magnificent one in *Lettres Françaises*, considering its definite tendency toward Communism; still, it could not refrain from writing about your book." Letter from R. Calmann-Levy to Koestler, 4 February 1946, Calmann-Levy Archives. We must remember that Jacques Decour and Jean Paulhan founded *Les Lettres Françaises* in September 1942. Though a Communist sensibility was present from the outset, it was "taken in hand" by the Communist party in the autumn of 1947.

14. *Action*, founded in September 1944, was increasingly directed by the FCP: "*Action* was a refuge for the intellectual Communists in discord with Jdanovism. But it was a short-lived refuge, and, through an elaborate process that escaped its participants, it became a strictly Communist publication." Verdes-Leroux, *Au service du parti*.

15. *J'ai choisi la liberté*, published by Albin-Michel in October 1947. On 13 November 1947, *Les Lettres Françaises* published an article entitled "What Made Kravchenko," supposedly written by a certain Sim Thomas and received from the United States. Extremely troubled by several similar articles published in the weekly, Victor Kravchenko accused both *Les Lettres Françaises* and *l'Humanité* of defamation. The trial took place early in 1949. The repercussions of the Kravchenko affair were even more pronounced in French society than those caused by *Le Zéro*. But one reaction cannot be understood without the other.

16. Phil Casoar mentions this interdependency in his preface to Koestler's *Oeuvres autobiographiques*. Pierre Debray-Ritzen assumes that "the publisher R. Calmann-Levy received a FCP delegation headed by Jacques Duclos in 1945. They ordered him to relinquish publication of *Le Zéro et l'infini* in France. The publisher went ahead with his plans." Arthur Koestler, *La Herne* (1975).

17. Koestler, *Hiéroglyphes*.

18. "I gather from an article by Randolph Churchill that Communist circles in France have tried to put pressure on you to prevent the publication and reprinting of *Le Zéro*. I would be grateful if you could give me full information about this affair. If you want me to treat the information or part of it confidentially, please tell me." A. Koestler to R. Calmann-Levy, 8 June 1946, Calmann-Levy Archives. R. Calmann-Levy's answer in June 1946: "About the issue concerning *Le Zéro*, we have never been pressured to cease publishing or re-editing, and all the stories in the French press are nothing but journalistic rumors." Calmann-Levy Archives.

19. Roger Garaudy, *Une littérature de fossoyeurs* (Editions Sociales, 1947).

20. Marc Lazar, "Les 'Batailles du livre' du Parti communiste français (1950–1952)." *XXe Siècle* 10 (1986).

21. Laurent Casanova, "Le Communisme et l'art," lecture given by L. Casanova at the 11th Congress of the FCP, 25–28 June 1947.

22. Jean Kanapa, *Le Traître et le prolétaire*. The title is an unmistakable allusion to

Koestler's *The Yogi and the Commissar*, published during the same period.

23. He pretended to have fought in the Spanish Civil War, but he has never been anything but a "petit bourgeois adventurer," "complacently released by Franco…at the intervention of Lady Astor" and the Vatican. Arthur Koestler, in fact, "deserted." A simple adventurer, Koestler "surrendered to the Phalangists, simply looking for a thrill and for the mark this gesture would make on his future undertakings." Kanapa, *Le Traître et le prolétaire*.

24. Further on, Kanapa continues: "[To publish Koestler is to favor] the return of the Nazis…because if Koestler attacks Communism and the Communists the way he does, it is because the Communists are the best defenders of our national independence." Ibid.

25. Martin Brionne, "Ni zéro ni infini," *Esprit*, 1 May 1946: 692–702. This catch phrase will be used as a gesture of defiance against the book. José Corti, for example, the well-known postwar Paris bookseller who was to become a publisher of famous books as well, fervently opposed Koestler's book because of his solidarity with the Soviet Communists and refused to sell the book in his shop, replying to customers who asked for it, "Je n'ai ni *Zéro* ni infini." The anecdote says a lot about the passionate reactions caused by the book, as well as the agreement with these reactions by a broad social segment, including a very prestigious bookseller who exercised censorship in this case, refusing to sell a book of which he disapproved. That such behavior was not always found shocking is an indication of the state of mind of that period, when people were quick to join some group and to accept the many signs that signified belonging.

26. "What I am trying to break down, with these all too brief lines, is the opposition Koestler has forced us into; I should like to say that for the Christian, humanity is not zero, and man alone must not be everything; that for the Communist all hope is not lost when a man is still someone, and that a singing humanity cannot be a mass of larvae. And while underscoring these points, I am trying to keep from misusing–as various extremists have done–Koestler's admirable book." Brionne, "Ni zéro ni infini."

27. "My bookseller told me a month ago that people were standing in line at Calmann-Levy's shop to buy *Le Zéro et l'infini*." Bertrand Astorg, "Arthur Koestler, prix Nobel 1960," *Esprit* 10 (October 1947): 378–98.

28. Concerning the way the book was received, it is worth quoting from the beginning of d'Astorg's article: "The book has caused a stir. It has had excellent reviews in the literary columns of the big dailies where the usual trend is to review only the dullest love stories. Its impact was immediately weighed in on a political scale: The RLP must recommend it to its members and *l'Aube*, to its followers. As for the Communist party, it sent out the signal to boycott and exclude it totally. Claude Morgan, in *Les Lettres Françaises* did not hesitate (just when we are celebrating the anniversary and the glorious celebrations of the Red Army) to sow discord (a scandalous book comes out…) and to affront the publisher by reminding him, with a certain amount of bad taste, that the Jews owed a lot to the glorious Red Army and therefore … the Calmann brothers would have been most astonished three years ago, in the London gardens of our delegation where they happily waited to obtain the rights for such an excellent novel, if they had been told at the time that the book would also result in them having their origins tossed in their faces." Ibid.

29. Ibid.

30. In *Hiéroglyphes*, Arthur Koestler refers to this. There is a delightful little book by Pierre Pachet on the same subject, a commentary on a sculpture by Jean-Louis Faure entitled *Jean-Paul Sartre and Simone de Beauvoir Refusing to Shake Arthur Koestler's Hand*, in Jean-Louis Faure and Pierre Pachet, *Bêtise de l'intelligence* (Nantes: Joca Seria Eds., 1995).

31. Michel Winock retraces the major political developments in Sartre's trajectory, together with his team on *Les Temps Modernes*, in *Le Siècle des intellectuels* (Seuil, 1997).

32. Maurice Merleau-Ponty, *Humanisme et terreur: essai sur le problème communiste* (Paris: Gallimard, 1947). Reprinted in 1980 with an introduction by Claude Lefort (Idées Gallimard).

33. This rupture is formalized in the publication of the *Aventures de la dialectique* by Maurice Merleau-Ponty in 1955 by Gallimard. In it is a chapter on "Sartre and Ultra-Bolshevism."

34. "The Marxist criticism of capitalism remains valid, and it is clear that today, anti-Sovietism includes the same components of brutality, pride, instability, and anxiety that were present in fascism. On the other hand, the revolution is now at a standstill: it is sustaining and worsening the dictatorial apparatus while renouncing revolutionary freedom for the proletariat in its Soviets and its party as well as the humane functioning of the state." Merleau-Ponty, *Humanisme et terreur*, 49.

35. "Political action must be judged not only from a moral point of view but equally according to the historical context and the dialectic situation when it is taken." Ibid., 121.

36. "However good-willed we may be, we act without a precise understanding of the objective sense of our actions, we build an idea of a future based only on probabilities, asking something of the future. We may be condemned for this, for events are unequivocal. A man cannot eliminate his own presence in terms of freedom and judgment ... nor can he contest the competence of the tribunal of history, because when he acts he involves others and, eventually, all mankind." Ibid., 158.

37. An example of the constant activity of the author-reader Maurice Merleau-Ponty is his discussion, in the preface to *Humanisme et terreur*, of the way his own ideas are received. He feels he's been misunderstood in his efforts toward a middle way. He evokes the "violent reproaches" he had to deal with because of his remarks about "this famous and little known book ... which has not been read," readers being carried away by their emotions. Merleau-Ponty points out: "When only a third of our study had appeared ... people who usually did not get involved in polemics...sat down at their desks and threw themselves into writing and, in a tone of moral reprobation, composed refutations lacking the merest trace of lucidity: sometimes making us say the opposite of what we were saying, sometimes ignoring the problem we are trying to state." Ibid., 60. The Communists had, in fact, accused him of justifying "a victorious Hitler," while the liberals claimed that he was justifying the Moscow trials.

Chronology

1905   Arthur Koestler is born in Budapest, Hungary on
              September 5 to Henrik and Adela Jeiteles Koestler, a
              prosperous, middle-class Jewish family fully assimilated
              into Germanic culture.

1914–15   Parents move to Vienna at the start of World War I where
              Koestler receives his early education. Following elementary
              school, he is enrolled in the *Realschule*, a school specializing
              in science and modern languages.

1922   Enrolls at the University of Vienna to study science and
              psychology, but postwar politics become his predominant
              interest. He is attracted to Zionism.

1924   Becomes involved in Zionist politics.

1926   Koestler makes his first trip to Palestine, leaving his studies
              incomplete, to live and work on an Israeli kibbutz.

1927–29   Works as Middle East correspondent for Ullstein
              newspaper chain of Germany. By June 1929, he leaves the
              Middle East and is sent to work at Ullstein News Service in
              Paris.

1930   Returns to Berlin in September and becomes science editor
              for *Vossiche Zeitung*, one of the Ullstein papers.

1932   Disillusioned with Zionism, Koestler secretly joins the
              German Communist party, but within a few months is
              found out and forced to resign his editorship. Goes to work

full-time for the Party, taking a series of assignments that eventually take him to the Soviet Union (1932–1933); back to Western Europe (1933–1936); and finally to the Spanish Civil War (1936–1937) undercover as an English journalist. During this time, he gradually becomes disillusioned with the party and the Russian revolution, and formally breaks with the party during the Spanish Civil War.

1934   Publishes *Von Weissen Nächten und Roten Tagen (White Nights and Red Days)*.

1935   Marries Dorothy Asher with whom he had been in living in Switzerland. Although at this time, he considers marriage a bourgeois institution, he marries because Dorothy's passport is about to expire. Their marriage lasts only a few months, but they remain good friends. During the Spanish Civil War, Dorothy manages to get Koestler released from one of Franco's jails.

1936–37   Serves as war correspondent in Spain for London *News Chronicle*.

1937   *Menschenopfer Unerhört* is published; republished as *L'Espagne ensanglantée* in Paris; and enlarged and published as *Spanish Testament* in London. Captured by Nationalists and sentenced to death, but freed following protests in London. Feeling betrayed, Koestler leaves the Communist party.

1938   Becomes editor of exile newspaper in Paris.

1939   Interned in French detention camp. Koestler's first novel, *The Gladiators*, is published in London and New York.

1940   Joins French Foreign Legion.

1941   Escapes to England after the fall of France. Koestler's second novel, *Darkness at Noon*, translated by Daphne Hardy, and *Scum of the Earth*, is published in London and New York.

1943   *Arrival and Departure* is published in London and New York.

1945   Becomes special correspondent for London *Times* in Palestine. Publishes *The Yogi and the Commissar* (and other essays) and *Twilight Bar: An Escapade in Four Acts* in London and New York.

1946   *Thieves in the Night*, a novel about life in an Israeli kibbutz, is published in London and New York.

1949	*Insight and Outlook: An Inquiry into the Common Foundations of Science, Art and Social Ethics* and *Promise and Fulfillment: Palestine 1917–1949*, his report on the creation of Israel, are published in London and New York.
1950	Marries his secretary, Mamaine Paget who, with her twin sister, was one of the prominent debutantes in England in the 1930s. However, within a year, Koestler and Mamaine are separated. *The God that Failed*, edited by R.H.S. Crossman, and including an essay by Koestler, is published in New York.
1951	*The Age of Longing* is published in London and New York. *The Accused*, by Alexander Weissberg and foreword by Koestler, is published in New York.
1952	*Arrow in the Blue: An Autobiography* (first volume) is published in London and New York.
1954	*The Invisible Writing* (second volume of autobiography) is published in London and New York. Mamaine dies after a prolonged illness.
1955	*The Trail of the Dinosaur and Other Essays* is published in London and New York.
1956–57	*Reflections on Hanging* is published in London in 1956 and New York in 1957.
1957	Becomes a Fellow of the Royal Society of Literature, England.
1959	*The Sleepwalkers: A History of Man's Changing Vision of the Universe* is published in London and New York.
1960–61	*The Lotus and the Robot* is published in London in 1960 and New York in 1961.
1961	*Hanged by the Neck: An Exposure of Capital Punishment*, by Arthur Koestler and C.H. Rolph, is published in London and Baltimore.
1963–64	*Suicide of a Nation? An Inquiry Into the State of Britain Today*, edited by Koestler, is published in London (1963) and New York (1964).
1964	Becomes a Fellow at the Center for Advanced Study in the Behavioral Sciences, Stanford University, California. *The Act of Creation* is published in London and New York.
1965	Marries his secretary, Cynthia Jeffries Patterson, twenty-two years Koestler's junior. Their marriage will prove to be his most durable and happy partnership.

1967–68	*The Ghost in the Machine* is published in London (1967) and New York (1968)
1968–69	Receives Sonning Prize from the University of Copenhagen and LL.D. from Queen's University, Kingston, Ontario. Organizes the Alpbach Symposium, *Beyond Reductionism: New Perspectives in the Life Sciences*, edited by Koestler and J.R. Smythies, is published in New York (1968). *Drinkers of Infinity: Essays 1955–1967*, is published in London (1968) and New York (1969).
1971	*The Case of the Midwife Toad* is published in London (1971) and New York (1972).
1972	*The Roots of Coincidence*, and a novel, *The Call-Girls*, are published in London and New York. Becomes C.B.E., Commander, Order of the British Empire.
1973–74	*The Challenge of Chance*, a book written with Sir Alister Hardy and Robert Harvie, is published in London (1973) and New York (1974).
1974–75	Becomes C.Lit., Companion of Literature of the Royal Society of Literature. *The Heel of Achilles. Essays 1968–1973* is published in London (1973) and New York (1975).
1976	*The Thirteenth Tribe. The Khazar Empire and Its Heritage*, Koestler's attempt to trace the origins of European Judaism, is published in London and New York.
1978	*Janus: A Summing Up* is published in London and New York.
1980–81	Koestler becomes one of the vice-presidents of the Voluntary Euthanasia Society, EXIT, of which he and his wife had been members. *Bricks to Babel: Selected Writings With Comments by the Author* is published in London (1980) and New York (1981).
1981	*Kaleidoscope* is published in London.
1983	On March 3, suffering from leukemia and Parkinson's disease, Koestler and his wife, Cynthia, commit suicide. *Stranger in the Square*, written jointly with his wife, Cynthia, is published. It is the third and incomplete volume of his autobiography.

Contributors

HAROLD BLOOM is Sterling Professor of the Humanities at Yale University and Henry W. and Albert A. Berg Professor of English at the New York University Graduate School. He is the author of over 20 books, including *Shelley's Mythmaking* (1959), *The Visionary Company* (1961), *Blake's Apocalypse* (1963), *Yeats* (1970), *A Map of Misreading* (1975), *Kabbalah and Criticism* (1975), *Agon: Toward a Theory of Revisionism* (1982), *The American Religion* (1992), *The Western Canon* (1994), and *Omens of Millennium: The Gnosis of Angels, Dreams, and Resurrection* (1996). *The Anxiety of Influence* (1973) sets forth Professor Bloom's provocative theory of the literary relationships between the great writers and their predecessors. His most recent books include *Shakespeare: The Invention of the Human* (1998), a 1998 National Book Award finalist, *How to Read and Why* (2000), *Genius: A Mosaic of One Hundred Exemplary Creative Minds* (2002), and *Hamlet: Poem Unlimited* (2003). In 1999, Professor Bloom received the prestigious American Academy of Arts and Letters Gold Medal for Criticism, and in 2002 he received the Catalonia International Prize.

ANNETTE EDWARDS PLATT was an Assistant Professor of English at Lamar University.

GORONWY REES has been Principal of the University College of Wales, Aberwystwyth and a member of the editorial board of *Encounter*. He is the author of *Brief Encounters* (1974) and *A Chapter of Accidents* (1972).

MARK LEVENE is Professor of English at the University of Toronto at Mississauga and is a Reader in History at the University of Southampton. He is the author of "'It Was about Vanishing': A Glimpse of Alice Munro's Stories" (1999) and "Tall Cows and Tapestries: A Perspective on the English-Canadian Canon" (1998).

SIDNEY A. PEARSON, JR. is Professor of Political Science at Radford College. He is the editor of *The Constitutional Polity: Essays on the Founding Principles of American Politics* (1983) and has written the introduction to *Progressive Democracy* (1998).

W. MARSHALL has been a Professor at the University of Southampton. He is the author of "Viewpoints and Voices: Serge and Koestler on the Great Terror."

HOWARD FINK is Distinguished Professor Emeritus of English at Concordia University in Montreal and Director of the Concordia Centre for Broadcast Studies. He is an editor of *The Road to Victory: Radio Plays of Gerald Noxon* (1989) and *All the Bright Company: Radio Drama Produced by Andrew Allen* (1987).

REED B. MERRILL has taught at Western Washington State College. He is the author of "Brain Fever in the Novels of Dostoevsky" (1976) and "Zorba the Greek and Nietzschean Nihilism" (1975).

WILLIAM PIETZ is an editor of *Border Fetishisms: Material Objects in Unstable Spaces* (1998) and the author of "Fetishism and Materialism: The Limits of Theory in Marx" (1993) and "The Phonograph in Africa: International Phonocentrism from Stanley to Sarnoff" (1987).

ANDERS STEPHANSON is Associate Professor of History at Columbia University. He is the author of "Regarding Postmodernism: A Conversation with Fredric Jameson (1988) and "Interview with Cornel West" (1988).

ROBERT SUTHERLAND is a Professor of Politics at Cornell College. He is the author of "Lying for the Public Good: Three New Case Studies" (1997) and "The Adam Smith Problem" (1987).

DAVID CESARANI is Parkes-Wiener Professor of Twentieth-Century Jewish History and Culture at the University of Southampton. He is the author of *The Jewish Chronicle and Anglo-Jewry 1841–1991* (1994), *Justice*

Delayed: How Britain Became a Refuge for Nazi War Criminals (2001) and editor of *Port Jews: Jewish Communities in Cosmopolitan Maritime Trading Centres, 1550–1950* (2002).

MARTINE POULAIN is an editor of the *Bulletin des Bibliothèques de France*, Paris. She is an editor of *Books, Libraries, Reading, and Publishing in the Cold War* (2001) and "Sociologie de la lecture et des usages en bibliothèque: Quelques Recherches récentes en France" (1991).

Bibliography

Abood, Edward F. "Arthur Koestler: *Darkness at Noon*." In *Underground Man*. San Francisco: Chandler & Sharp, 1973.

Abel, Lionel. "The Koestler Pardon." *New Republic* 191 (October 8, 1984): 28–32.

Atkins, John Alfred. *Arthur Koestler*. London: Neville Spearman, 1956.

Avishai, Bernard. "The Dangers of Devotion." *New Yorker* (January 6, 1997): 32–39.

Axthelm, Peter M. "The Search for a Reconstructed Order: Koestler and Golding." In *The Modern Confessional Novel*. New Haven: Yale University Press (1967): 97–127.

Bantock, G.H. "Arthur Koestler." *Politics and Letters* 1 (Summer 1948): 41–47.

Barnes, Julian. "Playing Chess with Arthur Koestler." *The Yale Review* 77, no. 4 (Summer 1988): 478–491.

Beadle, Gordon. "Anti-Totalitarian Fiction." *The English Record* 25 (Summer 1974): 30–33.

Blumstock, Robert. "Arthur Koestler: Hungarian Writer." *Hungarian Studies Review* 14, no. 1 (Spring 1987): 39–48.

Bokina, John. "From Communist Ideologue to Postmodern Rebel: Spartacus in Novels." *European Legacy* 6, no. 6 (December 2001): 725–30.

Calder, Jeni. *Chronicles of Conscience: A Study of George Orwell and Arthur Koestler*. Pittsburgh: University of Pittsburg Press, 1968.

Chiaromonte, Nicola. "Koestler, or Tragedy Made Futile." *Politics* 2 (September 1945): 266–70.

Davis, Robert Gorham. "The Sharp Horns of Koestler's Dilemmas: Difficulties of Reconciling Ends and Means." *Antioch Review* 4 (December 1944): 503–17.

Day, Frank. *Arthur Koestler: A Guide to Research*. New York: Garland, 1987.

Detweiler, Robert. "The Moment of Death in Modern Fiction." *Contemporary Literature* 13, (1972): 269–94.

Drucker, H.M. "Koestler's *Darkness at Noon*." In *The Political Uses of Ideology*. London: London School of Economics and Political Science (1974): 80–93.

Elkins, Charles L. "George Orwell, 1903-1950." From *Science Fiction Writers: Critical Studies of the Major Authors from the Early Nineteenth Century to the Present Day*. Everett Franklin Bleiler, editor. New York: Scribners (1982): 233–41.

Geering, R.G. "*Darkness at Noon* and *1984*—A Comparative Study." *Australian Quarterly* 30 (September 1958): 90–96.

Hamilton, Iain. *Koestler: A Biography*. New York: Macmillan, 1982.

Harris, Harold, ed. *Astride the Two Cultures: Arthur Koestler at 70*. London: Hutchinson & Co. Ltd., 1976; New York: Random House, 1975.

Hayman, Ronald. "The Hero as Revolutionary: Koestler's Novels." *London Magazine* 12 (December 1955): 56–68.

Hoffman, Frederick J. "*Darkness at Noon*: The Consequences of Secular Grace." *Georgia Review* 13 (Fall 1959): 331–45.

Howe, Irving. "Malraux, Silone, Koestler: The Twentieth Century." In *Politics and the Novel*. New York: Meridian Books (1957): 203–34.

Koestler, Arthur and Cynthia. *Stranger on the Square*. New York: Random House, 1984.

Koestler, Mamaine. *Living with Koestler: Mamaine Koestler's Letters, 1945–51*. New York: St. Martin's Press, 1985.

Mays, Wolfe. *Arthur Koestler*. Guildford: Lutterworth Press, 1973.

Merleau-Ponty, Maurice. *Humanism and Terror: An Essay on the Communist Problem*. Translated with notes by John O'Neill. Boston: Beacon Press, 1969; Westport, Connecticut: Greenwood Press, 1980.

Merrill, Reed. *Arthur Koestler: An International Bibliography*. Ann Arbor, Michigan: Ardis, 1979.

Mikes, George. *Arthur Koestler: The Story of a Friendship*. London: Deutsch, 1983.

Nedava, J. *Arthur Koestler*. London: Robert Anscombe and Company, 1948.

Prescott, Orville. "The Political Novel: Warren, Orwell, Koestler." In *In My Opinion: An Inquiry into the Contemporary Novel*. Indianapolis: Bobbs-Merrill (1952): 22–39.

Roland, Albert. "Christian Implications in Anti-Stalinist Novels." *Religion in Life* 22 (Summer 1953): 400–12.

Sayre, Nora. "Memories of Arthur Koestler." *Raritan* 19, no. 3 (Winter 2000): 19–36.

Siegel, Paul N. "Arthur Koestler's *Darkness at Noon*: The 'Logic of Revolution.?' " In *Revolution and the Twentieth-Century Novel*. New York: Pathfinder (1979): 110–30.

Sperber, Murray A. *Arthur Koestler: A Collection of Critical Essays*. Englewood Cliffs, NJ: Prentice-Hall, 1977.

Steele, Pete. "Darkness at Noon." *The Critical Review* 12 (1969): 73–82.

Strachey, John. *The Strangled City*. New York: William Sloane Associates, 1962.

Toulmin, Stephen. "Arthur Koestler's Theodicy." *Encounter* 41 (February 1979): 46–57.

Woodcock, George. *The Writer and Politics*. London: Porcupine Press (1948): 175–96.

Acknowledgments

"The Function of Rubashov's Toothache in Koestler's *Darkness at Noon*" by Annette Edwards Platt. From *McNeese Review* 23, (1976–77): 50–61. © 1976 by McNeese State University. Reprinted by permission.

"*Darkness at Noon* and the 'Grammatical Fiction'" by Goronwy Rees. From *Astride the Two Cultures: Arthur Koestler at 70*, edited by Harold Harris. Adapted from the introduction and appreciations in the Heron Books edition of *Darkness at Noon*. © 1976 by Random House. Reprinted by permission.

"Arthur Koestler: On Messiahs and Mutations" by Mark Levene. From *Modernist Studies* 2, no. 2 (1977): 37–48. © 1977 by the University of Alberta. Reprinted by permission.

"*Darkness at Noon*" by Sidney A. Pearson, Jr. From *Arthur Koestler*. © 1978 by Twayne Publishers. Reprinted by permission of the Gale Group.

"The Mind on Trial: *Darkness at Noon*" by Mark Levene. From *Arthur Koestler*. © 1984 by Frederick Ungar Publishing Co. Reprinted by permission.

"Viewpoints and Voices: Serge and Koestler on the Great Terror" by W. Marshall. From *Journal of European Studies* 16, part 2, no. 62 (June 1986):109–135. © 1986 by Science History Publications Ltd. Reprinted by permission.

"Orwell versus Koestler: *Nineteen Eighty-Four* as Optimistic Satire" by Howard Fink. From *George Orwell*, edited by Courtney T. Wemyss and Alexej Ugrinsky. © 1987 by Courtney T. Wemyss and Alexej Ugrinsky.

Reproduced with permission of Greerwood Publishing Group, Inc., Westport, CT.

"*Darkness at Noon* and the Political Novel" by Reed B. Merrill. From *Neohelicon* 14, no. 2: 245–256. © 1987 by Akadémiai Kiadó, Budapest. Reprinted by permission.

"The 'Post-Colonialism' of Cold War Discourse" by William Pietz. From *Social Text* 19–20 (Fall 1988): 55–75. © 1988 by Coda Press. Reprinted by permission.

"Comment on an Aspect of Pietz's Argument" by Anders Stephanson. From *Social Text* 19–20 (Fall 1988): 55–75. © 1988 by Coda Press. Reprinted by permission.

"Eternity in *Darkness at Noon* and the Consolation of Philosophy" by Robert Sutherland. From *Classical and Modern Literature* 13, no. 1 (1992): 31–43. © 1992 by CML, Inc.

"War, 1938–42" by David Cesarani. From *Arthur Koestler: The Homeless Mind*: 145–187. © 1998 by David Cesarini. Published by Heineman. Used by permission of the Random House Group Limited.

"A Cold War Best-Seller: The Reaction to Arthur Koestler's *Darkness at Noon* in France from 1945 to 1950" by Martine Poulain. From *Libraries and Culture* 36, no. 1 (Winter 2001): 172–183. © 2001 by the University of Texas Press. Reprinted by permission.

Index